HELL
in the
HEARTLAND

HELL
in the
HEARTLAND

MURDER, METH, AND THE CASE OF TWO MISSING GIRLS

JAX MILLER

BERKLEY
NEW YORK

BERKLEY
An imprint of Penguin Random House LLC
penguinrandomhouse.com

Copyright © 2020 by Jax Miller
Penguin Random House supports copyright. Copyright fuels creativity, encourages diverse voices,
promotes free speech, and creates a vibrant culture. Thank you for buying an authorized edition of this
book and for complying with copyright laws by not reproducing, scanning, or distributing any part of it in
any form without permission. You are supporting writers and allowing Penguin Random House to
continue to publish books for every reader.

BERKLEY and the BERKLEY & B colophon are registered trademarks of Penguin Random House LLC.

Library of Congress Cataloging-in-Publication Data

Names: Miller, Jax, author.
Title: Hell in the heartland : murder, meth, and the case of two missing girls / Jax Miller.
Description: First Edition. | New York : Berkley, 2020.
Identifiers: LCCN 2019056900 (print) | LCCN 2019056901 (ebook) | ISBN 9781984806307 (hardcover) |
    ISBN 9781984806321 (ebook)
Classification: LCC PS3613.I5374 H45 2020 (print) | LCC PS3613.I5374 (ebook) | DDC 813/.6--dc23
LC record available at https://lccn.loc.gov/2019056900
LC ebook record available at https://lccn.loc.gov/2019056901

Printed in the United States of America
10 9 8 7 6 5 4 3 2 1

Front jacket photograph by Anton Mayorov / Shutterstock;
back jacket photograph courtesy of Lorene Bible
Jacket design by Peter Garceau
Book design by Alison Cnockaert
Map by David Lindroth

While the author has made every effort to provide accurate telephone numbers, Internet addresses and
other contact information at the time of publication, neither the publisher nor the author assumes any
responsibility for errors, or for changes that occur after publication. Further, publisher does not have any
control over and does not assume any responsibility for author or third-party Web sites or their content.

My writing is forever dedicated to my children,
LA, K, AI & S.

This book is dedicated to Lauria and Ashley, forever young.

CONTENTS

SECTION 3: DRUGS

SECTION 4: LATER LEADS

SECTION 5: THE ARRESTS

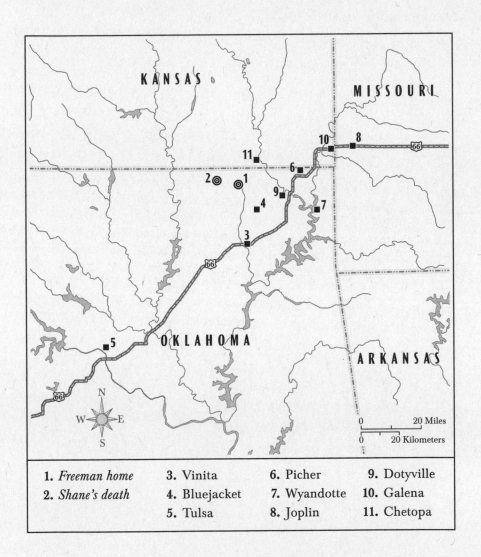

KANSAS

MISSOURI

11

10   8

6

2   1

9

4

7

3

66

5

OKLAHOMA

ARKANSAS

N
W   E
S

0   20 Miles
0   20 Kilometers

1. *Freeman home*	**3.** Vinita	**6.** Picher	**9.** Dotyville
2. *Shane's death*	**4.** Bluejacket	**7.** Wyandotte	**10.** Galena
	5. Tulsa	**8.** Joplin	**11.** Chetopa

While this book contains dramatizations and some names and identifying details have been changed to protect the privacy of individuals, this is a true story.

I was born on the prairie and the milk of its wheat, the red of its clover, the eyes of its women, gave me a song and a slogan.

—Carl Sandburg's "Prairie" (1918)

HELL

in the

HEARTLAND

The sheriff once told me this part of Oklahoma was haunted, that once you're a part of it, you can't ever leave. Here I am, walking along the edge of the Freemans' forty-acre property in the middle of the night and hoping not to be shot. I'm up against my own crippling anxiety and a backdrop of stars where in the winter of 1999 sat a small trailer that you'd never find by accident. In the pitch-black, from a dark and desolate dirt road I look up the hill, imagining how the home would have looked in flames, where inside were thought to be parents Danny and Kathy Freeman, their teenage daughter, Ashley, and Ashley's best friend, Lauria Bible.

God help them all.

Twenty years later, the Freemans and the Bibles remain without answer about what really happened that December night, strangled in the prickly weeds of rumor, rumors that include drugs, police corruption, serial killers, and the Second Coming of Jesus Christ himself. The secrets are out there in the Oklahoma prairie's whisper, her taunts. And as imaginary shadows move around me, I learn that while the prairie is playful by day, she plays tricks at night. Somewhere out there, closure might be found after all this time. If I've said it once, I've said it a million times: the prairie has her way.

But the stranger-than-fiction story of the Freeman-Bible case has hardly blipped on the radar of true crime, and it's hardly made its way out of Oklahoma and the intersection where Missouri, Kansas, and Arkansas almost meet to make crosshairs crookedly aimed at the gut of America. The fervors of youth are fading from those who stand today with questions, and those suspected to know where Ashley Freeman and Lauria Bible are now are taking the answers to their graves. Time is running out for an untold story, and I wonder who will be left to tell it when those closest to it are no longer here.

The taste of the prairie wind brings me back to being high, and a panic attack begins to spark in my chest. If I don't work this story, I'll have to sit with the unimaginable fear that found me only once I began this case. It is a hereditary monster that took the lives of the women before me in my family, including my mother, who will die from the effects of drugs in the midst of my investigation. Escapism. Fixation. While I get my demons from my mother, I take the diligence of my on-the-spectrum father and spend the next four years with the ghosts of Oklahoma.

Standing at the edge of the Freeman property, I go over (and over and over) what happened in the hours leading up to the fire and silently ask the girls where they went. But they don't answer, and instead, the hills whisper around me like they can smell my fear.

Like I said: the prairie has her way.

SECTION 1

THE FIRE

1

MOTHER, KATHY FREEMAN

December 29, 1999
The Day Before the Fire

S ummer is when I come to Oklahoma to meet the living, but I reserve winters for trying to acquaint myself with the dead; in the season when those I came to write about last lived, when it's still. I sometimes hear them better in the silence than from the survivors who still talk about them today. I may never get inside their minds the way I wish I could, or the way they get into mine. But I can at least feel the snow on my skin atop this hill where the trailer once sat, and wrap my fingers around the shoulder of an ax and wonder if our knuckles ache the same. In the lockjaw of winter, when memories of braiding watermelon vines and of blackberry-stained feet are long forgotten, Oklahomans carry on as they always have. They're hunters and gatherers by nature, canning and pickling, with freezers full of dove and deer, not just prepared but fortified for winter. They are, by default, a people who can withstand most anything.

Amidst the buzz-cut fields and dead-grass whistle, the white-tailed deer stand on their hind legs and pluck for persimmons' sweet orange flesh from the trees, which helps hunters track their paths. The folklorists tell me that cutting into the fruit at autumn's first frost is a way to predict the winter ahead. In 1999, the kernels were shaped as knives, foretelling of blade-twist winds (the spoon-shaped seeds mean heavy snow, while the fork-shaped formations forecast only dustings).

In 1999, blade-twist winds it was.

Kathy Freeman, age thirty-seven, paused momentarily to watch her breath hit the cold air hard. She was smoking more and more, to the point where the December air offended her lungs and the stains on her teeth were growing more prominent. The bleakness of winter brought with it a palette of homestead tans and doeskin browns, something lacking color, lacking life. Then a chop and a crack echoed down the hill when Kathy split another piece of wood. Outside the twenty-eight-by-fifty-six-foot mobile home, the air smelled like fresh coffee, bacon, and maple, an ambience of something cozy and all-American. Young barn cats played by the splinters, coming and going as they pleased, attracted to the smell of breakfast inside. Despite the temperature being thirty degrees Fahrenheit, Kathy kept warm by the sweat of her brow, wearing only faded Levi's and a T-shirt branded with the logo of the optometrist's office where she used to work. With breakfast still on the stove, she had just enough time to split a few more logs before returning, leaving the ax behind.

It was her daughter's sweet sixteen, there was much to do, and she was running behind on her homemaking chores.

She took the yard's chill inside with her, where a woodstove cooled just to the left of the front door. The home was small but nicely kept, toeing that fine line between cluttered and comfy. Kathy dropped an armful of firewood by the stove as she walked in, wincing at a splinter that found its way into her thumb's knuckle. She sucked on it, kicking off her worn Keds, which kept her feet cold, and dashed for the stove top, always the dutiful wife despite hating the cliché, for she also worked like a man with backbreaking endurance until her hands were nothing but two callused mitts.

The faux-wood-paneled walls were filled with display cases of Cherokee arrowheads, hundreds of points made of flint and bone, vibrant against red velvet and protected by glass, stained by the blood of the American Indians to whom this land once belonged. The open living room seemed to hang by the deer antlers that sprouted from the walls, with Ashley's laundry neatly folded on the couch. The TV was mistakenly turned to a soap, electric blue and amber light glowing through pan grease and unfiltered-cigarette smoke. On the floor was the family Rottweiler, Sissy, more nourished than any of the Freemans. The dog hardly raised her ears toward Kathy's moving about, half asleep for the lazy Wednesday afternoon.

Kathy added cracked black pepper and a touch of fresh milk to the fat drippings for the sawmill gravy, a Southern staple she was fixing for her husband for a late biscuits-and-gravy breakfast. Where the sausage smoke ended and Kathy's Natural American Spirit smoke began was clear from two different shades around her head, like a dual-toned halo. Her husband, Danny, had excused himself to go outside shortly before, halfway done for the day with whatever it was he was doing, living in a perpetual state of being in between odd jobs. Welding here, selling his own hand-picked wildflowers and willow branches to the florist there, whatever it took.

"My head's at it again," Danny often groaned, half excusing, half resentful. "Damn it anyway." He dropped a pat of butter into his black coffee and disappeared into the afternoon, swallowed by silver sun, never feeling the need to explain to Kathy where he was going or what he was doing. Then again, she never felt the need to ask. She didn't want to be *that* kind of farm wife, the kind whose floral dresses matched the wallpaper, the kind to put curlers in her hair before bedtime. God forbid. Gone were the calico-dressed women longing for their husbands out in the dust. Gone were the cowboys lit by a lantern's flame and navigating by the stars. Broken was the American dream and the barefoot girl that she used to be, playing in the bog and twirling red clover in her teeth. And she was just fine without all them frills. Between stirring the gravy and grabbing fresh eggs from their carton, she found a good ten seconds to find a sewing needle and go after that damn splinter.

Kathy had this natural-born killer's stare about her, one she was hardly aware of, what people refer to today as "resting bitch face." Her hair matched the fields that gave birth to her, just as wild, always catching the breeze. But 1999 was a trying year for the woman, her shoulders a fixed inch higher since her teenage son's death. *Murder!* she'd correct you if you mentioned it within earshot. *Cold-blooded murder!* Her eyes were but two swollen welts, the eyelashes plucked one by one out of nervous compulsion. Who could blame her?

Outside in the backyard, the blast of Danny's shotgun at the bottom of the hill, taking her attention from the splinter and over to the door of the refrigerator, where a lined piece of paper hung, a page she'd rewritten several times over earlier in the week. At the top, under a magnet made to look like a cow, in her tall but neat cursive, the words "ONE SHOT," a reference to the shotgun slug that had pierced her son's side.

> *My name is Kathy Freeman. I live west of Welch, OK—a Craig County resident all my life . . .*

She gave it a read, once over, with her hands on her hips and that inadvertent look of contempt nudging down the corners of her mouth.

"Ashley!" she called out over the stove top's bubble and hiss. "Grab yer breakfast, birthday girl. It's already after noon!" Kathy sucked hard on her cigarette, knuckles wide by chores never-ending and the pressing need to distract herself from seventeen-year-old Shane's death. *Murder, goddamn it!*

2

DAUGHTER, ASHLEY FREEMAN

December 29, 1999
The Day Before the Fire

Ashley Freeman had that adolescent thickness about her, one she was just starting to grow out of as the teeth in her head straightened into their adult positions. Her hair was dirty blond and homespun but tamed in a ponytail, her skin paler from bunkering in the shelter of "ay-kern" trees while wearing camouflage jackets that reversed into safety orange. She was just at the age when you could glimpse into what she'd look like as an adult, like her mother, but young enough that you could put your finger on exactly what she had looked like as a child. She was as country as country came. Photos often showed the girl, tall at five feet seven, sporting rifles and slinging the carcasses of various animals over her shoulder, proud like mink. Family bragged of her marksmanship and ate the deer she'd drag home from the hills, supper killed with unflinching precision. Sometimes, over the woodstove, Danny would make snack trays of turkey strips and deer steaks, paired with cans of Pepsi to wash them down, of which he could drink a six-pack in a day. Later, he'd make wind spinners from the cans and hang them from the gutters, to add flutter and rustle to their singing home. As a child, Ashley would watch the hypnotic silver and blue play against the sky on idle afternoons.

Like a good Oklahoma girl, she did her best to suppress her emotions, bred to see crying as weak but anger as strong. This is the Oklahoma way. But pain seemed to gnaw its way from the inside out, and in the past year, she'd lost a few pounds of that baby chub and the gold of her hair was losing its luster. Life had slapped her hard in the face, leaving a red mark of grief on her cheek that just wouldn't go away since her big brother's death. That afternoon, she arranged and rearranged the handpicked flowers of a bouquet, one made of hay from the yard, holly, Christmas rose, and fiery witch hazel sprigs, ready to replace the last bouquet from the side of a rural county road that had been stolen, plucked from the gravel.

The floral arrangement took her back to times when she and her father traveled together, over and under the nearby Oklahoma state lines between there and Kansas, Missouri, and Arkansas. They went anywhere the gas could take them to collect cattails and lotus pods and various wildflowers (cattails were their best seller at ten cents apiece to local florists). Ashley's mother would stay home to work at an optometrist's office while Shane continued on with his extracurricular activities and time spent with friends. Notwithstanding the cattails, which would fill the backseat at any given time, Ashley and Danny would arrange their handpicked commodities into spectacular sprays of sunroots, rattlesnake masters, and Indian blankets, displays of fire and sky wrapped in ribbon and sold for twenty bucks apiece, though you could get the price down to fifteen if Ashley was feeling kind enough. That was summertime, when red sunsets lingered over the fields after long days, hair tangling in the thick, hot wind of a speeding truck. She'd trace her hand over the passing fields and a dirty fingernail along the horizon, wishing for all the things that teenage girls wished for: the carefree heart, the white-trash kiss, reckless love. What little she could have known of growing up back then, walking in her father's shadow and eating fried pickles and pink lemonade on the side of the road to let the truck cool.

And now her sixteenth birthday.

It was the second half of winter break, one that lacked the vibrations of Christmas due to the weight of mourning. Ashley straightened the blond straw under her knee while listening to Billboard's Best of Country from her brother's radio. Because she had just moved up from her room to his, half of his furniture remained, though she couldn't bear looking at his *Sports Illustrated* calendar a second longer. She kept his football trophies and dusted them often, his worn Nikes at the foot of her bed, the blue-and-white Welch Wildcats football jersey he should have been buried in hung on the wall. She'd even spray his favorite Tommy Hilfiger cologne once in a while on her own flannel shirts just so she could feel him near.

Ashley ignored the thick smell of breakfast, appetite lost with her youth. She thought of a million things she'd rather be doing than turning sixteen, including, but not limited to, practicing for her driver's test.

"You know you're ready," her friend reassured her. "You've only been doing it since you were five."

"It's different when you're taking a test," Ashley replied. "You have to signal and all that crap. That's why Jeremy's been driving with me. Showing me all the formal stuff."

"Sure." The friend smiled, making quotation marks with her fingers. "'Formal stuff.'"

Ashley threw baby's breath at her best friend, sixteen-year-old Lauria (pronounced "Laura") Bible, who planted the flower behind her own ear.

The best friends had spent the day before preparing for the livestock showings for the county and state fairs, as part of the FFA (Future Farmers of America) and the 4-H Club, community-leadership and agricultural clubs to which they belonged. They knew all there was to know about roughages, dehorning, cattle parasites, castration, cuts of beef. These were country kids who'd spent the morning adjusting the gaits and training the coats of Ashley's goats, Jack and Jill. (Lauria had her own two pigs and a lamb back home.) They talked about seeding out the competition and making it all the way to the great Tulsa fair, which attracted more than a million visitors annually. Imagine, parades of antique tractors brandishing

American flags, pie-eating contests with sun-warmed blueberries exploding on clean cotton, demolition derbies, carnival rides, and bull-riding rodeos. The county and state fairs were the very embodiment of American life in the heartland. But back in the bleakness of winter, they trained with their sights set on summer. Ashley and Lauria wandered around the property that morning, gathering the leaves of dogwoods and bois d'arcs for the goats to eat as the cold made their rough hands ache. While the "crick" babbled at the bottom of the backyard, a weeping willow swished against the ground like the straws of a broom at the west side of the trailer. In fact, that was what helped Ashley decide on leaving her old bedroom on the east end of the house for Shane's on the west end: the branches that brushed against the windows and filtered dusk through strips of light like honey, a sense of security when the sun went down.

"Ashley!" her mother hollered from the kitchen. "Grab yer breakfast, birthday girl. It's already after noon!"

Ashley rolled her eyes—the picture of teenage disdain. Sometimes she wished that she didn't have to be the strong one within the family unit. Had it not been for Lauria's stability and her support, she wondered if she'd have been able to survive that last year of the millennium.

I spend years sitting with Ashley's family, friends, and neighbors, ambling her school hallways and stomping grounds, visiting classmates and teachers. I want to know what being Ashley Freeman was really like, and soon, another side of her emerges. Despite Ashley's outwardly tough persona, there was something tender about her. Back then, the kids in school knew that her family home wasn't the best, and the rumors as to why had long circulated, coming to a head with Shane's death. One friend tells of a time she forgot that Ashley was supposed to ride home with her from school and left without her, only for Kathy to show up on the doorstep with a sobbing Ashley, demanding to know why her daughter had been forgotten. While she could hunt for and field-dress a deer by herself, she required validation from others. Though she could lift any grown man, she'd dance in her room when alone. She was never able to throw away her favorite Berenstain Bears books and stuffed animals, yet took no issue in cutting the heads clean off turkeys. She had her feet planted in the manure and her heart in the clouds. There were the face she let others see and the face she reserved for behind closed doors, the real heart of her spirit she'd share with those closest to her, including Lauria.

"We're already late," Kathy yelled.

"Gimme a minute!"

Together, the friends got ready to leave, oblivious of their whole lives before them. Ashley slipped on her boyfriend, Jeremy's, high school ring and slipped into her sneakers, the soles dusty. Out there, the cricks and grain were stitched together with dirt roads that led off the beaten paths. That land breathed under their feet, heart pounding with hunger. In wait.

3

FATHER, DANNY FREEMAN

December 29, 1999
The Day Before the Fire

O ut here you'll find no one, and no one will find you, and that was exactly its appeal when Danny Freeman moved his family from rural Vinita to West of Welch back in 1995: father, mother, son, and daughter striving for a simpler way of living.

While Kathy prepared a late breakfast, and Ashley and Lauria got ready in the trailer, forty-year-old Danny Freeman wandered out back, sipping buttered coffee with a shotgun over his shoulder and hunting ancient arrowheads. This was how you'd find him most days. His shadow before him was long, and he couldn't catch up to it no matter how hard he tried, like he swore he could once when he was a boy. The sun warmed the quilted flannel on his shoulders. As he walked down the slight hill from his trailer to Big Cabin Creek that early afternoon, he paced along the edge of the river and listened for the familiar rasps of prairie rattlesnakes and water moccasins and other venomous pit vipers. To himself, he dared them to come out.

Danny eyed the land around him, bitter, feeling cheated by a little bit of everything: by the world, by God, by lawyers. He paced his way back toward a concrete dam at the top of the crick, where a feed bucket full of soybeans waited. With the sounds of the brook nearby, he spent the morning with fistfuls of the handpicked legumes, attracting rafters of wild turkeys. He even had the local game warden's permission to do so, provided he kept the routine up, lest they become dependent and later starve to death as a result. Danny agreed, feeding the birds every other day, just to listen to the whishing of their wings as they came close to him. They came with harvest-colored and copper plumage, Danny's eye catching on brief flashes of purple, red, and green.

But life weighed heavily on his shoulders, more heavily still since the death of his only boy, Shane. And Danny knew that death, once more, was lurking close, hiding out on the prairie. The sharp taste of paranoia lodged itself in the back of his throat, his shoulders winding tight. In those final days of 1999, Danny warned his friends, and warned his stepbrother, Dwayne Vancil, that she'd be a-coming, and that if anything were to happen to him, "you'd be best to look right here." Dwayne Vancil would repeat this exhaustingly over the years, asserting that in those last days, Danny pointed a finger hard into his stepbrother's chest and said, "If anything happens to me or my family, anything, look to the Craig County Sheriff's Office." Dwayne described that Danny's demeanor struck him as "fearful" and "absolute," traits rarely ever seen in Danny.

Some feared Danny's paranoia was a result of his overt marijuana use. Others feared he was right. Either way, rage seared just under Danny's skin, like sunburn at the back of his neck, mood fickle like fire. And perhaps, in many ways, the man was just . . . misunderstood.

After all, who could really understand a man who, once upon a time, had accidentally shot himself in the forehead?

It happened while he was cleaning a rifle, when the breech plug in the rear of the muzzleloader barrel blew back into his head and through his skull. With the plug actually lodged in his brain, Danny drove to the local hospital, waited two hours, got fed up, then drove two hours more to the city hospital, where doctors immediately rushed him in for brain surgery, replacing part of his skull with bone from his hip. The scar was a prominent badge in the middle of his forehead. So when people said that Danny was a tough guy, they meant just that.

Danny Freeman had inherited the rock-hard jaw and the bison-wide shoulders of the men before him, a lineage that emanated masculinity. Now alone, doleful, with an appetite for all things dwindling by the day, he wondered just how long it would take for him to waste away altogether. Unemployed with the exception of the odd welding jobs up in Kansas and cattail scavenges, he felt removed from the American dream of his ancestors. And the accidental injury caused crippling migraines and made steady employment an impossible feat to maintain.

He squatted on the dam, and nearing the bottom of the soybeans, Danny held the shotgun across his knees and pried his lips with a pipe. Fanned by the wings of turkeys, Danny could briefly forget it all, inhaling his grief into the depths of his lungs where it belonged, each hazy day blurring into the next. He'd rise and spend his days smoking, canvassing the riverbed for American Indian arrowheads, a hobby instilled in him since childhood. He didn't even have to search for them; they'd just catch his eye from the mire. He swore it was a gift inherited alongside that one-eighth of Cherokee hiding somewhere in his blood.

Despite the drug-induced sway in his gait, Danny shot his gun off and caught the leather belly of a cottonmouth snake. It was the same shot that took his wife's attention from the splinter in her thumb's knuckle back at the trailer.

The turkeys thundered into the air, yelping against the breeze. He walked over to the snake, tucked his thumb under its jaw like a trigger, and swung it into the creek. "Bastard," he muttered. Left with the gentle sounds of falling water, he returned to arrowhead hunting.

Then Danny, this epitome of all things virile, wept for his only son.

When Danny paused a few moments later, his eyes stung with salt as he scanned the unspoiled acreage that waved before him. Once gold from Indian grass and red with Oklahoma rose, today Welch was painted the color of sorrow. He smoked the burned resin of the pipe until there was nothing left. And when the waves of grief passed, as they always did, he swung the shotgun back over his shoulder and climbed the moderate incline back to the front of his house.

As he rounded the side of the trailer in the low winter sun, Danny watched his daughter unintentionally make the sign of the cross with her body spray, a cloud of pink in the afternoon light to smell like Cotton Candy Fantasy and hay. He passed behind her and rubbed the top of her head. "Happy birthday, Ash," he managed, just as Lauria followed from the front door.

The girls waited for Kathy at the bottom of the precast-concrete steps. Ashley zipped up her coat as Lauria looked under the bleached skull of a longhorn that hung on the front of the house. With the girls' backs to him, Danny stuffed the pipe deep in his jeans pocket and made his way up to the front door as his wife was leaving.

"We'll be back in a few hours," said Kathy as she blew the bangs from her face. "We'll bring back the birthday cake with us."

Danny stared her down, as he often did, and she hurried down the steps to avoid the familiar heat of his glare. Even before the night's events would unfold into one of the most far-reaching mysteries of the Midwest, there wasn't a person in town who hadn't heard of Danny's knee-jerk temper. Some even had their own accounts of how he had wound up with a scar in the middle of his forehead.

Danny leaned in the doorway and crossed his arms. "The big sweet sixteen," he remarked, and the trace of a smile crossed his daughter's face.

"You bet," Ashley responded.

Lauria left her 1989 blue Chevy Cavalier with Danny's truck and climbed into the backseat of Kathy's car. Danny watched them drive off down the seven-hundred-foot driveway into the December frost, passing by a JUSTICE FOR SHANE sign at the property's edge, decorated with a football signed by Shane's classmates and a few Beanie Baby bears and candles.

Pulling up only a moment after Kathy and the girls left was Danny's best friend, Charlie Krider, a bald man with a long beard and a bag of grass, to whom Danny waved from the front door. He came from Chetopa, the town just north of Welch but over the Kansas border, just eight miles from Danny's house as the crow flies but a twenty-minute drive on a rocky country road. Charlie parked in front of the trailer, trying to discern through dust the tail end of Kathy's car in his side-view mirror. "Perfect timing, I suppose," called Charlie as he exited his truck.

Danny repeated his daughter's words. *"You bet!"*

Charlie lifted his sunglasses and skimmed his eyes across the pastures for his red cattle. His fingers were shaped like spoons and the cold months chapped his lips. "Look at big mama cow and big daddy cow," he said as he spotted them across the property. "Too bad we gotta slaughter 'em."

Ready to partake in green communion, Danny dismissed the comment and thumbed over his shoulder for Charlie to start rolling a couple of joints without him inside the trailer. "I'm right behind you," he said.

But there was something anticipatory about Danny from those porch steps, looking after the road's dust from Kathy's car on the other side of the trees. He licked the aftertaste of dope from his lips and turned his attention to the empty ends of the road, away from his missus, where Danny watched a Craig County Sheriff's Office deputy's car crawl slowly along the edge of his property. The police officer looked out his window and up at Danny, and Danny stared right back. The deputy's car stopped. They watched each other without a word, the way Danny silently dared snakes out back. Danny cocked his head with a smirk and pointed his fingers in the shape of a gun, closing one eye and pulling an imaginary trigger at the deputy. The officer sneered back up at Danny, tilted his cap, and drove on after the girls.

4

BEST FRIEND, LAURIA BIBLE

December 29, 1999
The Night Before the Fire

With Ashley at her side, and Kathy driving, Lauria wiped the fog from the car window, scanning the neon lights of Route 66 as they ignited around her. The colors shone wet in her hazel eyes, streaking over the skin that maintained part of its tan from the long summer that now felt far. It was no wonder that Vinita, having been the first city in Oklahoma with electricity, felt brighter than other towns budding along the Main Street of America. Lauria's curly brown hair was shoulder length, and she came complete with a beauty mark stamped between her right nostril and upper lip like a maker's mark. Cozy in her blue-and-gold cheerleading jacket, which creaked with every movement, she settled, watching the sun shrink behind the historic art deco storefronts to the smell of car exhaust and deep-fried anything. The days were shrinking, with sundown at only a quarter after five.

The original plan was for Lauria to return home in rural Vinita that evening, but because they had a later start in the day than planned, and because Lauria wasn't allowed to drive after dark, they decided they'd later ask Lauria's parents to let her stay another night; since her house would be on the way to some of their errands, they'd stop there later.

The first stop was at a feed store to fetch food for Ashley's goats. Lauria helped Ashley and her mother pack the clover and alfalfa into the trunk of Kathy's Toyota before heading off to Pizza Hut in Vinita for Ashley's birthday dinner. Lauria was oblivious to the strands of straw stuck in her curls as they squeezed into a booth and enjoyed their dinner. Lauria and Ashley talked about fairs and cars as Kathy looked on in awe, wondering how the raptures of youth were so long ago. After they ate, they crossed the highway and went to Walmart. There, Lauria helped Ashley handpick her birthday cake: white frosting piped with blue. "Chocolate. No. Vanilla. No. Chocolate," Ashley argued with herself. Lauria, always the problem solver, offered, "Half and half," relieving Ashley of her indecision. Nighttime fell over Route 66 during the course of their errands and the neon signs kindled. The night remained cold and bitter and would feel this way in all the years since.

They then drove to the lightless outskirts of Vinita to the home of Kathy's mother, Celesta, and stepfather, Bill Chandler; Kathy would often haul water for drinking from there. (Contrary to several reports, the Freemans did have running water, suitable for laundry and toilets and showers; however, the water came from the Big Cabin Creek in the back of the Freeman trailer and was not drinkable. Therefore, Kathy made frequent visits to her parents' to collect drinking water for the family.) Lauria's house was only a few minutes from the Chandlers', and it was their next stop.

Kathy and Ashley waited in the car as Lauria ran into her house; the twinkling lights of the Christmas tree could be seen from far across the surrounding farmlands. Her father, Jay, had just returned from his job at an auto parts store in Langley. He was a nine-to-five man always topped off with a rugged baseball cap and plaid, a Midwestern man with Jack Webb–ish features and a thick, syrupy drawl. Hurrying so as not to keep her friend and her mother waiting, Lauria dashed for her bedroom, collecting a new set of clothes in her arm.

"Whoa, whoa, where's the fire?" Jay called out.

"My car's over at Ashley's, and we only just fetched the cake," she shouted down the hall. "Can I stay over just one more night? Pretty please?"

Jay gave in, always having a hard time saying no to his only daughter. "Well, now, you know you got animals you gotta take care of tomorrow, get around and take care of your show animals and stuff. You need to be home by noon."

Years later, Jay tells me, "Noon never came the next day."

Lauria squealed, rushing about and stuffing a couple of bottles of nail polish in her coat pocket. She was so rushed that she nearly bolted out the door without saying goodbye. But she stopped and turned around before planting a kiss on her father's cheek. "I love you, Dad." They were her last words to her father as she hopped down the steps of her porch, then skipped back into the idling car. The prairie, now dark, took her in with open arms, as it always had. It had something of the delirium of adolescence about it. And I'm sure Lauria's natural curls bounced off her shoulders, and I'm sure winter was kinder to her skin than to most people's. As they set off, Lauria's mother, Lorene, just on her way home from work, slowed her car to a stop beside Kathy's on the road where the Bibles lived.

"Dad said I could stay another night." Lauria grinned.

"Make sure you don't forget about the dentist's appointment in the morning. Be home at eight o'clock."

"I will!" Lauria shouted back the last words to her mother. Like with her father, the words "I love you" would be the last words Lorene heard from her daughter. Kathy smiled back at Lorene and slowly started to move the car forward.

The three of them made one more stop, this time at the Jack's convenience store in Welch, owned by the grandmother of Ashley's boyfriend,

Jeremy Hurst. They picked up some soda and invited Jeremy as a last-minute decision, which he accepted.

It was to be a night of modest celebration. They settled in, with Ashley and Lauria shifting near the kitchen table by Danny, and Jeremy Hurst following shortly after. Kathy took the cake to the counter and planted seventeen candles in it, including one for luck, using it to light her cigarette. With her back to the rest, Kathy glanced over at the piece of paper on the fridge. *One shot.* It took her attention long enough that she didn't notice the wax melting until she felt the heat under her face. She forced herself away from the letter, a manifesto of sorts, and set down her smoke, instructing Jeremy to turn off the lights as he came in.

The lights went out, and Kathy came with birthday cake ablaze. The flames of the candles sparkled in her beady but smiling brown eyes as she set the cake in front of her daughter. They sang "Happy Birthday to You," Lauria singing louder than the rest, as Jeremy took a seat and playfully pinched Ashley's side.

Ashley closed her eyes and made a wish.

The birthday candles were extinguished by breath, a breath as long as the prairie's. Now the unlit home could not be noticed against the nighttime outside, and the cheers of her family and friends rolled in short form from the hills. It is from here, from this jumping-off point, that it is anybody's guess as to what happened after, between a wish and the dawn's early light when the trailer was found in flames.

I've driven the route between Vinita and Welch more times than I can count, more times than I've visited my childhood home. Each trip is slightly brighter and louder than the last, to a place where it takes time for my eyes and ears to adjust. Coming here, to where they were last seen, isn't something I'm able to resist. I'm drawn. Obsessed. Manic. Sometimes I come up the driveway and think of the five of them here: Danny, Kathy, Ashley, Lauria, and Jeremy. Sometimes I imagine I am them. But as my senses adjust to deep, dark country, I light a smoke there on the Freeman property and imagine that I am the killer or killers who struck the first flame. I blow out my match, adding a pinch of sulfur to the pastures surrounding in the same way as Ashley blew out her birthday candles.

And then the prairie falls silent.

5

ONE BODY

December 30, 1999
The Morning of the Fire

Like the Freemans, Welchans Jack and Diane Bell lived in an area so rural that it didn't even fall within the city limits of any existing town. Instead, it was referred to as West of Welch; what locals called "the sticks." It was early morning, and their farmhouse was dimmed, so as not to wake their capricious teenage son. The home, only a few miles deeper into the country than the Freemans', was all long shadows, the smell of Scotch pine sap, and the emphysemic breathing of a percolator. In the stillness at the bottom of each exhale, the outside sound of handcrafted wind chimes made of hammer-flattened spoons and forks. Every house in Oklahoma seemed to harmonize with the wind.

The pickup warmed up outside. Only a few miles south of the Kansas border, the ranching town was starry and still as the married couple got ready for work. They were employed at the Eastern State Hospital for the Insane, located about twenty miles south in Vinita, where a working farm for the patients once served as an economic factor for the county. Jack dried his chest-length yellowed beard over the woodstove's heat as Diane fixed thermoses of chili and a side of leftover corn bread. His teeth ached that morning as he tied his beard into a single ponytail with three rubber bands, staring absently into the twinkling lights of the Christmas tree.

"Fetch the coffee," Diane whispered through the dark. Jack went to the open kitchen and filled two large mugs with Folgers. After Jack pulled the cord of the Christmas tree lights from the wall, they left, clad in their Carhartts and long johns, going on with the hackneyed "just like any other morning."

It was a wonder that the lightest breeze could find this town, and that morning, it crooned like a raw bow across a cello string, long and low. At approximately 5:40, Jack and Diane climbed into their Dodge pickup, not planning to fully wake until their tires reached the pavement of a God's honest road. The leather shifted under them, the radio tuned to the local weather.

"You unplugged the tree, right?" asked Diane.

Jack grunted, not a yes or no about him at that ungodly hour, ungodly because of the way he had tossed and turned the night before, prodded by toothache. They headed south over the vast stubble that was the landscape, serenaded by the soft scrape of tires on dirt, fiddling with the heating vents. Nothing but blackness for as far as their sleep-crusted eyes could see, but for the pockets of illuminated grit caught in the truck's headlights. Had they driven on just a little farther, they would have seen the familiar yellow signs inflamed in the lights, warning: HITCHHIKERS MAY BE ESCAPING INMATES—signs you'll still find in the area today.

As Diane sipped her coffee, she noticed a glow in the eastern sky just beyond a hill, a moving shade of tawny blotting out the stars. She nudged her husband's arm, pointing his attention due east to this little light that danced on the world's edge. For a split second, she wondered if it were the first flash of day, a brief panic at the idea of being late for work, but that couldn't have been right. Jack tilted his head and let a silent profanity fall down his ponytailed beard.

He turned the car east toward the light, his headlights streaking the hand-painted sign that read JUSTICE FOR SHANE at the end of the long driveway. The town being small enough, they knew the farm belonged to the Freemans, a family of four. A family of three now, Jack had to mentally correct himself, since the Freeman boy had been found near a ditch about ten miles west the winter before. Suddenly the couple was wide-awake, turning north up the moderate incline of the seven-hundred-foot-long driveway and edging closer. The Freeman trailer was engulfed in flames.

Jack slammed the gears into reverse and raced in the direction of the highway, stopping at the first house he saw: the Sherricks'.

Today, Wade Sherrick is a cattle rancher who lives at the end of that dirt road, he on the south end, the Freemans once at the north. "And you thought I was dead, eh?" he laughs when I mention that it took me three years to see him, because I had been misinformed; I thought he was an elderly man who'd died some years before. "Not sure what that says about me." It was only out of curiosity that I stopped my car by his barn in early 2019 when seeing two young men doing farmwork from the sheds. I knew by their young faces that they probably didn't have much firsthand information about the 1999 fire up the road, but I ask about the late Wade Sherrick, only to learn that Wade was alive and well, and just over there. Wade comes from the barn, winter pale from the shadows, middle-aged but still handsome in that callused-hand way you'd find around Welch. I follow him across the street to an office connected to his farmhouse, a cluttered room filled with agricultural newsletters and dusty trophies and belts from his days as a rodeo rider, a hobby that his two sons inherited (they all had a laugh at my thinking Wade was dead). I ask to wear his cowboy hat before inquiring about the morning of the fire. He and his sons are kind. Wade's wife, Kim, a local mail carrier, is working that day.

"Well, somebody's beatin' on the door," Wade says about the morning of the fire. "I could sleep through a bomb, but Kim wakes up and goes to the door. I stumble out and see it's that Bell."

———————

Back in 1999, the blue heelers stood by their masters, keeping quiet when the door opened to Jack Bell and the moonlit ranch behind him, one of Charolais and Angus breeds of beef cattle.

"Hey, I'm on my way to work," Jack calmly started. "But the Freemans' house is on fire up the road there."

Kim Sherrick called 911 at 5:50. At this time, Jack and Diane Bell continued to drive to their place of work.

They'd not speak of the incident publicly again.

Wade and Kim went to their children's bedrooms. They wrapped their six- and four-year-olds in the covers they still slept in, the parents slipping on their boots quietly in the dark by the front door with their sons' heads in the crooks of their necks. "It's five something in the morning. We get the kids up and throw 'em into the truck and get up there." The family of four squeezed into the cab of the family truck, summoned by the tiny light at the top of the road that shone red like the sun. The sleepy boys rubbed their eyes to inspect the sight ahead. When they reached the home, only half of the trailer was on fire (Kim remembers the east side while Wade remembers the west side). But the Sherricks couldn't leave their truck on account of the Freeman family dog, Sissy, a brute of a Rottweiler, jumping on the car doors and barking her jowls off. Helpless, all they could do was watch when a sudden swell of fire whooshed and washed over the other half of the trailer within the matter of a second. "We were, like, 'Whatta we do? Whatta we do?'" Wade recalls. Today, the Sherrick sons, now working on the family farm, remember not the fear of the fire, but the fear of the dog in their long-ago, hazy memories.

The Welch Volunteer Fire Department showed up at 6:10, twenty minutes after the call to police. The Sherricks knew the firemen as they came one by one, all of them bread-and-buttered on the same ol' farms. The pair rolled down the windows and shouted to them from the truck. "We told them that all the cars were accounted for," says Wade. "We knew that much about the Freemans." The Sherricks stayed for less than an hour, with Kim having to be at work by seven o'clock.

Wade closes our meeting by adding, "It was spooky."

Firefighters wrestled with the blaze for somewhere between one and three hours until it was extinguished, the trailer collapsing like paper under the pressure of the hoses' water. Elsewhere, as Welch began to wake at the edge of dawn, bored, fattened housewives coupled themselves to their home police scanners, few surprised, though ever fascinated, to hear about more trouble over at the Freemans' place.

The CCSO came to the scene soon after the fire department, sunrise trailing not far behind and with Sheriff George Vaughn at the helm. Vaughn's position as sheriff was an elected one as opposed to one based on academic or vocational merit, though he'd previously served as sheriff of the same county from 1969 to 1973 before being a twenty-one-year state representative (referred to by the *Oklahoman* in 1988 as one of the worst in the state at that time). He was tall and beer-bellied, and his expression, perhaps involuntarily, was one of sour certainty. Parts of him retained water, fingers like full rubber hoses and feet a little too wide for his shoes. He was fleshy and spoke slowly, albeit scrupulously, as though each slurred word had been carefully selected.

In these Midwestern towns, where sheriffs are elected for four-year terms, it's common to find that they come with their own posse. "Being a deputy for the sheriff's office isn't secure," one of my CCSO sources tells me. "You can come in with the sheriff and leave with the sheriff once his term ends. A lot of these guys are in and out before going back to the ranches and auto shops." Alongside Vaughn was a group of men from the CCSO, names synonymous with Vaughn's term: Undersheriff Mark Hayes, Lieutenant Jim Herman, Investigator Charles Cozart, and Deputy Troy Messick (though despite the titles, one wasn't afforded more training than another, as the positions were handpicked by Vaughn himself).

At the burning trailer, a volunteer fireman surfaced from the charred remains of the home, removing his helmet and gulping down fresh air. "There are fatalities." He pointed a thumb behind him as he informed the deputies. "Just the one, from what I see." Several more firefighters followed him out.

After firefighters discovered the body, CCSO deputies briefly poked their heads in, noting that the body was found near 7:30. At 7:33, the sun showed up to extinguish the stars, and the men returned to the front yard.

"Call Donna," Vaughn said to the officers beside him as he let his head fall, referring to Medical Examiner Donna Warren. "Then call the OSBI [Oklahoma State Bureau of Investigation]."

"The OSBI?" asked Investigator Charlie Cozart.

"That's what I said; we're standing down." The men stopped at their cars. Vaughn crossed his arms and leaned on his heels as he looked back at the smoke. "No one does a thing until OSBI gets here. We got too much bad blood with this family."

"Our hands are clean, boss."

Vaughn raised his eyebrows at Cozart. "That so?"

The single body found by the fire volunteers and only briefly observed by deputies was located in one of the bedrooms, lying facedown in the wrong direction on the bed. All trace of breakfast and open air had been tainted with the smell of burned flesh, which was caught in workers' throats for days to come. *You know that smell,* they'd say. *You know that smell outta nowhere.*

The fire had destroyed much of the body. The upper back and buttocks were burned to the muscle, and the feet and lower legs had been burned off. But most telling was the fact that the skull was shattered. Around the body's unrecognizable head, bricks were scattered about. The fire had caused the ceiling to collapse, and it was soon learned that on the roof were bricks from where Danny had left an unfinished roofing project in warmer months prior. Authorities initially assumed that the bricks, either by raining from above or by malicious strike, were the cause of this person's death.

And so this rumor began to filter from the burned trailer, down to the few Welchans who'd stopped their pickups and tractors at the edge of the property.

That Danny and his dadgum temper, it soon started.

At the end of the driveway, locals began gathering and stepping cautiously along toward the trailer site, peering up the incline to the curls of smoke. Police cordoned off the scene with yellow DO NOT ENTER tape. The rumor mills quickly started to crank, lubricated by chewing tobacco and tractor grease.

Many said they had seen this coming.

The CCSO kept to the front of the house, where three cars were parked; they refused to reenter the home until the OSBI arrived. The first was a white 1990 GMC flatbed truck that belonged to Danny Freeman. Then the silver 1998 Toyota Corolla belonging to Kathy. They were the only cars the Freemans owned.

"I'm guessing this third one belongs to the daughter?" one of the deputies asked.

"Christ almighty," Sheriff Vaughn sighed, looking across at the blue 1989 Chevrolet Cavalier. On the front, an airbrushed license plate read DRAGON WAGON, with bangles and curios hanging from the rearview mirror to match the Bluejacket school colors of blue and gold, the high school from the next district over. "No, but I think I know whose it is though." Vaughn shook his head, exhaling slowly as he spoke: "The Bible girl." He was referring to Lauria Bible, the best friend of Ashley Freeman.

The wood continued to hiss, an angry whisper about the dead. From the ashes there would be answers. From the ashes there would be questions. On this day, a single body was found.

The question was, which one?

6

ONE WOMAN, LORENE BIBLE

Today

I chose to write about the case in late 2015. Living for most of a decade in Ireland (though I was born and raised in New York), I spoke to Lauria Bible's mother for the first time in early 2016. It was nighttime, and a carnival spun brightly outside my office when I called Lorene, six hours behind me. I was newly wading the waters of nonfiction, a little apprehensive.

"To be honest, I have no idea what the hell I'm doing," I said to her. After all, I was just a writer with no law enforcement experience (at least not on the right side of the law) or any experience in investigating.

"Neither do I, but I just keep doing it anyway," she responded.

That single sentence would help me get through it all.

I come to Oklahoma, thinking that it'll be hard to write about the dead, but it has proven harder to write about the living, about those who'll have to read themselves through my eyes. This is most true for Lorene Joyce Bible. She is guarded. She holds her head high and listens more than she speaks. She is Lauria Bible's mother, and she is the only reason this case isn't forgotten on a shelf somewhere. Her maiden name is Leforce, and it's always felt apt to me.

I meet Lorene for the first time at the Bible farm, the cattle ranch that runs through her husband's family as the hay baler runs outside. I'm not the first person to sit face-to-face with her and ask her the tough questions about her daughter's 1999 disappearance, and I won't be the last. She sifts through a thousand photos of Lauria, knowing by only the feel of her hand which worn photo is the one she prefers the world to see—it is one of Lauria posing in her cheerleading uniform. It is the same photo that makes up Lorene's Facebook cover on the "Find Lauria Bible—BBI" page, where I first contacted the Bible family in early 2016. In the photo, Lauria looks like her father, Jay.

"The Bible Bureau of Investigation," Lorene explains when I ask what BBI stands for, "because we never stop searching." She comes from a large family, including Lisa Bible-Brodrick, Lauria's cousin, a woman who was raised like Lauria's sister, one of Lorene's own. She is Lorene's right-hand woman, especially in this new age of technology. This network of Lauria's relatives and friends comes with children who know their long-lost cousin or aunt only by word of mouth, by the stories and photos of those I interview today. They know her only as well as I do. But the Bibles are a people who have withstood the unbearable, a people who manage to find God's peace not when the clouds part but in the midst of the storm.

Lorene tells me she named her daughter after Laura Ingalls Wilder, author of the children's *Little House on the Prairie* series, part of which was based nearby. Having herself seen the tougher side of country living, Lorene holds the children's stories close to her heart. "It is still best . . . to make the most of what we have," Wilder wrote in *The Long Winter*. "To be happy with simple pleasures; and have courage when things go wrong." They are the kinds of principles that the Bible family clings to, the simplicity that gives birth to perseverance over the years. Lauria's mother added the "i" to her daughter's name to make it more distinctive, Lauria's own.

Like many witnesses years later, it remained silent.

Lauria is the only daughter of Lorene and Jay Bible and the only sibling of Brad, who is two-and-a-half years older. Her middle name, Jaylene, is a portmanteau of her parents' names. She came from a family built on Midwestern convention, of Sundays at Grandma Dixie and Grandpa Kenneth's, sit-down dinners with the family, of faith. Lauria used to babysit for several families in the Bluejacket–Vinita area, toting a large bag filled with coloring books and board games, making her the most beloved babysitter among children to the point that kids used to beg their parents to leave the house so that Lauria could come over.

Lauria materializes for me in Technicolor through those who can't wait to talk about her. How summer days were spent lighting firecrackers here on the Bible farm, putting them under the feed buckets and sitting on them, accompanied by hysterical laughter, pop and snap, and the smell of gunpowder under the white Oklahoma sun. How Lauria would walk barefoot through the garden rows, milk and black pepper and corn bread in hand as the pecans landed hard on the tarps across the yard (I even hear how she'd skim the cream from the top of Grandma Dixie Bible's fresh milk and pretend not to know who had done it).

"She certainly wasn't one to lay around," says her cousin Lisa.

"Let me tell you about Rambo," one of Lauria and Ashley's best friends, Sheena, recollects, laughing with tears in her eyes. She tells me of a time back in kindergarten class in Bluejacket, where most friendships are formed in the first few years of the local students' lives, and Sheena had just sat in front of Lauria. "You should have seen it. She was wearing a matching yellow windbreaker jacket and pants, a jogging suit. It was ridiculous, but it was fashionable for back then." She smiles. "She had one of those sweatbands around her head, looking like Rambo. I didn't know how to take her." Sheena describes the mischief in Lauria's eyes when Lauria wrapped her feet around the legs of her desk. With a raised eyebrow, and with Sheena pulling her head back to study the girl, Lauria leaned back and quickly lifted up her windbreaker and shirt, flashing her bareskinned chest at the stranger for a laugh. "I knew right then, I wanted to know this girl. She was wild." It was the start of an unbreakable friendship.

The stories that fill Lauria's short sixteen years are plentiful, as are

Lorene's boxes of her daughter's report cards and childhood drawings, which she regularly keeps in the trunk of her car when media appearances are steady enough. Despite this, I connect with Lauria best through her school binder, filled with Lauria's creative writing assignments written months before her disappearance. I carry them with me over time, over visits to Oklahoma, running my fingertips over the long-dried ink as though they're an epitaph on a gravestone. I hear Lauria better through the voice that continues here on paper than through her grinning in fading photographs.

"You say a bedtime prayer, and in the darkness, it's so peaceful, and you can rest," Lauria wrote for her creative writing class only weeks before the fire. On another page, she wrote, *"Each locust, steaming madly across the smoke-filled, gray sky. One by one they attack their prey, pounding them helplessly into the ground. Not one locust is slowed down or shot down. And when the helpless prey surrender, they are attacked and captured by the forceful locusts, who torture and kill their prey, sucking their blood until every last drop of blood is drank and the life of their prey is sucked right out of them. Every last breath gasped, a slow and painful death they had."*

Somehow, through her schoolwork, I find myself nostalgic for a childhood that I hardly remember. And I find I'm no longer connecting to Lauria, but I am connecting to her absence. Youth, lost.

Lorene watches me as I look over Lauria's belongings, stiff and of stoic ilk. Her yeses and nos are drawn out mm-hmms and uh-uhs, notes of observances and approvals with few words. There is a coldness to her, but it comes with understanding. The years against her haven't been all that kind, and she's adapted a tolerance to suffering. She talks about local events with her relatives as I sift through Lauria's things, memories that are not mine.

Glasses of iced tea sweat on the counter; the low sounds of farming equipment rumble outside on this clear summer day. We are far away from the cold, and far away from 1999, but I want Lorene to take me back. She fastens her stare on mine as we sit together in the kitchen. She is dressed in the colors of springtime, but her eyes are hard like times in winter—there seems nothing bereaved about her. I will never see her cry, and she will never get choked up or trip over a word. She has talked about her daughter and told this story a thousand times over, so when I ask about the morning of the fire, she remains still and composed.

"I was already working that morning," she starts, leading me back to 1999.

7

THE SCENE OF THE CRIME

December 30, 1999
The Morning of the Fire

News was spreading fast around the county, and the townspeople shifted their morning routines and steered toward the farmlands of Welch, where deputies continued to wait for the OSBI to arrive. Since the first few hours of the fire, no efforts had been made to search the trailer or the surrounding property for any person dead or alive, beyond the first, unidentified body in one of the bedrooms.

After the CCSO noted Lauria Bible's car at the scene, CCSO deputy Troy Messick made the drive from Welch to downtown Vinita, where he knew he'd find Lorene Bible. Messick was young, what Oklahomans call a boy's boy, and a newlywed. As he made the slow walk from his patrol car into McDonald's, where Lorene worked, he slowed his breathing.

Lorene had just received a call from her son, Brad. He'd heard from his girlfriend, who lived in Welch at the time, that there was a house fire at the Freemans'. They didn't know the severity and imagined only a small kitchen fire. Lorene immediately hung up and called the Freemans, but the phone just kept on ringing. A moment later, Deputy Messick walked in.

Messick and Lorene were already acquainted with each other; it was a small town and strangers were rare. "We need to go somewhere and talk," he said. Lorene remembers that his face was blank. She took him back to her office; she had been promoted to regional manager several years prior, having climbed the ranks since 1987. "Lorene, the whole house is gone. It's totally gone."

It would be a life-changing moment for any mother, but Lorene Bible isn't like most mothers. She is fixed in the Midwestern stoicism that reared generations before mine; in rural America, a *save your tears for the pillow* culture stands firm in the face of catastrophe. Crying is saved for the poets and the soft. More than once, I'd be embarrassed when getting teary-eyed for the victims in front of her. (One time I excused myself to bawl outside with the farm animals nearby, only to return to the house once I'd gotten it out of my system, for Lorene to watch me and say, "That's OK. I'll have my day. When I'm standing over the hole in the ground and looking down at my daughter, that's my day.")

Sitting with Lorene for the first time, a foreigner in her world, I feel confused when her reactions confound my expectations, or when her answers echo articles in the newspapers from years before. I struggle to understand what drove Lorene, what got her from one day to the next, how she resisted the draw of booze and hopelessness that has toppled so many parents in similar circumstances. But who am I to judge? If I had to describe Lorene in a single word, it would be "fearless." And how can she not be? Her worst nightmares have already come true, so what is left for her to fear?

Deputy Troy Messick continued. "They found one body, in the front bedroom."

Lorene knew that the front bedroom belonged to Kathy and Danny and said this much, assuming that the body must belong to one of them. Deputy Messick got on the radio and relayed to authorities still on the scene that Lorene had confirmed the room in which they found the body was the parents' bedroom.

"I had to get there" was Lorene's initial thought. There was no hypothesizing, no time for different scenarios to play out in her mind. "I just had to go and find my daughter." This single-minded urgency and resolve characterized Lorene's response to the tragedy in the weeks and years following the fire.

On receiving the news, Lorene called her husband, Jay, over at the auto parts store, just a fifteen-minute drive away. He picked her up in Vinita and, unable to get in touch with Celesta and Bill Chandler, the pair stopped off at the Chandler house and told Celesta that there had been a fire at her daughter's home. Celesta broke down, screaming and hollering, and refused to leave until Bill returned from a church meeting he was attending that morning at the Kingdom Hall of Jehovah's Witnesses. She insisted that they do nothing until her husband got home.

"I'm not waiting for Bill! If you're coming, then let's go. If not, we're heading on without you," Lorene shouted. And at that, they left—with Celesta in tow.

The three of them arrived in Welch at nine fifteen. Deputies stopped them halfway up the Freemans' driveway. Jay and Lorene watched the scene unfold the best they could; the blackened remains of the home were still smoldering and townspeople gathered on the road, looking up with curiosity. A number of eyewitnesses confirmed that the deputies of CCSO were "just sitting on their laurels" and watching, along with the citizens, a smoking pit of wood cordoned off with yellow crime scene tape. Once the CCSO made the choice to hand the scene over to the OSBI, they put their hands up and surrendered all responsibility.

Unofficial news quickly drip-fed from the home at the top of the hill and down to the citizens of the small town: that the body belonged to a woman. One fire department volunteer would tell me that he specifically remembered the body being facedown on the bed, that when he leaned the body over, he exposed a woman's naked breast.

But the body was too destroyed to know which female it belonged to: if Kathy, if Ashley, if Lauria, if someone else.

It seemed as though every Welchan gravitated toward West of Welch, with rumors of the fire running through the town like a virus. It was an extended game of telephone, with details shifting and morphing with each retelling. Neighbors and friends began to show up with whatever they had to offer to help. But for Lorene, the only question was what the sheriff's office was doing to search for the girls. Perhaps they had escaped and were hiding. Perhaps they were hurt and not far from the home. . . . Perhaps it was something worse.

From behind the yellow tape, Welchans stood atop the beds of their pickups and the wheels of their tractors. With a snap of a finger, they could hightail it into gear and swarm the place if commanded to. Some even picnicked at the edge of the property, mouths wet with sweet tea and gossip. In the space of a few short hours, there wouldn't be a person left in town who hadn't heard about the fire.

It didn't take long for people to suspect that Danny had finally gone off the deep end.

At around eleven, there was a tangible shift at the scene when OSBI agent Steve Nutter finally arrived. He was a tall, slightly stocky, owl-eyed man with wavy silver hair, known for sporting a ten-gallon hat and pointed cowboy boots. He came from the Ottawa County Sheriff's Office (OCSO), the next county over, where he was working on another case. Shortly after his arrival at the Freeman property, the investigation passed from the CCSO into the hands of the OSBI, with the CCSO only assisting from then on out. Nutter cast his eyes over the glowing embers in the front yard, looking back to the Welch Volunteer Fire Department, whose members had stuck around to make sure the fire remained contained.

Agent Nutter found Undersheriff Mark Hayes and CCSO investigator Charlie Cozart standing off to the side, speaking at a whisper. When he approached them, Hayes said, "We have a problem," and cited the bad blood between the Freemans and the CCSO that had formed in that past year. Mark Hayes was mousy but bright-eyed, as though welcoming anyone who made eye contact, a forty-year-old black-haired man with a thick mustache and round silver-rimmed glasses. To his side was Cozart, a brute of a man with his forearms decorated in tattoos, a wild mane on his face, and a near-finished smoke in his teeth at most any given time. "This has bullshit written all over it," Charlie observed, his chest inflated with apprehension as he put his cigarette out at the crime scene.

The townspeople's curiosity was beginning to spill over into impatience and anger, none of them strangers to the friction between family and county that had commenced upon the death of the Freeman son, Shane, earlier that year. They shouted questions from the driveway, demanding answers about who was inside the trailer and whether it was arson or an accident. Sighing, Nutter instructed the deputies to move the perimeter farther back, but that only sparked further irritation from the crowd and soon their voices grew louder, calling for more family and friends to join them, to watch the events unfold at the Freeman farm.

"Where is my child?" Lorene shouted to Nutter.

"Ma'am, you have to let us do our job. We're the experts," he answered.

"What about the cars?" the Bibles shouted. "Have any of you thought to look in their cars? What if they're in the trunks?!"

Nutter met the question with silence, in thought. He blushed and cleared his throat, moving swiftly toward his team; perhaps that was next on his list anyway. Hours after arriving on the scene, the OSBI commanded deputies to inspect the cars. Kathy's, Danny's, and Lauria's were all accounted for, and while nothing was noted in the trunks, Lauria's car keys were still in the ignition (not a terribly unusual thing for rural Oklahoma).

It wasn't the only thing overlooked, as Nutter and a couple of others on behalf of the OSBI also didn't thoroughly search the trailer. Not a piece of furniture was turned over; not a smudge of ash appeared on their clothes.

"The girls could have been hidden under a bed, for all they knew," Lorene tells me. "They didn't let any of us near the trailer, but they didn't do a thing themselves."

Meanwhile, Assistant District Attorney Clint Ward made a guest appearance at the scene. He was a well-built man with a crew cut and deep-set eyes, overly starched in a suit and tie, a politician down to the bone. He was only days away from leaving his position as the ADA before entering private practice with the new year. According to witnesses, he was seen and heard telling several Welchans, "Danny owed a lot of money in drug debt." Even before the investigators would wrap up, the notion that the murder and the fire were drug-related arson began to gain traction quickly, and according to several on the scene, it started with Clint Ward.

But when I first spoke to Clint Ward, he stated that he "thought Danny went off the deep end," admitting that Danny was a "loose cannon" and the "prime suspect." When asking about the rumors of drugs that would swirl around the case, Clint stated that he "didn't know Danny was into drugs," contradicting the accounts of firsthand witnesses I had on record. Clint Ward said that he thought that Danny "burned the place down and had taken the family elsewhere," when he observed the crime scene that first day.

"There was nothing to suggest that this was related to drugs," said Danny's stepbrother, Dwayne Vancil. "But this was all part of the conspiracy that started to transpire." And then, that first day at the crime scene, Danny's words kept replaying. *If anything happens to me or my family, anything, look to the Craig County Sheriff's Office.*

Arriving late at the scene due to a four-fatality accident that had held her up, Medical Examiner Donna Warren showed up at about three thirty. She disappeared into the debris, where the wall of the master bedroom still stood precariously upright.

The head of the waterbed pressed against the southern wall, with the upper body of the deceased female lying facedown across the bed with her head pointing west and feet pointing east. Her knees were off the bed, slanted, while the remains of her feet were on the floor. The waterbed had exploded and preserved the front of her body so it stayed mostly unburned, but the back side was charred. Her nightgown was also burned away.

The Bibles grew increasingly agitated outside and began to resist staying put with the rest of the onlookers. After a few choice words, the OSBI allowed only Dwayne Vancil and Lauria's father, Jay Bible, to search down near the crick to see if there was any trace of the girls. Agent Nutter permitted them to do so, provided they kept a certain distance from the crime scene.

At four o'clock, the body was hauled out by deputies and placed in the back of a white hearse that contrasted with the blackened home behind it. At the sight of the body bag, silence fell briefly.

But the silence didn't last long, and the bystanders began to rev back up in no time. In the crowd, ME Donna Warren sought out Lorene's face. They'd known each other, as Warren had once been Lorene's mother's primary physician, and Lorene waved her over.

"Who is that?" Lorene demanded in reference to the body inside.

Warren swallowed and leaned into Lorene's ear. "It's a woman who's bore children. And there's a wedding ring on her finger."

This confirmed for Lorene that the body in the house in fact did belong to Kathy Freeman.

"And you're sure that there's no one else in there?" Lorene searched for confirmation.

"That's what they're saying."

It should have offered relief, but it instilled in Lorene only a sense of panic she'd never let show.

Shortly after four o'clock, as dusk began to encroach, the burned body of Kathy Freeman was driven away from the premises and headed west with the sun toward Tulsa. Agent Steve Nutter wrapped up the investigation and called it to an end. He released the scene to Danny's stepbrother, Dwayne Vancil, and handed him a search warrant for the residence at around five o'clock, signed by Judge H. M. "Bud" Wyatt. The property, described in the search warrant as the "charred remains of a mobile home," was now out of the hands of the investigating officers and in the hands of the Freemans' next of kin. The warrant had been signed at 2:06, an hour and a half before the medical examiner even arrived at the crime scene and two hours before Kathy's body was removed.

"We're done," Nutter said to Dwayne as he started to leave.

"What do you mean, you're done?" Dwayne demanded.

"There's nothing else that can be done here," continued Nutter. "Listen, some neighbor reported Danny driving through a gate with the girls in his white pickup truck over where the pond's at."

Dwayne was surprised—that was where Danny and he had been raised, but Danny's vehicle had been accounted for. "Well, then, I'll go up there and look for him," Dwayne suggested. "Won't do him any good if I have authorities with me. I'll be able to talk to him if he has the girls."

"No, no, it's dark," answered Nutter. "We're liable to get someone hurt tonight. Why don't you run up there in the morning and see if he's there, and then you can call me if he is?" Agent Nutter went on his way.

It was interesting to me that based on what the OSBI knew at the time, they'd be so quick, not just to wrap up the investigation, but to hand it over to someone who could potentially have been a suspect.

Seeing that Nutter was on his way out that night, the Bibles approached him. "What about the girls? Aren't you going to search for them?"

"If Danny's got the girls, then it's just best that we let him cool off," Nutter told them. "It's getting late. We'll look for them tomorrow."

One of my sources in law enforcement tells me that at the time, he feared Danny was actually hiding out there in the shadows or the trees, watching it all unfold with a high-powered rifle. This transpires as a common thread: a number of police officers believed that Danny was more than capable of an ambush on authorities, and it clearly unnerved them, this image of Danny, bitter in the shadows, white-knuckling a firearm with each one of them in his sights. Even before the events of that night, they all knew he wasn't a man you wanted to be up against.

Dwayne turned to Sheriff George Vaughn, Undersheriff Mark Hayes, and ADA Clint Ward with tears of indignation in his eyes and said, "If in fact you think that Danny did this and you think he's up there waiting on you with the girls, holding them captive, you all better get yourselves locked up on the top floor of the courthouse, because as sure as anything, Danny will be coming to kill you. If he did all this, there is no doubt in my mind." Anger coiled around Dwayne's sternum. After all, it was no secret that his stepbrother had long taken issue with the authorities and how they'd handled his son's death and the subsequent investigation that past year.

The officers exhaled and began to recede, and the gold of the sun darkened to its last spit, like a flame cut off from oxygen. Winter squeezed what was left of the day from December 30, and still, no first attempts had been made to find the girls, beyond a brief check of the stream out back by Dwayne and Jay Bible. After the cops disappeared into the night, several men brought their geldings and began to comb the property via horseback. The lone headlights of several four-wheelers swept the dark undulating pastures in the distance, the echoes of men calling for Danny and the girls emanating from the shadows.

Fear could have paralyzed any parent at this point, shrouded by night without an inkling of where to look—the sudden hollowing of a person's soul brought on by helplessness and shock and grief and fear. But not them. Not the Bibles.

The OSBI made appointments to meet with Lorene and Jay that evening, penciling them in to reconvene at the sheriff's office in Vinita between six thirty and seven thirty.

But unbeknownst to the Bibles, as they stayed behind and formed their own search with what little light was left, was the tip that had been called in. It was the first viable lead and the only one for authorities to go on. The man who called it in was an acquaintance to most in the area. He called the law and claimed that he had seen Danny Freeman at a gas station, filling up a white Ford pickup with the two girls in the truck. "Danny isn't going to give the girls back," the man told dispatchers. "He won't give them back until you give him the man who killed his son."

It was the only lead they had—but the OSBI insisted they wait until morning to pursue it.

Darkness fell too fast for the families, leaving the hills of the prairie black and blind. The smell of the smoke chained itself to the night, and nothing much could be done until the first, agonizing break of day. It felt far. So, acting on what he learned from Nutter, Dwayne Vancil went to the old cabin where he and his siblings were raised, hoping to spot Danny, knowing that if anyone could calm him down, it was he. Jay and Lorene went to their scheduled interviews.

The lobby of the sheriff's office in Vinita was full of people, the smell of fire stuck in their flannel and their eyes open but tired. Authorities split them up into groups before interviewing them individually, questions aimed at Danny's affairs. *Who have you seen come in and out of there? Did you ever witness Danny doing drugs? Did you ever see Mr. Freeman with large amounts of cash on hand?*

"Our hands were tied," Lorene says to me. "They questioned all of us individually. They asked us about Danny's dealings, what kind of stuff he was into, and that's it. All we could ask was, 'What are you doing to find the girls?' They said they were working on it, that they were making plans to, but they didn't. Nobody was searching for the girls but my family. The authorities were done with the case." According to Jay and Lorene Bible, Agent Nutter later informed them that he was in the process of entering the girls' information into the National Crime Information Center (NCIC).

Years later, Nutter would tell me, "I believe the sheriff's office put out a missing-persons report immediately."

It was here that authorities told the Bibles that their prime suspect was Danny Freeman, informing them that it was their belief that Danny kidnapped the girls and was now holding them hostage. Of course, this notion had stirred in all their minds throughout the day.

The night ended with more questions than answers. Imagine the shock for a family without any information. The sickness in their stomachs swirling and sleep an impossibility without knowing what had happened to their daughter and her best friend. Each minute that passed was an unbearable strain, their faces numb with distress. It was a wonder a person could muster the strength to breathe, let alone take over the investigation— but that's exactly what Lorene Bible was about to do.

8

THE PRIME SUSPECT

December 31, 1999
The Morning After the Fire

It was the last day of the millennium. The pink morning light appeared to create a film upon the cold creek, while roosters perched themselves on the Kansas state line, announcing the new day. But for Lorene and Jay Bible, daybreak came like the pains of childbirth. Their skin still tingled with shock after a night of being relentlessly interrogated by OSBI agents in Vinita and fighting with them to get out there and look for the girls. And now it had been over twenty-four hours since Danny, Ashley, and Lauria had vanished, and still, not a single attempt had been made by authorities to search for them.

The married couple made their way up the driveway toward what little was left of the Freeman home, shaky arm in shaky arm, with sunrise to their right. They were intent on sifting through the earth for their daughter one grain at a time. Sleep was far from them; steadfastness took the wheel. A dutiful wife, a father in mourning, a sporty girl doing her best, and a playful friend who loved life, all gone, with nothing to show for it but a blister in the earth.

Lorene and Jay reached the top of the driveway, where the now open crime scene climbed into view. There wasn't a marker or a streamer of yellow left behind. "Where the hell is the crime scene tape?" Lorene wondered out loud.

Looking around, Jay answered, astonished, "They left this all wide open." All remnants of law enforcement had disappeared, a lull in the hottest stage of an investigation. All the while, it was assumed, Danny—a man who'd lost his grip on reality—was out there with Lauria and Ashley, his hostages, bunkered in the wooded area, waiting for the police to hand over the man who'd killed his boy in exchange for the girls. The familiar rafter of turkeys arose, hungry without Danny to feed them.

While Lorene retained her stone composure, Jay handled himself differently. Over the years, he'd bubble over at the seams, eyes spilling every time he talked about his little girl. Where his wife always had her footing and found her place in the investigation, Jay felt at sea from the beginning.

"Come daylight, we're figuring there's going to be a SWAT team going up here," Jay tells me of that second morning. "That we're going to find out where this cabin is and see whether Danny's got the girls or not. And that didn't happen." Hopes for action were replaced with the singing prairie wind and the smell of fire.

Up the road, Dwayne Vancil had waited all through the night at the cabin where he and Danny were raised. It was being used as a hunting cabin, where a man and his two young sons were up early to hunt deer. To Dwayne's disappointment, there was no sign of his stepbrother or the girls. Compared with Lorene's self-control and Jay's grief, Dwayne expressed his urgency in the form of rage. Getting back in his car to meet the sunrise at Welch, he huffed hard from his nostrils. "Where the hell are you, Danny?"

Back at the scene, Jay walked carefully around the yard, where the barn cats played with a part of an unrecognizable something. The feral mixed breeds added a little life to the property, which was otherwise still in the frostbite of morning, hungover from the events of the day before. When he heard Ashley's Rottweiler, Sissy, whimper from where the house once stood, Jay turned to her. "I know, girl. I know." Upon inspection, there was a large, fresh knot above Sissy's brow, stained with dried blood. Jay wished then that Sissy could talk, could point them in the right direction. The dog let out a low cry, standing now in the same spot where the master bedroom had stood, where the body of Kathy Freeman had been removed in a black plastic body bag less than a day before. (Eventually, Sissy would be adopted by distant friends, only to be put down after attacking and killing their chickens.)

The Freeman trailer stood on axles and wheels, and most of the flooring had fallen through to the ground, except for the master bedroom. There, the flooring was mostly intact. "That waterbed had burst and soaked all the carpet and stuff there," explains Jay. As a result, the master bedroom was more preserved than the other rooms, and Jay tiptoed around the debris, "looking for any pile of ashes big enough to be a human body folded up in a fetal position." A brown rug lay in tatters in the corner, and the air was cold and damp.

Lorene squatted down at a separate part of the trailer, overturning pieces of wood and other debris. The smell of death still lingered, and the cold found its way to the roots of her hair. Into Lorene's ears, the gentle sound of the creek water ran slow, unsuitably calming. In the ashes, a framed wedding photo of Danny and Kathy.

With Sissy at his leg, Jay surveyed the unburned floor of the master bedroom. He found what he described as something that looked like a bowl of hamburger meat. "I thought, *Wait a minute.*" He hesitated, squinting down at it. "Lorene?" he called out.

Lorene rose from the broken glass and soot, ashes wet from the fire hoses. She commanded her knees not to buckle as she reached her husband. Following his gaze, her whole body braced for impact as her eyes alighted on a second body. The sight took their breath away.

At about this time, the sun made its first appearance, still cold on their faces as they peered down. They then stared at each other, dumbstruck. "How the hell did the police miss this?" Lorene breathed. It had taken them less than a minute to stumble across a second body. Every theory about how Kathy had died, and every theory about why Danny took the girls, faded for a moment. Shocked by the sight of the burned body, Jay turned away and stared into the rising sun. "We have to call the sheriff's office," he said, unaware that he was crying until his words hit the air. By his feet, the barnyard cats continued to play with what he saw, bringing his gaze back to the ground, was in fact a human nasal bone.

The feet of the second corpse were almost under the corner of the waterbed, partly concealed by the deflated mattress, and the upper body was partially covered by a carpet. While the cause of Kathy's death remained unknown, and was still generally thought to have been a brick or bricks, the cause of this person's death was evident to Jay and Lorene. "We knew right away that they were shot in the head, so we figured Kathy must have died this way too." Years later, Lorene says to me, "Nothing from the jaw up. It was all gone." What was left of the head was in the doorway, faceup, an arm propped up in the doorframe, and cowboy boot prints largely believed by both the Bible and Freeman families to be those of OSBI agent Steve Nutter were clear on the torso (the families assert that Nutter was the only person on the scene wearing cowboy boots). The fire had burned much of the charred body's clothes right off to expose the genitalia, so they were immediately able to tell it was the body of a man. On top of that, the metal wiring used to reconstruct the sinus cavities sprouted from what remained of the face and skull.

Within moments of arriving on the scene, Lorene and Jay Bible discovered what authorities had managed to miss the day before: the body of their prime suspect, Danny Freeman.

9

DAY TWO AND THE BBI

December 31, 1999
The Morning After the Fire

I have hung the autopsy reports of Danny and Kathy on a nerve in my brain that acts as a clothesline; I can mentally see the outlines of the ME's body diagrams like paper dolls. The diagrams are scribbled on with the examiner's pen, representative of where charring was present all over the bodies, tighter ink lines at the heads, where the skulls were destroyed and mostly gone. Because she died in 2004 of cancer, I would be unable to interview Medical Examiner Donna Warren about her examination and findings. But I sleep through mornings and spend rainy afternoons reading over the external examination of Danny Freeman, which would be written days after the fire. Based on the ME's evidence, it was deemed that just prior to his death, Danny's right collarbone was broken, and the shotgun blast entered under the left side of his jaw by the third molar.

Also telling was evidence brought in with Danny on a separate cart that included pieces of men's brief underpants, portions of the waistband of sweatpants, a shirt, some remnants of sneakers, and part of his upper jaw.

It was soon learned that Kathy had been shot in the head from behind, while Danny was believed to have been shot while facing his killer. Both were dead before the fire started. This is precisely what Jay and Lorene Bible came across when showing up at the Freemans' burned trailer to look for clues about their daughter's whereabouts.

Lorene and Jay raced up the road, incapable of finding a signal on their cell phone near the trailer (few in 1999 even had cell phones, though Lorene had bought one the evening before in light of the events, a phone whose number hasn't changed in twenty years). After driving one mile south, they made it through to 911. From there, they waited for the CCSO to arrive, and this time, the Bibles decided they were taking control. No more waiting for authorities to search for the girls. No more standing back behind the yellow tape while deputies sat there and watched the home cool off. No more trust.

"There's a body here," Lorene said to dispatchers.

"How do you know that?"

"Well, there's a body."

"You're at the Freemans'?"

"Yes. We're at the Freemans'."

This is the part where I can safely say that the shit hit the fan.

Deputy Troy Messick, who'd delivered the news of the fire to Lorene the day before, was already at the office in Vinita, and he'd be the first to arrive back at the crime scene. He left his coffee and sped over to the Freemans'. Once there, in reference to the OSBI, he commented the same thing to Lorene and Jay that was already on their mind. "How the hell did they miss this? I thought they were supposed to be the experts."

Wary of locals listening over their police scanners, and they surely did, Messick spoke carefully into his radio when he called in to confirm the body, nearly dumbstruck with disbelief. "What I was sent out to do is confirmed."

"Can you repeat that?"

"What I was sent out here to do is confirmed."

Back at the property, as Deputy Messick called in for backup, Jay found Danny's two front teeth still attached to the gum but detached from the jaw in the grass of the front yard, where the outdoor cats continued to chew at his bones. "Animals had been eating on his body. That's how gruesome it was, you know," says Jay. "But that started day two for us."

At around this time, Dwayne Vancil, who had failed to glean any clues as to Danny's whereabouts from the hunting family up at the cabin, returned to the property. He was waved over by the Bibles and found himself looking down at his stepbrother's body in the wreckage. "I felt like I knew right away what'd happened here," said Dwayne. "Danny told me where to look if something happened to him. Well, it did, didn't it?"

The CCSO returned between seven and seven thirty a.m.—I imagine a little red-faced—and began to cordon off the area once again with crime scene tape. From there, they called the OSBI back and waited. Aware of the scrutiny this monumental oversight would undoubtedly bring to the bureau, OSBI agent Steve Nutter returned with ten to twelve more agents in tow to oversee the rest of the investigation.

Deputies asserted that what they were doing was going to be a repeat of the day before.

"Oh, no, it won't be!" Lorene exclaimed. Despite several attempts to clear the Bibles from the scene, Lorene was having none of it. "I ain't leaving here today, boys. You can tie your tape to the mirror of my vehicle, but we're not moving. I'm not going to be in your back pocket today. I'm going to be in your front pocket. We're not leaving here until we know that this place has been searched thoroughly this time."

The OSBI objected, trying to explain to her that she needed to let them do their job.

If maybe for the first time, Lorene raised her voice. "I stood down that road yesterday and let you do your job. There were *nine* of you who told me that y'all were one hundred percent sure that there wasn't another body in here. So we're not leaving till we take this sucker to the ground."

When the OSBI continued to try to affirm their authority, she stubbornly reminded them that they'd already released the crime scene over to Dwayne the evening before. "You had your day. Now it's mine."

From here, it seemed that every man, woman, and child in town came to aid the Bibles in their crusade to find the girls. By nine o'clock, they were already lining the driveway leading up to the trailer, waiting on the Bibles' command to storm the trailer, like lightning waits for God's permission to strike.

Medical Examiner Donna Warren arrived late, having been held up at yet another fatal car accident. Wide-eyed, she came onto the Freeman property for the second time in twenty-four hours. "What the hell happened here?" she asked one of the deputies. "Who found the body?"

The deputy hung his head and pointed at Lorene, who only stared back at Warren in the fixed-gaze demeanor that makes Lorene the imposing figure that she is.

"This is bad," said Warren. "This is real bad."

No gun was found within reaching distance of Danny, ruling out any suspicion of a murder-suicide. Soon after, his body was removed. At this, the Bibles sprang into action.

God Himself couldn't have stopped Lorene from going into the crime scene. She figured that any evidence left behind would have surely been destroyed by the fire. And since authorities failed to find an entire body in the small trailer, she couldn't trust them to find anything relevant, anything that might point them in the direction of the girls. It was now up to the families. Agents from the OSBI and deputies of the CCSO, about twenty-five in total, stood back as Lorene took over the crime scene, along with approximately a hundred fifty volunteers under her command storming the trailer: distant relatives and high school friends of the girls, neighbors and strangers alike. Even staff from the local funeral parlor came, erecting a canopy tent about fifty feet from the trailer to hand out sandwiches and drinks.

"It was a sideshow," Lauria's cousin Lisa admits. "There were so many people there who helped us, but not everyone. Some were just nosy, even letting their kids run around. I even remember people calling out mothers not to let their three- or four-year-old kids let loose to find another body, God forbid." Some even came and parked on the property just to watch it all unfold, refusing to help at all.

For the first time in recent memory, Welch came to life. The resistance to authority brought on by Lorene, Jay, and Dwayne spread through the residents like a fever. They came by horseback and tractor, insulated in their flannels and with cups of breakfast blend to pepper the dirty blond prairie. Locals withstood the cold and the chaos, restless in spirit and in mind. They came with thermoses of coffee to keep alert those who'd stayed long, and others came with bottles of water to wash the taste of char from their mouths.

The many agents of the OSBI watched, contained, like boys kicked out of their classrooms, their buttonlike eyes lined at the sidelines of the crime scene. The family directed neighbors to rip out the floorboards until hitting the air between the trailer and the ground. A line of nearly one hundred people formed down the long driveway, equipped with makeshift sieves, an assembly line to receive handfuls of clumpy ash, sifting for something, anything, that could be a clue. Many bones from the animals whose heads were mounted on the Freemans' walls were found in the debris. They didn't know exactly what they were looking for; they were hoping only to recognize it when they found something.

With her face blackened by wet ash like war paint, Lorene overheard one of the agents say that she was letting everyone destroy the crime scene.

"It can't be messed up any worse than you did yesterday," she called over her shoulder. "So if you're going to be a part of this, you're just going to have to do it our way." Lorene went through the larger pieces of rubble first: what remained of the couch, the chairs, the icebox. If the girls had been lost in the fire, they were going to find them, come hell or high water. While Lorene stood as the head of the crime scene, Jay and Dwayne were a two-man command center working from the Freemans' yard, where they organized a grid search on the forty-acre property, including volunteers who came via horseback, some even taking their canoes to the creek in the back. It took all that they had not to rip off their own skin out of sheer determination, urgency, and frustration.

"Look no further than right there," said Kathy's mother and stepfather, who'd sat in their parked Astro van at the end of the driveway, looking up at the action. They locked their eyes on the men in uniform, and burst out in abrupt accusation. "They're the ones who did this, and they're all going to burn in hell for it too." But few seemed to mind the couple, who'd always been known for barking like crows, made of wild tales and batty superstitions.

Dwayne kept an eye on Sissy the Rottweiler, who went to the end of the driveway several times and howled in only one direction, where the road met the driveway to create a T intersection. It was assumed, and accepted today, that the lump with the dried blood on top of Sissy's head was the result of the butt of a shotgun. Even as he organized the searches, Dwayne became convinced that the girls must have traveled in the direction of Sissy's whimpers. As a regular visitor to the Freeman home, he also recognized that something was missing from the house—the hundreds of arrowheads and their cases, absent from the walls, along with several buckets full of other arrowheads and tomahawks.

I ask Dwayne if he thinks the arrowheads could have been the motive. "I think they were more of a trophy," he answers.

Lorene and her volunteers cut the axles on the trailer, and together, they pulled the entire home apart. It would take several more days, but there wasn't a piece of ash any bigger than a small stone that went unturned. Later in the afternoon of that second day, Lorene found her daughter's purse at the north wall, where Ashley's bedroom (formerly Shane's) used to stand. Inside the purse, Lauria's ID and Christmas cash, totaling about two hundred dollars. She also found Lauria's partly burned pajama top in the remnants of Ashley's bedroom, which suggested to her that the fire had started prior to Lauria and Ashley's getting ready for bed, or that someone made them change out of their pj's into something else.

Family and volunteers also found thirteen guns belonging to the Freemans, placing them out in the front yard, one by one. It occurred to everyone that any one of the guns could have been the murder weapon, but on the front lawn they'd stay for at least a week, none of them collected as evidence by the agents or officers nearby.

The possibility of one of the guns being the one used to kill Kathy and Danny remains unexamined today.

Evening was closing in; damned be the short nights of winter. But the Bibles refused to let darkness threaten their efforts to find the girls. Thanks to the Rural Electric Cooperative, a nonprofit electricity producer owned and operated by the people of northeastern Oklahoma, lights were hung around the property to make this little corner of the pitch-black countryside sparkle and glow through the night next to the veils of the plains. Another local brought light plants, illuminating the property like the football fields of local Friday night lights.

Once again, at the close of day, the authorities left.

While the world celebrated the new millennium, and Y2K turned out to be a lemon, the search for the girls at the Freeman property continued into the third day, and into the year 2000. Far from the confetti and noisemakers and hangovers, Welch became a well-oiled machine, functioning without sleep, too distracted to acknowledge the world's ringing in of New Year's Day.

Jay Bible said the good Lord put it in his heart to call the radio station and appeal for help, and because of it, there were nearly five hundred volunteers on the scene that third morning. This time, the grid search expanded to a five-mile radius, with Jay and Dwayne delegating small groups to different sections of the property. Each small thing they stumbled on was marked by volunteers, who'd shout out for word to get back to Jay and Dwayne so that they could collect the evidence themselves. It was the family, and not law enforcement, who laid down the evidence markers.

That morning, there was no sign of law enforcement returning at all.

In the afternoon, Lorene enlisted the help of a family friend to make missing-persons posters for both Lauria and Ashley at their office supply house. After picking the flyers up, Lorene drove to an acquaintance down at the Vinita Police Department to confirm that the girls had been properly entered into the databases of the NCIC, as OSBI agent Nutter said he would on the evening of December 30.

"The girls aren't in here," the acquaintance replied after pulling up the database on her computer.

"That's impossible," answered Lorene. "Steve Nutter said that he was submitting all the info. You mean to tell me there's no alert out there for them? No one is out there looking for the girls?" For Lorene, it was another dispiriting sign that she was on her own, that law enforcement was not acting in the best interests of her missing daughter. "Well, what the hell do I have to do to get the girls in there and their faces out there?"

The acquaintance advised Lorene that she had to go to the sheriff's office herself, that she'd have to sign for Lauria, and that there would have to be a next of kin there to sign for Ashley. At that, Lorene stepped outside the station and called Celesta, pleading with Kathy's mother to go to the sheriff's office and sign for her granddaughter.

Kathy's mother, Celesta, and stepfather, Bill Chandler, were an unusual couple. They kept to themselves, isolated in the nameless outskirts of Vinita with dozens of cats and dogs in a small trailer, which you could smell from the road. The couple was paranoid, perhaps rightfully so, given their family's history, but it went further than that. Years later, they tell me about the helicopters that nearly crash into their house each week and the devices in their walls. They would stay half-dressed throughout the day and scan the skies for spying planes. When I sat outside with them for several hours one particularly hot afternoon, Bill spent the entire interview spraying hundreds of flies with some household chemical spray. It was because of this paranoia that Celesta initially refused to cooperate with

Lorene and sign for Ashley to be entered into the NCIC database. "She was screaming and hollering, like she always does," said Lorene. "But I told her I didn't care what she thought, that she just needed to get here." With Lorene not taking no for an answer, Celesta submitted, meeting Lauria's mother at the sheriff's office to sign for Ashley. The girls then were officially entered into the database and listed as missing.

Lorene raced back to the Freemans', and handed out the flyers to various individuals and groups who ventured on out of Welch to circulate the girls' faces as far and wide as they could. At this point, local media started gathering. The girls' school photos started to adorn telephone poles and storefront windows. Large magnets with their faces were affixed to the sides of interstate trucks. Phone booths displayed the flyers.

A couple unaffiliated with the police came with a pair of scent dogs and offered to help. Led by their owners, the dogs started at Lauria's pajama top and Ashley's pillow up by the trailer and hightailed it down the driveway. Everyone on the scene stopped what they were doing for that heart-stopping moment, spinal fluid like ice water at the sight of the bloodhounds chasing the smell of the girls. The hounds went fast, skimming their snouts across the cold ground and past hundreds of volunteers. At the end of the driveway, they turned in one direction and sped along the edge of the property. It was the same direction in which the Rottweiler Sissy had howled. At a ford in the stream, floodwater from the creek forced the dogs to stop. At the water's edge, the dogs continued to look on, barking and howling, noses pointed in one direction.

On that third day, at about four p.m., Agent Steve Nutter arrived on the scene to check in. He was described as strutting from his car with his white ten-gallon hat and cowboy boots, looking more like an oil tycoon than an agent for the OSBI, and he asked Lorene, "So, what'd you all get done today?"

She didn't take to his smugness. "We've done a grid search five to ten miles out. We've got people driving out there and getting the word out.

Now we're getting their faces out there with these flyers. *And* they're on the NCIC."

"That's because I put them in there."

"No, you didn't!"

"How do you know?"

"Because I went to town, and I had them look for me. And guess who wasn't in the system. I had to force Celesta Chandler down there to the sheriff's office and sign for Ashley while I signed for Lauria. That's how the girls got there."

Nutter's blood pooled in his face. "Well, no. I was about to," he stuttered.

Lorene gestured to one of the young cameramen to film Nutter as she began to give him a tongue-lashing. "This guy's getting you on tape. You did nothing, nothing, to find my child. Another day . . . they could be in Canada, in Mexico. Hell, they could be overseas at this point! You said you were going to enter the girls into the NCIC, but guess who did. *I did.*"

Years later, I'd get one of my law enforcement sources to pull up the missing girls on the NCIC databases, which aren't open to the public. The date of submission supported Lorene's timeline; they were entered into the system on January 1, 2000, three days after the fire. It did not align with Nutter's belief that the girls were entered into the system the night Kathy's body was found.

Among the hundreds of volunteers who came to aid in the search were two private investigators, named Tom Pryor and Joe Dugan, who'd heard of the murders on a local news program. Abandoning his trust in law enforcement, Danny's stepbrother, Dwayne, hired them on the spot, paying them one dollar to take on the case. The private investigators accepted.

Tom Pryor had been an investigator in law enforcement for twenty-eight years before running his own private company for fourteen, while his partner, Joe Dugan, was a bounty hunter and a friend of Pryor's for thirty years. They referred to themselves as a dynamic duo, also sporting ten-gallon hats. As soon as they went on the clock, they joined the search party and began combing the property. At the end of the driveway, about fifty feet from the road, Tom Pryor came across a car-insurance-verification card, one belonging to a woman who sounded familiar to no one. Studying the card, Pryor glanced around him; it didn't seem to have come from the ashes, and it was far enough from the trailer that it struck him as peculiar. PI Pryor had been at this game a long time, and the insurance card of an unknown female this close to a rural road might be nothing—or it might be something.

Pryor walked back up the incline of the driveway, past the dogwoods and bois d'arcs where Ashley and Lauria had collected food for the goats only days before, and asked around for who was in charge, at least on an official level. After a moment, he found Agent Steve Nutter. Introducing himself, Pryor held out the card. "This might be of some interest to you. Might be nothing, but every little thing counts in these things, don't they?"

Nutter looked down at Pryor, curling his lip. "Why don't you leave this investigation to the big boys, eh?"

"Well, I just thought—"

"We don't need any PIs coming around here, screwing things up for us. Keep it up, and I'll have your license revoked so fast, you won't even know what hit you."

At a loss, Pryor pulled out his wallet as Nutter turned and walked away. His partner, Joe Dugan, moved over toward him. "Whatcha got there?"

"I don't know," answered Pryor. "But I think we'll find out."

The days went on without any answers, and those days became weeks, became years, became decades. Today, there is no doubt in Jay's, Lorene's, or Dwayne's minds that Lauria and Ashley did not die in the fire.

Welch defrosted into springtime, there to distract its residents with its warmth and the seasonal obligations of its farmers. Life simply went on for everyone. Still, light didn't dim for the families who bound themselves to the pasturage of Welch. Their eyes stayed wide and their focus was kept narrow but far-reaching.

Almost two decades later, that's never changed, nor has the sealed-lipped land that offers no closure. But time continues on against their will. Time is something that people don't feel until it turns against them. Where it's thought to heal all, for the parents of any missing child it only tears the cut wider; sands of time become grains of salt to an open, bleeding wound.

I wonder after all this time, sixteen years later, if there is even anything that can be found.

SECTION 2

CORRUPTION

10

THE INITIAL THEORIES

Today

I have a defect of the mind. I love the same Lord that these people do, but this is what He gave me. It is a shadow that lurks on the sidelines of my mind, trailing me all throughout this research. It stalks. While fear finds me in Oklahoma, I'm not sure it's because of Oklahoma. I'm not talking about the word "panic," which is so often loosely thrown about today, but the paralyzing terror that makes you vomit where you stand and unable to speak. It is an inherited psychosomatic disorder only compounded by my immersion in a case filled with death and fire.

It is hell.

Forgive the sweats and shaking hands, or the mad dash to the closest bathroom to get sick, or my sitting without speaking until I can bring my heart rate back down. I begin to lose confidence, and if not for the wit that I just manage to keep, those closest to me will start to wonder if I'm back to old habits. Sure, I still miss the needle in my arm all these years later, but I fight to work with the demons at bay. Fighting, I'll learn much later, would be the very thing that encourages the shadows of my mind to lurk, ready to pounce without warning. Panic.

Working the case through this lens wasn't easy, but I'm a person who fixates; I'm not naturally designed to let go, and I'm shit at multitasking. So off to Oklahoma I went, over and over (and over) again. *Isn't this the very definition of insanity?* And then I try to escape, ending back in the prairie, lost in prayer and surrounded by killers who aren't really there. Then the frustration of being able to see the wind but not the tangible flesh of the girls turns hope into bitterness and the earth's sweetness into decay, like the taste of blood when left too long on the tongue. I fix my gaze to the distance, off into the pecan groves ahead.

"Puh-cahn," Lorene Bible will forever correct my pronunciation of "pee-can." "It's puh-cahn. How many times will I have to tell ya?"

What the hell are my frustrations compared with those of a woman who has spent the past two decades searching for her daughter and her best friend? And then my sense of hopelessness becomes a sense of wonder. While the story of the girls' disappearance brought me here, it is a mother's plight that keeps me.

Over the next few years, I receive information in random bits, mostly due to the fact that it takes time for people to sit with me, to speak to me. "What is it that you do when you're in Oklahoma?" people ask me back home.

"Ninety-nine percent of my job is gaining trust," I say. "The other one percent is investigation, research, and sunblock."

The sun is so bright that my memories are in shades of hot white and platinum, and the nights so dark that it's like having amnesia. I don't know where the fuck to start.

"We don't say those kinds of cusses here."

"So what kind do you say?"

"Well, shit, I don't know."

These are not my people, and I am not theirs. But something keeps pulling at me to come here. It's an itch, a hunch, a fight with the husband. "We didn't even think you'd come," Lauria's cousin Lisa admits. I'm not the first person to show interest in writing their story. But now it's been sixteen years. . . . The girls have been missing for as long as they'd walked this earth.

Today, two prominent theories stand a foot above the rest: corruption and drugs, the Bibles believing the latter, two theories that have divided the two families since 1999. I will walk between them, edging along a great divide and listening with each ear. I have my days when I'll latch my hooks into one, and then I have days when I'll latch my hooks into the other. *"What's your theory, Jax?" "Depends on my mood."* It sometimes feels like a balancing act, an unsteady one that sends my brain spinning.

"Much of those first couple of weeks were just chasing up the leads of drugs and Danny's doing and dealing of drugs," Lorene contends. But in my talking to Lorene so many times, it's difficult to distinguish whether she's referring to marijuana or methamphetamine, as they seem synonymous to her. And while not even the Freemans dispute the fact that Danny was an avid grower and smoker of weed, the meth angle was thrown around loosely as being the route by which Danny brought trouble to his home . . . perhaps murder.

It bears noting, however, that no evidence of drug use was discovered at the crime scene, and I've never been convinced that meth had anything to do with the murders (though I remain open-minded). Furthermore, Danny's and Kathy's toxicology reports were never included with the autopsies I received from the state, which could have been indicative of whether or not the couple was actively using methamphetamine and/or marijuana. I was first told by the state that they'd been lost, as was the case for reporters before me, then later told that they were not subject to open record (they would be the only Oklahoma autopsy reports out of the two dozen I receive that don't come with toxicology).

This is something I also discuss when first meeting Wade Sherrick and his sons, the ranchers who lived at the end of the Freemans' road and who called 911 on the morning of the fire. "It was pretty well known," Wade concedes. "Cars would come back and forth this road, at all hours." On the long dirt road, between where the Sherricks and the Freemans lived, was a small, easy-to-miss, and rickety house that looked like something from the *Grapes of Wrath* era. I would pass the house countless times and hardly notice it exists, as do others. There is a total of only three residences on the road. "I'm not sure if the traffic was going there or to the Freemans', but we'd always heard rumors. Everyone here kinda knew about it."

"Do you know who lived at the other house?"

"No," they answer. "No idea."

While rumors of Danny's dealings in drugs have long circulated, and I will examine them closely throughout my work, they're usually assessed separately from the notion of cartel involvement, which pops up now and again. Back then the Mexican cartel had small influence in the county, where mom-and-pop meth labs still sprout around the mushroom farms of nearby Miami and Commerce, where many Mexican immigrants found employment starting in the early 1990s. But Lorene knows everything there is about this case, and she is quick to dismiss these.

"So, in your mind, do you have any doubts that the Mexican cartel could have been involved?"

"They weren't," Lorene answers.

"How do you know?"

"I have my ways."

Lorene's curtness is something that takes getting used to. She doesn't mince words, never slips. If there is something she doesn't want to answer, she'll stare into my eyes and meet me with silence, or never answer a text. There's never an *"I'd rather not say"* or *"No comment."* Just an arresting silence as impenetrable as her belief that Danny Freeman's dealings with drugs had everything to do with the murders.

"So how did the rumors of the cartel begin?" I ask.

"Danny's missing hand," she admits. "The rumor was that his hand was cut off"—like a signature, something telltale.

When I read Danny Freeman's autopsy report today, it is not possible to know exactly how his hand disappeared, whether by fire or with intent.

It did not, however, show up separately from Danny's body, with the other parts of his body rolled in on the cart, including a lower leg below the knee and the other foot, which were assumed to have been burned off, and parts of Danny's nasal bone and upper jaw, which were shot away.

"This is something the authorities looked into?" I ask.

"No, it was something that *I* looked into." She makes sure I know as much. "Like I said, the authorities were done with the case." It would take some time, and trust, but Lorene will eventually go on to tell me about her own encounter with the cartel in 2000. It was the dead of night when she and the small posse of people she'll never reveal rolled along the lifeless back roads just under the Kansan border in a pickup truck. No one spoke as she drove. They rode slowly, and everywhere around them was the shushing of switchgrass. She knew that somewhere nearby, a local cartel kingpin waited with his own posse for Lorene to arrive. She doesn't divulge how the meeting was set up, but Lorene parked the truck with steady hands. She and the man she was meeting, a well-known, violent drug dealer, kept the cars running and left their comrades behind as they exited their vehicles, walking toward one another in the brazen headlights. They came face-to-face, breath crystallizing in the cold night air.

"How do you know I won't kill you?" the kingpin asked as he tilted his head and scanned Lorene.

"How do you know I won't kill you?" she coolly responded, and it was a response that could only have come naturally from a woman like Lorene Bible.

The nocturnal intensity between them faded, however, once Lorene began asking him all the questions she had come equipped to ask. In the end, Lorene felt satisfied that the cartel had had nothing to do with the girls' disappearance. "That's not their nature. He told me so," Lorene tells me. "They'd have no qualms killing people over drug debt, but to abduct two girls as retribution would just be too risky for them."

And just like every other time I ask Lorene if she was scared in this situation, her answer is always the same, delivered with the familiar fixed stare. "Just another day I look for my daughter."

It is a sunny afternoon when I sit in a bright, air-conditioned office with now-retired OSBI agent Steve Nutter in the Northeast Regional Office of the OSBI in Tulsa, just an hour and a half southwest of Welch. With him is OSBI agent Tammy Ferrari, an attractive round-faced woman with long highlighted hair and a background in law enforcement; she's from Fort Smith, Arkansas, near the eastern Oklahoma border. Ferrari leads the investigation today, but speaks less than Nutter, not having been there for the initial stages of the 1999–2000 investigation that I'm here to discuss.

"This one was unique to me," starts Nutter, "because after you process the scene, which is the first thing that gets gone, you start looking for leads, and for the first week, there were no rumors in an entire county in Oklahoma about this homicide. None whatsoever. And generally speaking, in cases like this that I've worked in northeastern Oklahoma, I spend the first week or two just chasing down false rumors. That was what was very unique about this case."

This contradicts the information I have at hand, but it is not my objective to trip anyone up. I don't hunt witches, and I don't come just for the truth. I come for people's versions of the truth. I come for what some think I want to hear. I come for their lies. So when Nutter tells me that there were no rumors, I don't confront him with articles and with the statements of those who've said otherwise over the years. I never felt pressed to say, "Gotcha," and become some arrogant know-it-all, and I want to keep this line of communication open. If I call him out, he'll end this. Besides, lies can be just as revealing if you already know the God's-honest truth.

My list of theories didn't stop at the cartel. After Danny's body ruled him out as the prime suspect, and when murder-suicide was dismissed when no gun was found near him, one of the earliest theories was that Lauria and Ashley had killed Ashley's parents themselves. While this angle was largely dismissed by the family, especially since Lorene found Lauria's purse containing two hundred dollars inside, it continues to course slowly through website forums today: that the girls are playing out some happily ever after on the white sands of the Mexican Riviera, that they are criminal masterminds who had the stomach and the psychopathic streak to execute Danny and Kathy in such a violent fashion.

"Anything is possible," Nutter answers in response to the idea of the girls being killers. "But the Bible girl would have eventually called her mother. Their bond was so tight that she could not avoid calling. And when she didn't that first year, that told me she wasn't gone by her own volition."

Another theory that soon arose in those initial days was that it was a random passerby, though most agree that the Freeman trailer wasn't a place that one just stumbled upon. The trailer was too pushed back from the desolate road, a road you'd never come upon accidentally—anyone lost would have turned back in the direction from which they had come long before reaching there.

It's important that I look at these secondary theories before really tackling the angles of drugs and corruption, which survive imagination today. But the relatives of the Freemans remain vocal in their belief that this was a murder instigated by one or more employees of the sheriff's office, just as Danny had warned Dwayne Vancil in the days before his death. "Danny told us where to look," the Freemans say.

"There's been some speculation of possible drug use," interjects Agent Tammy Ferrari. She explains that it's not necessarily the case that the murders occurred because of drugs, but that many of the people with information over the years are or were active in the drug scene. "A lot of these people involved in drugs, they're turning up dead." But there's not much more the agents care to say on the topic.

When law enforcement failed to find the body of Danny, it only fueled for the Freeman relatives what they'd already suspected: that Danny was right about the sheriff's office being involved in the murders, that corruption was in all of it.

"The next day, when Danny's body was found, he was found under six to eight inches of ash," explains Nutter. "I and other people probably walked right by it a couple of times. And even after we dusted the ash off, you could not recognize it as a human body. That's the only explanation I have."

But this goes against the statements of the Bibles and Dwayne Vancil, who all saw Danny's intact corpse that morning. Nutter also seems to shift the blame of not finding the second body on two fire marshals who were at the crime scene prior to his arrival. "The fire marshal said that they had searched the debris and had found— The only thing they found had been a body located on a bed in what was later determined to be the bedroom of Danny and Kathy Freeman." And while the OSBI, the DA's office, and other branches of the law will spend years referencing an assumed fire marshal's report, no one can recall such an investigation taking place. What the families learned about the fire came largely from the information of a local retired fire marshal who went to the scene only after catching wind of the action, and he was not there in an official capacity. According to Nutter, and no one in the family has ever argued against this, gasoline was used as an accelerant to start the fire: arson.

"I can find no record of the December 1999 fire in Welch," said the state fire marshal's office in May of 2017. "Apparently we were not called to do an arson investigation."

In January 2018, I contacted the assistant state fire marshal himself. "I searched our records, and we did not investigate a fire in Welch, Oklahoma, on December 30, 1999. By state statute, the state fire marshal must be requested by the local fire chief, police chief, or sheriff's office to conduct a fire investigation. No such request was made to the state fire marshal's office."

Pressing once more for confirmation in the fall of 2018, I requested some further information and requested that they look into all dates, in case of some clerical error. Their response was a curt one. "Like the previous e-mail stated. We were not called to that fire."

According to family members' opinion, partly based on the hypothesis of the retired unofficial marshal, the path of the accelerant went around the kitchen table, was tossed into the living room, and set by the killer(s) at the woodstove just at the front door of the trailer. A later conversation saw a former volunteer from the department say with certainty that the accelerant started on Kathy's body. Without a report, I'll never know.

"I used to think I could handle anything," Nutter says toward the end of our meeting. "When I retired, I wanted to live in the country. Well, now, after I worked these years with the OSBI, I want to live in a town where if something happens, at least there'll be a witness."

With this, my meeting with Nutter and Ferrari concludes. It will be the last time I speak with either one of them on the record, and Nutter's last public interview.

I wanted to get a take from CCSO officers on the scene as well; however, no one wanted to speak with me those first couple of years—my interview with Nutter comes three years before I'd meet with then CCSO undersheriff Mark Hayes, who, in 1999, took serious issue with the way Nutter quickly abandoned the scene.

It's a biting January afternoon when I meet retired undersheriff Mark Hayes at his home, which has been creatively converted from a barn at the top of a hill in Big Cabin, Oklahoma. I'm so far in the country that my car stereo can't find a radio station, and a tinge of fear starts as a prickly sensation in my scalp—my anxiety is charging. Inside, his home is cozy, adorned with cuckoo clocks and old, rustic tools on the walls. A woodstove keeps us warm. He is kind and welcoming, and he doesn't mask his feelings toward Nutter. "There are a lot of great agents in the OSBI," Mark tells me. "And why and how we got this one will always be beyond me. Nutter started wrapping up the scene so fast, I said, 'How are you done already?' He told me there was nothing more that could be done, but that wasn't true. I even pointed out a shotgun shell right in the driveway. He shrugged it off." Hayes gives a dry laugh. "If you can't tell, I'm not a fan of Nutter."

It is the first time I hear about this shotgun shell, one referred to by Hayes as being "fresh." Then I think back to the thirteen guns never collected from the front lawn.

According to Hayes, Nutter rolled his eyes and told the others to bag the shotgun shell, "if it makes Hayes here happy."

"I'll tell you why Nutter *really* rubbed me the wrong way," Hayes continues. "He was acting like we were partners, like we were friends. But it didn't take long to realize that he wasn't being buddy-buddy with me. He was treating me as a suspect."

"Were you a suspect?" I ask.

"Sure, I was," he answers. "They made me and my brother take polygraph tests, asking us if we murdered Kathy and Danny, if we had anything to do with abducting the girls."

"And this was because of your previous dealings with Danny?"

"That's right." He nods. "From when my brother shot Shane."

I knew that, according to the Freemans, the killing of seventeen-year-old Shane Freeman lay at the heart of this story, and before I could examine the theories of drugs that continue to cumulate over the years, it was best to start on the boy who had been shot and killed less than one year prior by CCSO deputy David Hayes.

11

SON, SHANE FREEMAN

Less than a year before his parents' murders, seventeen-year-old Shane Freeman's hazel eyes matched the dusk of January 8, 1999, when he waited by the broken-down truck he had stolen a couple days before. Several Welchans, even though they knew he was wanted by police, stopped their cars as they passed, asking if he needed any help, upon seeing the truck was disabled, with one front tire pointing straight and the other pointing outward. "No, thank you; help is on the way," he politely answered them all with a nervous smile and with a storm stirring in his head. The chill locked the smell of cologne and gun smoke in the air around him, a smell you can still catch on Welch boys today. Shane inherited his handsome parts from his father, took with him that hand-me-down temper he never wanted. As he waited by the disabled truck west of Welch, about ten miles from the Freeman trailer, he waited for death, just minutes away, on the snow-dusted prairie.

I visit Kathy's parents on the outskirts of Vinita in 2017. Their trailer is tucked far back in the shade of coffee trees and surrounded by cattle ranches. In the front, by the road, a large sign that reads JUSTICE FOR THE FREEMAN FAMILY stands all these years later. As I walk up the driveway, I hear the blaring of daytime television. The door has nearly a dozen varieties of locks. Answering is a shirtless Bill Chandler, whose bald head is scabbed over and partially bleeding. Before I can finish introducing myself to him and explain who I am, Celesta pushes Bill out of the way. "It was the police who killed my family! They deserve to burn in hell," she barks, using both her hands to come down the steps of her home. Celesta is an elderly woman with an incomplete bottom row of teeth, and is braless in a matching gray sweatshirt and sweatpants on a hot day. "Shane might still be alive if Danny treated him better."

But she has her reasons for not liking Danny, reasons that include a 1985 assault and battery (misdemeanor) charge against Danny after he attacked Bill Chandler for accidentally mowing over Danny's marijuana plants. Despite this, Celesta was quoted in the *Joplin Globe*, a daily newspaper out of Joplin, Missouri, saying, "There was only one thing wrong with Danny, and that was his temper. He was one of those guys that would say things to Kathy and the kids both that hurt their feelings. But he wasn't a killer."

Sadly, Celesta and Bill go on to blame Shane's death on the White House, the ancient history of Ireland, and the Obama administration (though once Trump took office, they shifted their blame to him). The loved ones, the survivors of the Welch murders, are deteriorating as fast as their little, once prosperous farming towns. "The sheriff's office killed my whole family," Celesta repeats each time we speak. As we sit outside her trailer in a few flimsy lawn chairs, it's hard not to look at a blue 1985 Chevrolet pickup truck parked at the side of her trailer. "That's the one Shane took," she tells me. She doesn't have to explain it to me. I already know what she's referring to, just like she knows why I look at it.

"May I?" I gesture my desire to take a look at the truck.

"Go ahead."

Sitting alone in the pickup, I trace my fingers along the steering wheel, grip the blue leather, and begin to talk to Shane. I ask him what set him off, what made him run, what made him tick, what really happened in the moments before his death. There's something sacrosanct about sitting in the very spot that Shane, a boy I've spent years familiarizing myself with, panicked and fled in the days before his death. I breathe in the old leather; the truck still starts, and when I turn on the radio, a staticky gospel sermon plays. I try to find some rock and roll but end up with only fire and brimstone. I touch every part of the truck he would have touched, from the armrest to the door handle, trying to imagine what raced through his mind that night. I want to sit with him and watch.

Tell me what happened, I silently request of the dead.

It's easy to picture Shane in one of the many trucks he'd steal for joy-rides. Beer bouncing in the bed, midnight in a Midwestern summer, when the winds are warm and the skies spangled with stars bright enough that you swear to God you can hear them burn. He was five feet seven and a muscular 169 pounds, with short brown hair and a clean shave, garnished with a stud in his ear. The soft scrape of tires on dirt overpowered by the revving of a V-8 and a late-nineties song. With the dust sticking to his sweat, and cooling off under the condensation of a beer can, he rode off into the witching hours of Route 66. Scanning over one sleeping town after another, Shane had all the swagger of adolescent defiance, powered by hormones and adrenaline.

Among classmates, friends, and family, people's opinions differ in trying to peg just who Shane Freeman was. Perhaps his personality changed in the company of each one. He was the rebel without a cause, yet people were charmed somehow by his capacity for reckless abandon.

"Joy!" he once called out to a girl among a group of locals hanging out in the parking lot of the Pizza Hut in Vinita, his head and arm hanging from the driver's-side window. "I'm gonna marry you one day. You best believe it."

Another girl called back, "You said the same thing to me last week!"

"I did?" He smiled. "Dunno if I can make an honest woman outta you, though."

Despite the playful tales exhibiting Shane's charisma, others described him as shy and reserved. I get much of my information from Shane's best friend, Justin Green, an athletic man who has since moved out of state, though we talk often.

"Shane was very athletic. Funny, outgoing, when he didn't—how do I say this?—when he didn't have his family life on his mind," admits Justin.

"Shane was handsome as anything," most people I talk to will agree. "And he ran faster than anything." These are the two attributes that most remember him for today: dashing looks and tree-trunk legs. "He ran like you wouldn't believe, go hell for leather." And Shane seemed to know this much about himself. When watching the show *Cops*, he always commented on how he'd outrun them all.

"All the girls wanted him. They'd follow him anywhere he went," says Justin.

On many occasions, I drive to the godforsaken section of the country road where Shane died. Each sporadic passerby stops to see if I need help; then I ask about Shane. "Sure, I remember him," says one passerby. "The boy ran like lightning."

But rumors of Shane's home life are buzzed with whispers of a quick-tempered father and poverty. Shane gloried in rebellion, with a striking contempt for authority. "Let me ask you this," says Justin. "Wake up on a Saturday morning, and you have a choice: go fishing or hunting, or go play some basketball and meet some girls at the county fair? Shane would grab a basketball. Danny hated that."

In writing this book, I always hesitate over how best to faithfully describe Danny. As with Shane, there seem to be two sides to who Danny really was. No one ever argued that he didn't have a knee-jerk temper, but it appears to have come and gone, and there were periods of tenderness and calm too. Of the lightheartedness of his and Ashley's ambling through the pastures and gathering up every beautiful flower from the fields to sell. Of his soulful connection to the birds in the backyard. Of looking to the waxing moon as a sign of good fortune, before it doubled over into the crick.

But then there are the stories of Danny's anger. Justin Green alleged that one winter's day, when he and Shane had fallen asleep on Shane's bed, they were woken by Danny's closed fists raining down on them, and he called them faggots and cocksuckers. Waking into this red-hot reality, the boys, still in their pajamas, ran out of the back of the trailer while Danny stormed out of the room. When he returned, it was with a high-powered rifle. Danny ran outside and jumped into his pickup truck to chase the boys into the creek amidst a hurricane of homophobic slurs and profanity, shooting the gun in their direction as they braved the cold waters of the stream.

It was the very stream where Danny would later feed the wild turkeys and lament for his firstborn child.

The boys, shaking and cold in the creek, believed that Danny was prepared to kill them that morning.

Even Sheena, the friend of Lauria and Ashley who recounted the Rambo story to me earlier, said that Ashley confided in her, telling her that Danny had once thrown Kathy through a wall. "I wish I did something then," Sheena said.

But other friends contradict Danny's tales of horror. "I never saw anything like that," says one. "I always knew Danny as very kind. In fact, when I read something that I wrote at Shane's funeral, Danny just cried and held me."

During one visit to Welch, I visit Danny Freeman's friend Albert "Ally" Lynn at his farm. He talks about the kind of friend Danny was. "He was older than me. I was about nineteen," says Ally. Though he was closer to Shane's age, Ally describes Danny as the best friend he ever had. "One time, I came over from work, and I was tripping on acid." The friend laughs through his crying. "Danny, he was always tsk-tsking me. That's who I was. That's who he was. And we went on the pee-ro [pirogue] and went gigging that night. I was tripping. We loved doing those kinds of things together." Gigging, a sport found in the Ozarks. Many an evening could Danny and Ally be found smoking grass in a pee-ro, a flat, shallow watercraft. Ally would row from the stern while Danny took the bow, skimming across the black waters of the crick with a flashlight out back and through clouds of mosquitoes and the sparkle of lightning bugs, looking for the glowing orange eyes of frogs at the water's surface, before using a long prong to pierce through them, and bring them home to cook frog legs over the fire. "Sometimes we'd go out to where Shane died, just me and him, and he'd just cry and cry," Ally continues. "Before they died, me and my wife made plans with Danny and his wife to drink blue tarantula margaritas and light off fireworks on New Year's in memory of Shane."

Others who knew Danny, including Lorene Bible, said his rage stemmed from the time he accidentally shot himself in the head. "That muzzle in his forehead gave him some mean streak." The migraines kept his temper bubbling just beneath the surface.

"Shane wanted something better," says Justin. "He wanted to get as far away as he could so that he couldn't become his dad. I think that was his worst fear."

Like his sister, since their preteen days, Shane had known how to hunt and field-dress game like squirrel, rabbit, and deer, when it was in season. He'd stroll aimlessly on the back roads with a rifle bouncing on his back, not minding the animal blood on his pants (nothing about this picture would ring peculiar to Welchans anyway). The days were quiet, outside of his gunshots, as he kicked "ay-kerns" and the taste of oak filled the air. By summer, the countryside shimmered. By winter, it was stark, and for most teenagers like Shane, it was the most boring place in the world.

March of 1998, which many claimed was when Shane's troubles became evident to locals, probably wasn't when Shane first brushed with crime, but it would be, at a family member's insistence, when the involvement of law enforcement was initiated. In fact, the then sixteen-year-old's small-time crimes were so regular that when something in town did go missing, the first thought was *There goes that Shane Freeman again.* For reasons not entirely understood, his burglaries were usually contained to friends' houses, where he would shower and eat. During one burglary, he got his hands on a red emergency light.

"I regret ever bringing law enforcement into the family." It was Dwayne Vancil who'd remorsefully bring in the police. It all started when Dwayne and his family were out of town in Branson, Missouri. When Dwayne returned home, he found his truck caked in mud, and the gas tank nearly empty. Without thinking twice, he knew it was Shane, who had permission to access Dwayne's shop while they were away. Shane had broken the locks of Dwayne's house and taken the keys. And I'm sure Shane loved every second of spinning doughnuts in the fields wet with melted snow; I can imagine him lying on his back in the bed, whistling at the stars, smirking at his own delinquency. In the end, I'm not so sure he'd take it back.

Dwayne drove straight to one of Shane's friends' houses, where he knew Shane was sleeping over, and all but dragged him by his ear all the way to the sheriff's office. "I filed a report down there," Dwayne said. "We wanted to scare a little bit of sense into him before he could run into some dangerous consequences." Waiting there at the Craig County Sheriff's Office in Vinita were Shane's parents. Together, they explained the troubles they'd been having with the teenager: the local burglaries, the lifting of trucks, the sneaking out. They even arranged to give Shane a tour of the local jail, to show him where he might end up if he didn't get his act together. At first, the intervention seemed to be successful. They even went through the Oklahoma Department of Human Services (OKDHS), where they attended family counseling: Shane, Danny, Kathy, and even then fourteen-year-old Ashley. It seemed to improve Shane's behavior, at least for a short while. But after a couple of months, Shane capitulated to the itch that could only be scratched by petty crime.

In the late summer of '98, Shane was helping Danny on a job across Welch, at the home of a family acquaintance. With the garage door open,

Shane saw the opportunity to steal a length of telephone cord, which he continued to steal on multiple occasions over several workdays (for reasons unknown, Danny had recently stripped Shane of his phone privileges). That defiant spirit in Shane emerged on the morning of August 20, 1998, before school, and Shane snuck some of the phone wire to improvise an ad hoc line from his bedroom to a phone box on the side of the trailer home. His father found out.

While rumors churned about the way Danny treated Shane, there was a faction that defended him. "He was strict with Shane, but the kid was out of control. Danny only did what he had to do to try and get him in line. He may have spanked him here and there or whipped his behind with a belt, but he didn't abuse him," Danny's stepsister, Chris, once told me when I visited her in Louisiana. It's worth noting here that a majority of Oklahomans favor corporal punishment, with paddling still allowed in the state's public schools if parents sign a permission slip. Shane's family feared that if they couldn't get him on the right track, then the cops would do it for them—or, worse yet, a righteous gunshot from a homeowner aimed at their teenage trespasser would.

But then again, who isn't invincible at age sixteen?

That August, Shane's junior year had just started, with his basic studies in session for the first half of the school day before he was bused over to vo-tech (vocational school) at the Northeast Technology Center about a half hour away in Afton, where he studied autoservice technology, a fancier term for "mechanics." But that August day, when Shane arrived at Welch High School after his father's punishment, a track coach found Shane "oozing blood" from his gym shorts as he entered the hallway. Sure, he was the popular jock who would high-five his friends in the hall and had all the girls chasing after him, but he was also a hurt and angry boy shrinking with humiliation when faculty had him recount what had happened.

According to the Craig County deputy who took Shane's statement, Shane reported that Danny "hit him with a telephone cord approximately thirty times, along with slapping in the face and punching him with his fist three times." The officer also noted that Shane's buttocks were "black-and-blue and bleeding."

After this, Shane did not return home. In response, Danny met with CCSO deputy Troy Messick at Roscoe's convenience store, where Ashley Freeman worked part-time, and reported Shane as a runaway. Still in the town of Welch, Shane moved in with his best friend, Justin, and his family; Shane was close with them all, and Justin's mother had long been like a second mother to him. That night, before Shane could settle in, police brought Shane into the sheriff's office to make an official statement before returning him home with Justin.

By all accounts, Shane was happy living with this new adoptive family. He continued going to school, and if only in small slivers, those months on the brink of his turning seventeen provided happy memories for Shane.

On September 2, 1998, an arrest warrant was issued for Danny Freeman, charging him with "Injury of Minor Child (Felony)." Clint Ward, who reportedly announced that the Freeman crime scene had drug debt written all over it, was then the assistant district attorney. According to Dwayne Vancil, Danny felt like the DA's office was letting the case go too far for someone who was only trying to correct his son's behavior, that the commotion surrounding the event was BS. That day, Danny was arrested, then released on five thousand dollars bond, a small fortune for a family with the barrel-scrape income you'd find in Welch.

In court during a preliminary hearing on October 20, 1998, Shane Freeman was quoted as saying the only words I ever find directly attributed to him: "I was talking to someone I wasn't supposed to. He caught me and tried to find a belt and couldn't, so he got the telephone cord and used it." Soon after, on November 6, 1998, Shane turned seventeen.

Thanksgiving came before the Freeman family could realize just how close they were to the holidays. Shane's grandfather and Danny's father, Glen Freeman, drove up with his wife (Danny's stepmother and Dwayne's mother) from Louisiana, a twelve-hour journey. Accompanying them were ice coolers of crawfish and crabs, dirty rices and gumbos. I imagine the faint whiff of Cajun spice filling the Freeman trailer as they took turns putting every meat and side into one large bucket and letting everyone pick their favorite parts of a jambalaya holiday. Shane made a guest appearance, wearing a smile, splitting the holiday between the Freemans and the Greens. While the rest of the family went on with their casual conversations over dinner, Shane noticed a tinge of worry behind Ashley's eyes. He squeezed his sister's knee under the table and leaned into her ear. "Everything's OK, Ash," he reassured her. "I love where I am." Ashley, doting on her big brother, smiled back at him. "You don't be worrying, all right?"

"Me? Worry?" She crossed her arms and jokingly puffed her lips. "About you?"

"Come here, brat." He pulled her in and rubbed her scalp with his knuckles before their arms comfortably landed wrapped over each other's shoulders.

That Thanksgiving Day, November 26, was the last day he'd see his parents, sister, and extended family.

Around this time, Justin Green's mother rented an apartment for the two boys to share. It was minimal, at best, but it was a Christmas dream come true, furnished with the hijinks of two teenage boys eager to be grown-ups. Though life was seemingly easier for Shane, he took with him his demons. "He had a lot of issues," says Justin, "because of the hand he'd been dealt in life." The burglaries in Welch continued, though Shane was consistently attending school. His life was punctuated with what were later perceived as manic spells and bouts of depression, and the pleasures of living without supervision were short-lived. But some people in town maintained that the only reason he committed those crimes was to get away from his father, that jail was a better alternative to an eggshell house and an explosive father.

A week and a half after Christmas, on January 4, before he was due to go back to school after winter break, Shane took Justin's truck without permission, along with a large gun (Justin claims not to know from where he got the gun). He showed up at Grandma Celesta's house at eight fifteen a.m. in a frantic state, saying that if he didn't get somewhere in thirty minutes, he'd be killed.

"Who's going to kill you?" Celesta asked. But he wouldn't say. Instead, Shane repeated himself, pleading with her for the keys to her pickup. Celesta hesitated. "Well, whatever's at you, you shouldn't have that gun. It's only gonna get you in trouble."

Shane sat inside the trailer and held his head in distress. "They're going to kill me if I don't get somewhere." Giving in, Celesta handed over the keys and watched Shane drive away, not knowing it'd be the last time she'd see her grandson. I will never learn if Shane was only trying to scare his grandmother into giving him the keys to the truck, or if there really was someone who was after him. . . . Whatever it was, Shane's cool started to unravel.

"Pick a song," I ask of Justin Green, trying to get him to paint a picture of his best friend. "What was his favorite song, something he may have played?"

"'Truly Madly Deeply' by Savage Garden," he answers.

"You're so full of shit."

"'Tootsee Roll'?" We have a laugh.

What followed was a four-day-long crime spree that seemed to illuminate Shane's mental state—he tried, in the end, to run off, presumably for Louisiana, where his grandfather and his aunt lived, but he didn't make it far. In these short, crime-filled days, he became a fugitive and earned the name "the Red Light Bandit."

After Celesta gave Shane the keys to the blue 1985 Chevrolet pickup, the very one I'd sit in, Shane wound up in Afton—about a twenty-minute drive northeast from his grandmother's—where his mechanics class at the vo-tech was, but he never attended class. For the next few days, Shane's whereabouts are disputed; he was on the run, in and out of hiding and not in regular contact with any one person. Bursts of mania and indecisiveness plagued him as he rampaged his way through a sweat-stained crime spree that came to an abrupt halt half a week later.

When I asked everyone I interviewed, no one close to Shane had a guess as to what sparked his spree.

"It was DHS," Justin admits to me, disclosing this twenty-year-old secret that seemed to elude Shane's family and friends alike. According to Shane's best friend, the cause was the Oklahoma Department of Human Services coming to their new apartment the morning he went on the run. "Danny couldn't stand that he wasn't at home, under his control, so he kept fighting to get him back." Being that Shane was still seventeen years old, he was not legally allowed to live on his own, so a social worker came, telling Shane that he had to return home. "And that just wasn't happening."

It is also hypothesized that social workers were planning to place Shane in foster care.

At some point in the chaotic intervening days, Shane found an unoc-cupied animal-control vehicle in Craig County and swiftly stole the offi-cer's jacket and ticket book. It gratified the desire for that high, the thrill, but he was also teeming with the nerves and anxiety that he had difficulty coping with. He also still had the red light from an earlier, undated burglary.

On January 5, when Shane was next seen, he visited one of his girl-friend's houses and left at about five thirty p.m. Several attempts by me to reach this girlfriend went unanswered. Later that evening, Shane attended his girlfriend's basketball game at her school in Afton, leaving at ten forty-five. Overnight, a cold front fell over Oklahoma, bringing with it a terrible winter storm that brought golf-ball-sized hail and winds that took down signs. Out there on the pitch-black back roads that Shane had to drive to reach his next destination, he somehow weathered the floods and ice and howling gusts; he seemed preconditioned to weather most things that life could throw at him. Around then, Shane was entered into the NCIC and reported as a runaway.

On Wednesday, January 6, Shane was spotted by several locals in Blue-jacket, driving his grandmother's truck.

Later that evening, between seven and seven thirty, seventeen-year-old Sabrina Chivers and her girlfriend were driving up the 3500 block of North Main Street in McAlester, about one hundred fifty miles from Welch, when the flashing of a red light caught her attention in the rearview mirror. Unsure how they could have warranted the attention of a cop, the girls pulled over. A young officer approached the driver's-side window and bent down to eyeball Sabrina and her friend. "Hello, ma'am," he began. "License and registration, please."

Sabrina did as she was told. The officer thanked her, and she watched him in her side-view mirror as he returned to his vehicle with her documents, then sat in the truck for a few minutes before returning.

"Ma'am, could you walk with me back to my vehicle?"

Apprehensive, Sabrina looked over to her friend, convinced that something was off. But she obliged. As traffic continued on the main street, Sabrina climbed into the passenger seat of the truck. She stared at the cop as he pretended to talk into a police radio on the shoulder facing away from her. "Do you have any alcohol in your vehicle?" he asked her. She shook her head. "All right, wait here, ma'am." The officer exited the vehicle once more, leaving Sabrina in the truck. She watched him search the back-seat of her car for a moment before he returned to her.

Noticing how remarkably young he looked, Sabrina cleared her throat. "How long have you been on the job?"

"Two weeks," answered the officer.

"And what's your name?"

"Deputy Shane Freeman, ma'am."

Shane decided that Sabrina was free to go, but as she made her way out of the truck, a police officer pulled up to the scene, after a passing motorist thought that the whole thing looked suspicious and alerted the cop. Shane punched the blue pickup into gear and engaged police in a pursuit up Main Street and into the outskirts of McAlester. He weaved heavily but precisely through traffic, riding on and off the shoulder at high speeds until the storefronts dwindled and the road headed into the trees. There, he braked hard in the middle of the street, jumped out, and continued to run from police on foot. The Oklahoma Highway Patrol and a K-9 unit were summoned to help search for the boy in the Gaines Creek area, just east of McAlester between Seven Devils Road and Robbers Cave State Park. McAlester Police sergeant Cecil Day was quoted in the *Tulsa World*, saying, "He went into a wooded area, bailed out of the truck, and took off in the woods. We went after him with tracking dogs and lost him."

I contacted the McAlester Police Department, and they explained that they didn't keep records that old.

Those old jokes Shane had made about outrunning the police on *Cops* turned out to be an accurate prophecy.

Back at the abandoned truck that belonged to his grandmother, police recovered two loaded guns. For unknown reasons, police believed that Shane was still armed with a .357 Magnum revolver. But Shane braved the forests, scratched by brambles and bare twigs, and took shelter. Overnight, he found another truck, with the keys left in it, one belonging to a man who passed away of old age in 2008. It was a 1989 Ford F-250 XLT four-wheel drive. It was reported stolen from the small town of Krebs, Oklahoma, on January 7. After stealing the Ford, Shane made the decision to leave Pittsburg County.

Even today, nobody can know for certain why Shane opted to return to Craig County instead of continuing southeast toward Louisiana, which his family assumes was his intended destination.

Shane needed supplies, and back on home territory, the next house he decided to raid, on January 7, belonged to the Bible family. He'd spent the night sleeping in his truck on a rural driveway across from the house, until Jay and Lorene each left for work. According to Lorene, he entered the house at about nine a.m., ordered several pornos on pay-per-view, ate from their refrigerator, took a shower, and selected a few things to take with him. He stole some blankets, but most of what he took came from Lauria's room, including her pillow and bedspread, sixty-seven dollars, a shirt, and gym pants. Lauria was reported saying her mom would have killed him just for eating leftover fried chicken off the good china.

He also took several guns from the Bible home, and he left at about three thirty that afternoon.

"He took with him enough ammo to hold off Coxey's Army," said Lorene. She filed a statement along with her husband, Jay, at the Craig County Sheriff's Office.

"None of these farmers were worried," Danny was quoted saying in a January 1999 article in the *Tulsa World*. "He was a well-mannered kid. . . . He did some stealing, but he just wasn't violent."

On January 8, 1999, Shane wore a camouflage jacket, blue denim jeans, and sneakers. Near the intersection of 4430 Road and 40 Road, about ten miles from his home west of Welch, Shane's stolen truck finally broke down. Out there, it was eerily quiet, with no sign of mankind until he'd hear the tires scrape from far away. Bleak in winter, the surrounding fields were filled with crows and Limousin cattle, frostbitten straw, and a chill that found its way into the marrow of his bones. Icy winds hoisted and dropped. Shane was good at thinking on his feet, and he went across to cut a section of nearby wire fence, to see if he could rig the tie rods back together. At this time, a local farmer, Terry Layton, whose house you could see if you squinted hard enough without the January wind in your eyes, called the sheriff's office in Vinita to report the location of the Red Light Bandit.

Arriving on the scene at precisely 4:20 p.m. was CCSO Deputy David Hayes, the older brother of Undersheriff Mark Hayes. Mark Hayes, therefore, was his older brother's supervisor. Operating on the basis that Shane was a fugitive and thought to be armed, David took with him his dash-mounted shotgun from the patrol car, which he parked in front of Shane's truck so that the vehicles were facing each other.

David Hayes had only been with the sheriff's office for two days.

Reports will vary over the next few days, months, and years, but the official report is that within the very minute of David Hayes's arrival, Shane, standing at the driver's-side door of the truck, reached into his waistband behind him, raised his hand, and pointed a gun at the deputy. David went on to raise his shotgun and pump it upon seeing that Shane had a pistol pointed directly at him. He advised the boy to drop the gun and reportedly found himself "looking down the barrel."

Then, at 4:20, less than a minute after Hayes arrived at the scene, the sound of a shot fired.

Today, in the wider community, more often than not, Welchans seem to have forgotten about the boy's death. *Sounds familiar. I think I remember something like that.* All that exists from immediately after Shane's death is a brief article in the *Tulsa World*. While roaming the halls of his high school, I dig up a short piece when sifting through the school's dusty yearbooks. In there is a black-and-white picture of Shane as an infant playing with a toy pickup truck.

> My grandchildren. I had six—an even half dozen. A boy and girl, a girl and boy. Then a boy and girl. I told everyone each of mine has two. Now one of mine is missing from my sight, but never from my heart and never from my mind. I can always hear "Hi, Grandma" anytime I choose, from the special first one. Love, Grandma Chandler.

On another page, the high school version of an obit reads:

> Shane Freeman was born on November 6th, 1981, and died on January 8th, 1999. He moved to Welch in 1995. Shane played football and basketball and ran track. He was also a member of FHA [Future Homemakers of America] and TSA [Technology Student Association] and was a student at vo-tech, studying autobody. No

matter what, Shane always had a big smile on his face. He was always the center of attention with his funny jokes and outgoing personality.

No official obituary could be found.

Nor police report.

Nor autopsy.

It was just the beginning of hell for a family who sought answers regarding the death of their only son and brother, a hell that would boil over between the Freemans and the police until the Freemans' untimely deaths at the end of the year. And standing here, west of Welch, is my way of sifting through the relatives' emotions, which seem to cloud the memories of Shane. On this rural road, the redness of anger toward deputies and the green of sickness over what happened a year later dissipates, and I can see Shane for exactly who he was, who he should have been: a seventeen-year-old boy with his whole life in front of him.

12

THE ALLEGED COVER-UP OF SHANE FREEMAN

I swim through starry oblivion nights, humming the song "Oklahoma!" where the waving wheat can sure smell sweet. I wonder why Oklahoma wants to kill me, as I'm nearing a dozen panic attacks a day. I remind myself to breathe from my belly when the light-headedness comes. *Inhale for four seconds, hold for four, exhale for eight.* It sometimes feels like a watering can against a forest fire. And then I shake off the smell of meth and the warnings coming my way to remind myself of the girls' laughter I've never known and their olly olly oxen frees. I sit and obsess over the changing stories of the addicts who deny all knowledge and the cops who think I'm stupid to even try. And maybe I am. But at least I'm here, and very few seem to be in a story that hardly makes news outside the small, gossip-slick towns of Oklahoma. I wonder why.

"I advise you to tread carefully on your project," a member of law enforcement publicly writes on my Facebook wall, and never communicates with me again.

"They won't think twice about killing you," says another source.

But who are *they*?

The calls with the heavy breathing and the cryptic messages from obviously fake Facebook accounts come about a year after I start this project.

I struggle to describe this all-consuming fear of my own body while in the midst of it, of the way it betrays me. It is that stigmatized nervous breakdown that is the rot of my family tree. The sweats, the racing heart, the painful flu-like symptoms, the horrible fuzzy head, the feeling that I am being poisoned to death, the cold-shock mornings that chain me to the bed, the loss of appetite, the shitting and vomiting that lead to my losing thirty pounds in one month. My sour stomach cramps, the pins and needles all over my body, the nonstop peeing, the heart palpitations, the inability to take a much-needed deep breath, and the dreaded scalp-prickling headaches. I don't understand what's happening; I've always been strong, fearless. I've jumped out of planes and faced loaded guns without flinching, so why is this happening now? Why am I dying? And why can't anyone tell me what I'm dying from?

A shadow follows me everywhere I go, a figure of a monster in the shade of every distant tree on the plains, in the blind spots of Oklahoma's bright sky. His name is Fear, and he's always ready to pounce. Still, I can't leave, not until I can see some possible semblance of resolution of the case of two beautiful girls whose voices I concoct in my broken mind, and whose families will wait until the end of time to find them. And in the times I want to walk away, I remind myself that there are two families who don't have that option. *They* are the ones familiar with the actual sound of the girls' laughter, and the feeling of the girls' hair on their chests from when they held them so long ago. In these minute reminders, I want to siphon some of Lorene's strength, that maternal drive fueled by a mother's first look into her daughter's eyes and the last words she heard her speak.

I come to learn that there is no real difference between being brave and pretending to be brave. Maybe a cure will present itself tomorrow. Maybe tomorrow. Maybe tomorrow.

Hope.

At night, the trailers of northeastern Oklahoma are tiny specks in the distance, single spotlights to mark their existence against an encompassing realm of stars. I look out at them and imagine it'd be nothing for the sky to just suck them up through a straw. By day, the flaxen pastures are end-less, impossible to distinguish one acre from another. There are so many places to hide, so many hidden things, so many places to hide a body. I think to myself that Lauria Bible and Ashley Freeman could be anywhere and nowhere at once.

"I don't know why I connect to Shane more than anyone else in this story," I say to my husband. Of course, I grow to love the missing girls in the way artists love their work, but they are different from me, wholesome, and good, and I'll always struggle to empathize.

"Maybe that's because you were just like Shane when you were his age," he says.

Of course, he is right.

So little is documented about the death of Shane Freeman, so I go to the archivists in Vinita, a group of elderly women who speak in tongues of conspiracy and murmurs in the back of the library (they've since moved to the back of a funeral parlor, I'm told). *Meet us in the graveyard at night,* they request, cautious of people listening in on our conversation. Though I'm sure there are places other than cemeteries to ensure privacy, I think they like the air of spookiness surrounding the idea. We flip through piles of scrapbooks they've spent years collecting while they twist their necks to glance over their shoulders. They're a living, breathing microfiche col-lected. I could spend years here in black and white, as these ladies have, but I'm only here for so long. I take as many pictures of the articles as I can on my phone to read later.

Over time, I listen to several competing narratives of how Shane died at the hands of CCSO deputy David Hayes: that he was shot once in the chest or four times in the back, that he died on the side of the road or he died while climbing a nearby fence, that Shane wasn't armed at all, that he witnessed deputies doing something illegal and was killed for it. Without any surviving records and without an autopsy report, it seems unlikely that

I'll ever find out the truth, and David Hayes hasn't publicly spoken of the incident in twenty years, not even once. But I'm not the first person to come across these roadblocks: I read articles of a public dispute over Shane's death between law enforcement and the *Joplin Globe*.

Before I'd get to hear the Freeman family's side of things, I sit with then CCSO sheriff George Vaughn, the man initially in charge of the investigations into both Shane's death and the murders of Shane's parents. I get the opportunity to speak with Vaughn several times before he gets too sick to leave home on his own. Nearing his eightieth birthday, today he is the pastor of a community Baptist church, prefacing that he has Alzheimer's disease, forewarning of vague recollections. . . . Maybe so. He is heavyset, his movements painfully slow. Despite this, he speaks clearly.

"David Hayes was a seasoned officer," Vaughn says. When not sipping his mocha, he passes his cane from hand to hand like a tic, as though wavering between choices, maybe variations of the truth. Each time we meet, he defends David Hayes, stating that the shooting of Shane Freeman was *justifiable*. "My officer did as he was trained to do."

All I have of the dispute between the *Joplin Globe* and the sheriff's office are phone shots of black-and-white articles from the graveyard girls dating back to 2002, when George Vaughn was no longer in office. He was voted out the year following the murders in Welch, and fifty-two-year-old Jimmie L. Sooter took office in January 2001. The debate started when the *Joplin Globe* filed a Freedom of Information Act (FOIA) request for an investigative report into the 1999 shooting of Shane. It seemed that the timing of the public-record request aligned with the inauguration of a new sheriff. Only one month after taking office, "Sooter had said his policy was to deny all open-records requests. He also said he believed that the records from the Shane Freeman case were missing," according to the *Joplin Globe*. When the paper noted that the new sheriff was "violating the Oklahoma Open Records Act," Sooter referred to the article as "deceitful," citing the sheriff's office's efforts to locate the records and claiming that he was falsely accused of such a violation.

After some back-and-forth between the newspaper and the CCSO, the *Joplin Globe* looked to District Attorney Gene Haynes, whose role it was to ultimately decide whether or not to bring charges against David Hayes and/or the sheriff's office on behalf of the state of Oklahoma for the killing of Shane. According to the *Joplin Globe*, on April 11, 2002, DA Haynes personally wrote the following response:

> Several weeks ago I received a letter from your paper complaining that Craig County Sheriff James Sooter had refused your request for information about the shooting death of Shane Freeman by Deputy David Hayes. As a result, we asked Sheriff Sooter to try and locate the report of the case so we could send you the information that is required under the Oklahoma Open Records Act. Sheriff Sooter informed us that he was unable to find any records of the case. As you know, the shooting of Shane Freeman occurred during the term office of the previous sheriff, George Vaughn. I believe the reports of the shooting may have been lost during the changeover of sheriffs and that Sheriff Sooter honestly cannot find them in his office.

It wouldn't be the first time that this line of defense—evidence becoming lost during the course of sheriff changeovers—would show up in this case, and it was an excuse I'd curse frequently.

Former sheriff Vaughn asserted that the records had been in his office when he left the job. Even from his near-finished mocha in an ice-cream parlor in Vinita, he maintains this. "Well, it's protocol, really," he says. "Whenever there's a police-involved shooting, we call in the OSBI." This was another place for the *Joplin Globe* to reach out to in its continued attempts to obtain the investigative report.

But when the *Joplin Globe* asked the OSBI for these records, OSBI spokeswoman/public information director Kym Koch publicly cited that because of confidentiality clauses, all OSBI reports were protected by state law. She did, however, acknowledge that the DA's office was in a position to release such documents if it saw fit, with legal records more subject to the public's petitions than the state's investigative documents with the OSBI. This seemed to push the blame back on the DA's office, and soon, the Oklahoma Press Association intervened, urging all officials to do their best to locate the report. After this, DA Haynes's secretary "located copies of Vaughn's records," much to the skepticism of the community.

Under the pressure of an increasingly dubious public, DA Haynes admitted that they had found approximately fifty pictures of Shane's crime scene, as photographed by the OSBI. He also publicly blamed the CCSO for their loss, adding that they'd also found "two rolls of exposed film as evidence obtained at the crime scene," as well as a videotape of the crime scene made by OSBI agent Dennis Franchini. Despite this, there is no public evidence of these items today.

Now-retired OSBI agent Franchini kindly declines to comment when I reach out to him, citing state statutes.

In 2002, the public dispute between the *Joplin Globe* and the DA's office ended when the newspaper received a twenty-nine-page investigative report on Shane's shooting death, which included ten pages of reports from the CCSO, seven pages from the McAlester Police Department (Shane fled on foot from one of their officers after a car chase a couple of days before his death), and twelve pages of autopsy and medical examiner's reports, along with a personal note from Gene Haynes. However, the *Joplin Globe* never released its findings, and when I contact them to inquire about the report, they refer me to the investigative reporter, who is also unable to locate his findings.

Having contacted all pertinent agencies, I am left with not much more than some newspaper archives, and my thumb up my ass. I have no official reports saying how Shane died and no statements, and the sequence of events immediately following the shooting remains unknown to me, outside of alternating rumors that range anywhere from troubled kid to Clyde Barrow incarnate.

Have you checked flight records? The graveyard girls tilt their heads down to look at me over the rims of their glasses.

In an effort to track down the investigative report with the DA's office, now headed up by Matt Ballard, I encounter more disappointment. "After a search of our records, we are unable to locate any documents responsive to your request. The report you are referencing—if it ever existed as a record in our office—was apparently created 15 years ago and by people who haven't been employed in this office for many years. Our staff undertook a diligent search to attempt to locate any open records responsive to your request, but did not find any," writes the chief of the civil division on behalf of the DA. I am astounded that its very existence can be called into question when the authors of the report are former employees of that same office.

Further attempts to personally reach DA Gene Haynes go unanswered.

In the days of this dispute, Haynes adamantly stood by David Hayes's defense after reviewing all the evidence made available to his office: he announced that they had "determined that the shooting death of Shane Freeman was justified." He declared that while David's eyewitness statement is the only eyewitness statement available, the evidence and autopsy records support it. "I could find no evidence on which to base a criminal charge against David Hayes."

This is the official record as it stands today.

In 1999, Danny Freeman did not agree with the claim of self-defense—and by the time I reached Oklahoma, there wasn't a person familiar with the case who didn't believe that in the wake of his son's death, a "full-on war" developed between Danny and some of the deputies of the CCSO, which included Deputy David Hayes, Undersheriff Mark Hayes, Deputy Troy Messick, Lieutenant Jim Herman, Investigator Charles (Charlie) Cozart, and Sheriff George Vaughn. All of these men were present at Shane's crime scene, and with the exception of David Hayes, these very men would be present at the Freeman fire in December 1999 as well.

David Hayes was merely off duty when the call of the fire came in.

But it wasn't just Shane's death and the controversy surrounding it that later led people to believe that the police had had some involvement in the murders of Kathy and Danny. Not only was the timing deeply suspect, but in the months following Shane's death, Kathy and Danny were exploring their options with the hopes of filing a wrongful-death suit against the county.

The couple, who had two years to file, was murdered nine days before what many people I spoke to mistakenly believed was the final filing deadline, just one year after Shane's death.

13

BOYFRIEND, JEREMY HURST, AND POP POP, GLEN FREEMAN

I come to Welch at night alone. The "ky-oats" are loud in the hills. I can smell a trace of fire, as though it's a memory, but it's a hazy memory, and I try to fill in the gaps. Can anyone really know what happened here? I suppose if they did, I wouldn't be here, where night comes as a wave from the hills, and I'm suffocating in the smoke.

When my nerves slacken, so does the prairie. I listen.

"It was just like any other night," Jeremy tells me. Jeremy Hurst, Ashley's then boyfriend and the last known person to see the Freemans alive, becomes one of my first sources, and he is the first person to bring me to this spot, which I revisit so many times over the years. He is short, a Bluejacket boy with ice-blue eyes under the cream-colored rim of a Stetson. He tells me that on the night of Ashley's birthday, he gave her a necklace, a heart-shaped pendant on a silver chain with her birthstone, turquoise, now listed in the *last seen wearing* section of Ashley's missing-person flyer, as is Jeremy's class ring. "I loved her," he tells me.

Today, Jeremy is a truck driver who tends to his family farm, still pressed into the ranches of Bluejacket. We talk in his pickup truck after leaving the convenience store where Ashley used to work in the center of Welch (it was called Roscoe's back in 1999, though the store's name changes several times in my years here until finally being demolished). It was one of those regulars' joints that sell pork rinds and heat-lamp chicken, from where I would leave with the smell of grease stuck in my hair and clothes for the rest of the day. Jeremy and I also pass where his grandmother used to run her store across the street, where he was invited one last time to be with his girlfriend and family on the night of the murders. Jeremy doesn't even look in that direction, and I don't ask for the sake of small-talk bullshit.

"Are there regrets?" I ask him.

Not blinking, he looks out to the road ahead as we drive toward West of Welch. "I wonder. Maybe if I was there . . . maybe there was something I could have done."

For the ride that takes us from one end of Welch to the other, the very route the Freemans daily took, Jeremy and I talk about the night he last saw them. "We all ate cake and drank soda, and there really wasn't much more to it," he tells me, an account that remains unchanged over the years and also corroborates what the medical examiner's report showed in the stomachs of Danny and Kathy. "When I left at about ten o'clock, Ashley and Lauria were just hanging around, watching TV," he says. "It was a hunting show." In our side-view mirrors, nothing but dust—what's behind us no longer exists. Before us, the blond vertigo of summer-lit prairies.

Jeremy and I also discuss his getting the news of the fire the morning after while putting the cattle away on his family farm. "My grandmother was the one who told me that there'd been a fire. I didn't know there was a body until later on. But I just blanked out. I can't say. I jumped into my pickup truck and got to the trailer as fast as I could." It's the very path we're on at this moment. "When I got there, one of the deputies smirked and said to me, 'Looks like someone's gonna be spending New Year's Eve alone.' I couldn't believe he'd say something like that to me. My feelings were all over the place. But soon after, they took me behind the trailer, where they questioned me."

Over the years, Jeremy and I grow close. He'll invite me to his wedding, and I'll eat corn-battered catfish with his wife and daughters. Maybe, when we first meet, I should be a little more apprehensive about jumping into the truck of the last person to see four people alive, but I enjoy the view of the countryside and the smell of fresh-cut hay in the air flowing through the truck's windows. "At one point, the agents came over and asked to see my guns," says Jeremy. "So I showed them, and they saw they were collecting cobwebs. They told me to clean my guns and left." We sit the rest of the way in silence, and I feel inspired by the land around us. The quietness is comfortable.

"By God, that tore him up," Jeremy's mother once told me as we sat on the bleachers at a Bluejacket football game that Jeremy refereed across the field. Before us, *Friday Night Lights* and a line of cheerleaders dressed in virginal white radiated from the sidelines, the very squad in which Lauria cheered years before. Around us, bake sales and coolers of lemonade, and a raffle for an honest-to-God .22 caliber rifle. "It was just tragic," Jeremy's mother continued. "Jeremy hides it. He's always joking and smiling. But it was just so hard for him."

But back during the drive into the heart of West of Welch, I am surrounded by pure gold so that I'll see the same color imprinted behind my eyelids later that night when trying to sleep in a blanket of aloe vera gel. I dream of being a scarecrow, static and exposed in the middle of the prairie. My head throbs from the raw sunlight as the day wears on, arms tender with sunburn.

As Jeremy and I drive up through the surrounding ranches, we rise suddenly to a view of hills and trees that had been obscured by the blinding sun. It's as though the land picks up a pulse, and nestled in those hills is the Freeman farm.

Jeremy slows the truck near a pair of stone-and-wire pillars at the end of the Freemans' long driveway. Also on the other three corners of the forty-acre property, the structures were erected by all four Freemans, evidence of their labor, of their existence. A pair at the driveway and three more across the way, the pillars seem to represent the two friends, and the other three Freemans I already know to be dead. It is here, Lorene Bible will tell me, that she comes when she wants to pay respects to her missing daughter.

While I'm not a bashful woman, and I have no issue with knocking on strangers' doors, I'm warned about Danny Freeman's father, said to have settled on the property. "You go up there, you're askin' for trouble."

When the truck stops and the engine dies down, the sounds of the countryside are clear and beautiful; the shade stops the hisses of the sun and the vultures circle overhead. Vultures, at every subsequent visit, always seem to circle over West of Welch. At the top of this hill is a light-colored trailer, newer than the Freemans' was before it was reduced to nothing.

The day starts to ease toward dusk, and my eyes keep wandering up to the trailer, to the windows sparkling like flames in the softening sun, and I try to catch a glimpse into the past. And then, as I'd half hoped and half feared, a group of small dogs appears at the top of the hill where the trailer home sits, barking.

"Have you met Danny Freeman's father?" I ask Jeremy.

"I have not."

The heat has left me smelling like bone broth as I wait for a man who I've heard will kill me if he feels the need. Soon, a revving four-wheeler comes crookedly downhill toward us, driven by a cowboy in white. I don't want it to seem like I'm up to anything shady, so I move farther up the hill to meet him, stopping at the barbed wire fence until he arrives. From where I stand, the trailer is up ahead, a little to the left at my ten o'clock; Glen loops around so that he pulls up to my two o'clock. I quickly realize that this is so his mounted rifle points straight at me, which doesn't bother me so long as his hands are off of it. He comes in a white cowboy hat and with a collie at his quad's side, plaid shirt starch stiff. In the shade of his hat, the man's face bears distinctive burn scarring, dappled like lacework, and a portion of his nose is missing. I reach over the barbed wire fence and shake hands with Danny Freeman's father, Glen Freeman.

We shuffle through some small talk, Glen hesitant to speak on the record or move past this grassy spot, where I continue to speak from the dirt road's ditch over barbed fencing. After about fifteen minutes, I convince him to let us up to the property, where I hope to see the spot at the top of the hill where the Freemans once lived. He gives us permission to drive up onto his land, revving his quad back uphill as I hop in the back of Jeremy's pickup truck. The temperature begins to drop as we make our way up the driveway. It is my first visit to the Freeman farm. For reasons I cannot explain, there in the back of the pickup, the sight sticks with me; seconds of memory stretch across sunbeams from the hills and shimmering fields. It's easy for me to see why Danny Freeman chose here as a place to plant roots with his family all those years ago. This was the sight they saw when settling in after long days of work, the view of coming home. It is peaceful. But knowing what I know, I find it is also chilling.

It will be my first of countless visits here.

"The problem is," Glen begins before I can even hop out from the back of Jeremy's truck, "nobody wants to hear that this had to do with the sheriff's office."

Glen is as stern as they get, an obsolete type of the John Wayne era, always full of tales of glory days delivered in a low, hoarse voice. "I once punched a man so hard in the gut that it reached his spine, had his head in the toilet for hours" is one of many. At eighty years old, he is slower than he likes to see himself, white hair thin over a patchwork of liver spots and burns and topped with a Stetson. He explains that the scars are surgical on account of skin cancer as Jeremy and I follow him into his trailer.

Because of his partially missing nose, he sniffs often, a near-constant nasal drip he has to stop and wipe. He admits that his appearance makes him self-conscious. "People would rather think I'm a crazy old man up here." Through the back door, we go outside, where the Freeman trailer used to be.

It is the first time I hear the prairie sing.

The old sheds built by Danny still stand outside, pens full of goats and rams—a wild turkey nearly feels symbolic. Glen's trailer is only a few yards south from where his son's trailer sat; all that's left of the latter today is a rectangular mark at the top of a slight sun-dried hill. Here, the grass is slightly discolored, with a utility pole and the same weeping willow on the burn's west end. Just downhill at the back were the sounds of the stream spilling over the concrete dam where Danny used to feed the turkeys and leave to go gigging for frogs. It is where the most circulated photo of the girls was taken sixteen years ago. Standing at the site of the former trailer, I feel a chill run through me that reminds me of being on hallowed ground, that sacrosanctity that shakes me: on this small patch of ground, there was life, there was a family, there was death. For the first time on this trip, I bless myself.

"You're standing right around where they found Danny's body," Glen says at one point with no visible emotion. The weeping willow that once grazed Ashley's window is green and lush, rustling at my side where strips of sunlight whip across the former crime scene. As Glen walks me through the layout of the house, he talks about the case as if he's talking to himself. "I think Kathy was across the bed that way because she was going for a shotgun I bought them, which they kept at the head of the bed," says Glen. "God help them if she got her hands on it."

"Them," I comment. "You think it was more than one person?"

Glen nods, clarifying that it would have been damn near impossible for one person to kill two grown adults and hold the two girls hostage, while making the several trips it would have taken to get the many frames of arrowheads from the walls and out of there. Whether the arrowheads were a trophy or a motive, most of the people with direct knowledge I talked to over the years believe that Danny's arrowheads seemed to have had something to do with the murders, and Glen was firmly in that camp, as were the Bibles, who viewed them more as a killer's opportunity than a motive. The worth of the arrowheads varies, depending on whom I talk to, ranging anywhere from a few hundred dollars to forty thousand dollars.

Arrowheads come up around many corners of my research, and I think back to my conversation with former OSBI agent Steve Nutter when I met him in Tulsa. "The family was concerned about the arrowheads. I, a little bit less so," Nutter said. "Not to say that I wasn't concerned, but less concerned than they were. I went to college in Emporia, Kansas, which is what they call the Flint Hills of Kansas. I was in a fraternity, and as all fraternity boys, we sometimes went to the country with kegs of beer and we'd build bonfires. And I know that flint explodes when it's hot."

Lacking fire marshal reports and/or any reference to the arson investigation, I'll later have a discussion with my friend Aaron Roper, whom I met in Oklahoma in the early days. As Oklahoma as they got, he was a knowledgeable man, and a former fire-operations specialist for the US Fish and Wildlife Service. "You would have found evidence of something. Rock and glass don't disintegrate," Aaron explained in regard to the dozens of frames of arrowheads in the Freeman trailer. "A house fire will burn at eleven hundred degrees. Not even gold will melt at that temperature. You would have found scorched arrowheads or melted glass." I enjoyed playing devil's advocate, trying to prove each opposing argument. But Aaron seemed to base his facts on science, and not fraternity keg parties, and while he acknowledged the same thing that Agent Nutter did, that flint might crack in extreme heat, he claimed it wouldn't have disappeared. "Flint will burn at twenty-two hundred degrees. It takes eight hundred to cremate a body. The kind of heat you're talking about to make the arrowheads and the glass cases disappear is the type of heat to come from nuclear heat."

"The family remained fixed on those arrowheads," Nutter said in our conversation. "I'd follow every lead related to the arrowheads. They'd call and say, 'Hey, so-and-so has got some arrowheads. It might be Danny's,' and I'd go out and see. But just never went anywhere with it. I don't see it as a significant thing."

During that same interview, now lead OSBI agent Tammy Ferrari chimed in. "We're still getting leads on arrowheads," she said. "We still have tons of people call in on arrowheads."

Back inside Glen Freeman's trailer in Welch, Danny's father houses several dogs and even more rifles, many lying around on his tables and couch (I've learned this is not uncommon in Oklahoma). Like his son, Glen has built up an impressive arrowhead collection, which he shows me over several occasions. "I'm eighty years old now," he tells me. "I don't know if we'll find the truth before it's my time to go." We speak for hours; Jeremy Hurst stays mostly quiet on the couch—when Glen speaks, you're best off listening. By the time I finally come up for air, the sun is gone beyond the Flint Hills to the west.

Today, what came of the missing arrowheads remains unknown.

"Do you ever get scared?" I ask him. "Being up here all by yourself, knowing that the killer or killers are still out there somewhere?"

Glen moves swiftly for an eighty-year-old man, and a gun appears from under the arm of the recliner in which he sits, and I'm staring down the barrel of his pistol. "You see this, Jack?" (He'll never be able to pronounce "Jax.") A rush of wind shoots up my sternum to my brain, that familiar jolt that warns of panic, but I am not scared. Anxiety can floor me sometimes, but I'm not a fearful person as a rule, and I know to keep still, to keep calm. "Someone comes up here, this is what they're gonna get," he continues with the gun pointed at me from across the room. I can tell Glen doesn't mean this gesture to be menacing—or at least not to me specifically—but Glen propped in the chair, pistol in hand, will always feel like the most accurate portrait of the man I can imagine. It's not the intent of his mind that scares me, but the unpredictability of an old cowboy's mitts. "But *you* oughta be scared, Jack." Glen slowly eases the pistol back to its resting place. "You would be if you knew what you were dealing with."

It's more than a year after I met Glen Freeman for the first time. Autumn in Oklahoma, when the days smell like fire and the nights smell like rain and the sun smelts like gold casting into the ingots that are the American prairies. I spend hours getting lost on the back roads west of Welch; Indian Country, the old-timers call it, but I always trace back to the two stone columns. The Freeman property becomes my home base, and every place in Welch from then on exists only in relation to the homestead. *So-and-so lives ten miles north of the Freemans'. That one lives six miles west of the Freemans'.* With so few landmarks on the blank canvases of northeastern Oklahoma, it has to be.

One particular autumn day, I find Danny's stepbrother, Dwayne Vancil, and father, Glen Freeman, under the awning of Glen's trailer. I'm peculiar to them, with my bottle red hair, ripped jeans, and Echo and the Bunnymen shirt. *Would you believe the kids are buying their jeans like that nowadays?* Standing next to them was Chris, Danny's stepsister, whom I'd met a couple of times before. She is attractive, with long silver-streaked hair and dark skin. Like her father, she is stern, strong, never one to let her eyes stray from mine. Like everyone here, she wants justice. But unlike her father, she is willing to let her grief show with tears when recounting the days of her family's murders. Today, she is up from Louisiana, where I'll visit her not long after to ride airboats over the alligator-infested bayous.

"Come inside," she says, nodding toward her father's trailer. Leaving Dwayne and Glen outside, she takes me to a box she dug up from her father's belongings and wordlessly hands me several letters. None of them is addressed to anyone in particular; rather they are statements, seemingly declarations of facts. One of them is a handwritten letter by Kathy's mother, Celesta Chandler, dated the fall of 1999, a couple months prior to Danny's and Kathy's murders: nine pages detailing what went wrong with Shane's death, the investigation, and the year following. These pages survived because Kathy, fearing for her safety, left copies in the care of her close friend DeAnna Dorsey and with Danny's stepmother and Glen's late wife (the mother of Dwayne and Chris).

On the second letter, the words "ONE SHOT" are scrawled at the top of the page. This letter, which has not surfaced in this case before now, was penned by Kathy Freeman in the days before her burned body was discovered.

I take photos of the words before I can read them.

The letter reads like a testament to the betrayals and tragedies her family suffered, and holding those pages in my hands, I can't help but wonder if, in those final days, Kathy knew she was going to die.

14

THE LAST LETTER OF KATHY FREEMAN

I take the letters of Kathy Freeman and her mother, Celesta Chandler, back to my motel room, where I knock back a cup of cold coffee that's been sitting there since before I left this morning. My stomach hates me for it. A storm outside, the sky detonates; my heart palpitates with the anticipation of dissecting the letters. In recent months, my body hasn't been able to differentiate between enthusiasm and fear, so my excitement becomes a dreadful, sickly episode. I go over the same sentence over and over and over again. I hide the phone and take a deep breath. I do the opposite of instinct, since it hasn't helped. Instead, I dare this thing to do its best. Suddenly, the breath reaches my belly. I start reading once more.

According to the first letter written by Mrs. Chandler, in 1999, "A few weeks after Shane's death, his father, Danny Freeman, met with a criminal lawyer in Tahlequah, Oklahoma. His name was Tim Baker. He seemed interested in the case until he spoke to (ADA) Clint Ward."

I make the ninety-mile drive south and track Mr. Baker down in Tahlequah, the capital of Cherokee Nation. Now retired, Baker claims he can't recall ever meeting the Freemans back in 1999.

Likewise, upon reading this to Clint Ward, he comments, "I know Tim Baker and he is a good attorney. I don't recall having any conversation with him [about this case], though." I also track down a third lawyer, suggested by the family, in Tulsa who is also unable to recollect meeting with the Freemans.

In her letter, Celesta Chandler alleges that attorney Tim Baker sent a letter to the Freemans that read, "The case would be too hard to win . . . the deputy [David Hayes] will never change his story."

"The thing was," says Lorene when I ask her opinion on the death of Shane, "Danny sought out several lawyers, and every one of them told him that he didn't have a case. And he just didn't want to accept that." Lorene seems a little more sympathetic to Kathy's plight. "As a mother, she was just trying to understand what happened to her son."

I take my work to a large window that flashes in lavender and silver, my world fractured by lightning. But now I read what Kathy wrote in the days before her murder, the very declaration that hung from a cow magnet on her refrigerator. And as I read her words, I see a frustrated woman, a devastated woman, a woman hell-bent on justice for her son.

I see a mother.

> *My name is Kathy Freeman. I live west of Welch, OK—a Craig County resident all my life. My complaint is with the Craig County Sheriff's Department. My son, Shane Freeman, who had just turned 17 on November 6, 1981, [sic] was shot and killed by Deputy David Hayes on January 8, 1999, with a shotgun within seconds of Deputy Hayes arriving on the scene. The location of the shooting was a dirt road out on the prairie approx. 14 miles west and 8 miles north of Welch. The shot entered in the back of Shane's left elbow and enters the body 2 inches to the left of his nipple. I want the angle of the shot explained. Shane was shot at 4:30 pm but we were not notified until 10:15 pm by Sheriff Vaughn.*

If the law did everything right it was still wrong. The whole community of Welch and surrounding area knows this was wrong and they also want something done. Everyone that knows Shane believes that he wouldn't have pulled a gun. David Hayes took drastic measures and he along with the whole Sheriff's Dept. needs to be held accountable.

The Craig County deputies have a bad attitude and they think they can get away with everything. They have been defensive from the start, harassed us, and tried to intimidate us. The following list is actions taken by the county that I feel is suspicious or odd.

I am taken by her words, and suddenly, there is no more storm, either in my head or outside. It's just Kathy and I, as if I'm sitting with her at her kitchen table back at the Freeman trailer, woodstove on, her world icy and black. Her pen to the paper, her words are anger-filled lacerations.

Kathy goes on to list eight things that she believes are proof of wrongdoing by the Craig County Sheriff's Office. The very first thing she lists is, "Flowers and wooden cross at road site were removed by county." It seems that over time, crosses and the bouquets made by Shane's family, namely by his younger sister, Ashley, were plucked from the side of that country road where Shane had taken his last breath. When I speak to the Freemans years later, they all feel certain that it was cruelty on the part of the sheriff's office, which usually saw the tributes removed within a day of their being placed.

"The county didn't want any sign of sentiment," says Danny's stepsister, Chris. On top of the floral arrangements and memorials, all throughout Oklahoma, there were hand-painted signs created and erected by classmates reading JUSTICE FOR SHANE. They too were removed without a trace. Nearly twenty years later, I will see an original one in the front yard of Celesta and Bill Chandler.

I imagine Kathy writing the letter through the smoke of a cigarette and light one for myself as Kathy continues.

The second item on Kathy's list reads: "Road graded immediately."

I try to get the records from the Craig County Commissioner's Office to no avail, but I wasn't really expecting that they'd have records of a road grading from nearly twenty years ago. According to family, the resurfacing of the road took place the day after Shane was killed. "A friend of mine called me and said they were grading the road," Dwayne Vancil will tell me years later. "I called bullshit. So I go out there, and sure enough." Less than twenty-four hours after Shane's death, the road where Shane was shot was graded from one end to the other, the top layers and stones shaved by the construction blade. The Freemans feel certain it was to get rid of evidence. Bearing in mind that it was the middle of winter, the middle of nowhere, the middle of where an investigation should have been conducted, the family says they cannot understand why there'd have been an urgent need for such a project.

"Six hours before we were notified by sheriff" is third on Kathy's list. The delay in informing the family would have been immediately apparent when the autopsies and statements of the officers on the scene were in their possession. According to media reports, Shane was shot at 4:20 p.m., and the family wasn't notified until 10:15.

I knew this information could be corroborated by Freeman family friend DeAnna Dorsey. A Welchan and one of Kathy's closest confidantes, DeAnna worked as a nurse at Craig County General Hospital in Vinita. According to reports made by the Freemans, DeAnna learned of Shane's death while working a shift in the ER, when Shane's body was brought in for inspection by Medical Examiner Donna Warren. Shocked by the news and hoping to offer her support to the family, DeAnna headed straight to the Freeman trailer. But once there, she was surprised to realize that despite it now being several hours since the shooting, the Freemans had yet to receive the news. DeAnna couldn't find the words to tell them. Since most reports say that DeAnna was there when Sheriff Vaughn delivered the news of Shane's death to his parents, I knew she would have been able to confirm or deny Kathy's charges, as well as the Freemans' continued assertions that upon Sheriff Vaughn's delivering the news, he'd told Kathy, Danny, Ashley, and DeAnna that there was "no gun visible," that Shane hadn't been armed at all.

Those three words will be repeated in nearly every subsequent visit I have with the Freemans. "When Vaughn came up to the trailer, he told them, 'No gun visible.'"

According to Danny's father and siblings, the story changed to Shane's having a rifle. About a week after that, it changed one last time to Shane's having a pistol.

DeAnna Dorsey could have also chimed in on number four from Kathy's list: "Sent body to Oklahoma City before we were notified." I am not sure if this is a legitimate claim of wrongdoing here or what the due process ought to have been, so I speak to my friend, a former-sheriff-turned-coroner and current teacher named Darren Dake out of Cuba, Missouri, to clarify.

"The family is not required to ID the body prior to a police investigation or autopsy," Darren tells me. "In fact, if the police were familiar with him and/or they ID'd him through a driver's license, then the family doesn't have to ID him at all." When I inquired about possible reasons Shane might have been sent to Oklahoma City as opposed to the nearer medical examiner's office in Tulsa, which was another concern of the Freemans', he said that this was commonplace. "It stands to reason that the local office may not have had the resources to do the autopsy or had sent the body to a bigger office and out of local jurisdiction since it was a police-involved shooting."

Despite Kathy's claims in the letter, however, I am not able to verify that Shane's body was taken to Oklahoma City. Without an autopsy, and with the medical examiner Donna Warren having passed away years prior, it is virtually impossible to know for sure, unless I can speak to nurse and friend DeAnna Dorsey.

The fifth item on the list is, once again, something that could possibly be confirmed by her. "Sheriff lied to hospital that we had already been notified."

But sixth on the list is the most damning, if true. And while this information isn't well-known around the community, the remaining Freemans bring it up regularly. Kathy's phrasing is a little unclear, but she referred in the sixth point to an event that occurred one February afternoon, a month after Shane's death. "Shane's father [Danny] was stopped on Main Street of Vinita, because he drove through Big Cabin on his way home from work. Held shotgun on Danny. He was told if he took off on foot then he would shoot. His truck was searched and took him to the courthouse. Sheriff let David Hayes yell and scream at Danny."

Big Cabin is the name of a town thirty miles south of Welch, more specifically, where shooting officer David Hayes then lived, and where I'd meet his brother, Undersheriff Mark Hayes, at his converted barn.

Kathy's mother's letter is slightly more detailed about this incident. "Feb 9, 1999, a month after Shane's death, Danny was stopped because he came to Big Cabin. He had a shotgun pointed at him, was handcuffed, and his truck was searched. The deputies took him to the office and rant and rave about him being a no-good father. Sheriff George Vaughn saw and watched as this was going on and never tried to stop it. Other officers were present."

It would have been a small spectacle for a town like Vinita: a car full of deputies in front of the old KFC handcuffing Danny before traffic. I had first heard about this specific incident from former sheriff Vaughn during one meeting with him over tea (coincidentally, Jeremy Hurst walked in on us in the middle of our interview). When I asked about the alleged arrest of Danny, Vaughn claimed that "Danny had been stalking David in Big Cabin," and that Danny would sit "down there in his car close to [David's] house. Best that I can remember we called him in and talked to him and told him, 'That's not to be done.'" Vaughn switched his cane between hands.

Undersheriff Mark Hayes also recalled that Danny, at one point shortly after Shane's death, had arrived in the town of Big Cabin, where his brother then lived. Danny pulled his truck up to a group of kids playing in the street "and asked these children if they knew where the deputy was who shot his boy." One of the kids' parents called the sheriff's office. "We proceeded to go toward Big Cabin to see what was going on, and as it turned out, we met Danny at his vehicle on Route Sixty-six, this side of Vinita. We pulled him over, and he agreed to follow us to the sheriff's office."

Waiting at the sheriff's office were Deputy David Hayes, Investigator Charlie Cozart, Lieutenant Jim Herman, and possibly others, all part of Vaughn's entourage.

According to several family members, Danny explained that the deputies took turns screaming at him, getting in his face, making threats toward his family. The deputies claimed they were *the law* and that no one would believe Danny if he tried to blame them for anything. Relatives said the deputies threatened to kill his entire family. According to Danny's brother, Lonny Freeman, when Sheriff Vaughn came in to see the deputies surrounding Danny as he was handcuffed to the chair, Danny called out, "Why are you letting them do this to me?" Sheriff Vaughn didn't respond and walked back out of the room without a word.

By these accounts, this detention may have been a violation of Danny's constitutional rights.

"I think Danny was reading them," Danny's stepsister, Chris, once said. "I don't think Danny thought they were all bad there at the sheriff's office, but he wanted to sift through which ones were and which weren't." She went on to describe how it took Danny, a man known to never take any lip from anyone, all that he had not to fight back. "They wanted Danny to react. They wanted to have a reason to lock him up and throw away the key."

"It was a tit for tat," said Lorene Bible. "Danny was threatening David Hayes's family, stalking his kids and all, and the sheriff's office was fighting back."

Some said that Danny was out for blood.

Others said he was out for dirt.

It wasn't much of a stretch to believe Danny's account of how he had been mistreated by CCSO officials, since it was well known, and well proven, that corruption plagued several sheriffs' offices in northeastern Oklahoma in the eighties and nineties: a Wild West mentality and a long, dark history of sheriffs caught up in scandals, sheriffs implicated in murder, sheriffs murdered (Sheriff Harkins of neighboring Ottawa County was stabbed to death only two-and-a-half weeks before the Freeman murders). There is a steady stream of alleged corruption and people with firsthand accounts of police wrongdoings, and I spend four years talking to people with the wildest of tales. "I watched Deputy So-and-so OD in my living room, needle still in his arm. I must have been about ten years old, watching my mother try and revive him" is just one of many stories I'd hear (and that same Deputy So-and-so did confirm this). At first, I chalk some of it up to rumor and bad feeling, but there are countless accounts, many well documented in newspapers after arrests or trials of the officers, of police engaging in drug use, illicit sex, and unlawful harassment.

"Neither side was blameless," said Lorene in regard to Danny Freeman and the CCSO.

But Kathy isn't the only one related to the case who brings up the police provocation. One account of police harassment comes from Jeremy Hurst, Ashley's boyfriend, who remembers a spring afternoon when he and Ashley stopped at a store in Welch. They collected several bags of chips from the shelves, elbowing each other playfully, blue eyes smiling back and forth, when they noticed one of the familiar deputies enter the store. The deputy neither shopped nor looked around, just watched the couple. And when Ashley and Jeremy left, the deputy followed, getting in his patrol car and crawling behind them. "We weren't speeding or nothing," says Jeremy. But the deputy pulled them over, asked about where they were going and what they were doing. Jeremy confirms that these instances occurred almost every time they went out. "We weren't doing anything wrong."

I spend a good amount of time spider-webbing over the four-state area, listening to dozens of claims from family and friends of police harassment of the Freemans at their rural home. I hear how in the witching hours, deputies came out there to the middle of nowhere to ignite their spotlights up at the trailer: blinding white light spilling into the windows enough that it moved the Freemans from their trundles and caused the dog to have a conniption. And of the many times Ashley got off the school bus to find deputies parked there, watching, where there was nothing but back roads and farms. Sometimes she'd be nearly crying with anxiety. And by most accounts, this consistent harassment was led by CCSO investigator Charlie Cozart.

"He was the ringleader of them," many say on both the Freeman and Bible sides. "The sheriff didn't run the deputies. Charlie and the Hayes brothers did."

According to the letter written by Celesta Chandler, "Officers from the department started parking their cars in front of the Freeman home, on the county road in view of the Freemans." It appeared that Kathy had never been alone in having a grievance with the sheriff's office.

Returning to Kathy's letter, the seventh thing that she writes is: "Road signs west of Welch went up suddenly (because ambulance couldn't find location)." The family looked to the county for answers as to why there had been street signs missing from the country roads. It was their belief that the ambulance got lost on its way to the scene because of the lack of signs, which resulted in the ambulance showing up one hour and twenty minutes after the fatal gunshot was fired. Without a police or investigative report, I have no idea still.

The eighth and final thing listed is, "Wouldn't let EMT in to help. She lived close by the scene," referring to a Welch woman who stopped and tried to help Shane at the scene. There wouldn't be, however, any violation here if Shane had already been pronounced dead (which he had) and had the area been secured as a crime scene.

Signed by Kathy at the bottom of the page, a slogan of sorts: "One cop, one kid, one shot."

An almost identical slogan was coined by Danny in the *Tulsa World*: "One cop, one shot, one seventeen-year-old kid."

According to Celesta Chandler's letter, Kathy and Celesta attended a community meeting at the Public Service Company of Oklahoma building in Welch on October 6, 1999, two-and-a-half months before the murders. There, residents made several complaints about the sheriff's office. The Freemans were instructed by someone (by whom would be cut off at the bottom of the letter and never discovered) to put their complaints about the CCSO in writing and have them notarized.

The letter, perhaps inevitably, is a product of emotion, hearsay, and—at times—conspiracy theory. But throughout my investigation into this case, I consistently find that where there is smoke, there is fire.

I can see Kathy Freeman rising from the kitchen table and slapping the page onto the refrigerator with the cow magnet, unaware that she is only days away from being shot to death.

In speaking with former undersheriff Mark Hayes previously, he told me that in February 2000 he and his brother passed the OSBI-mandated polygraph tests taken in light of the Freeman fire. The tests were administered by the OSBI about their possible involvement in the deaths of Kathy and Danny and the disappearance of Ashley and Lauria.

"I thought it was a good idea from the beginning," Undersheriff Mark Hayes said in regard to the polygraphs as we sat in his home. "For whatever reason, Shane made a choice that late afternoon, and the deputy reacted as he had been trained."

I look at a *Tulsa World* article from February of 2000 titled "Rumors Spur Tests in Case of Two Missing Welch Girls," with a subtitle that reads: "Two brothers, a deputy and an undersheriff, pass polygraphs [*sic*] exams regarding the disappearance of two girls." But the reports of the men passing the tests seem to be claimed only by the Hayes brothers themselves. The same article also states, "An OSBI spokeswoman [Kym Koch] cited confidentiality rules and would not comment Tuesday about any polygraph tests." This leaves me confused.

As of today, I have never seen an official report pertaining to the results of the polygraph tests, nor am I any more aware of what questions were asked.

It is undeniable that there was heat on the department at the end of Vaughn's term, partly because of the implications of police involvement in the murders of the Freemans. To add fuel to the flames, in August of 2000, it was discovered that CCSO investigator Charlie Cozart, the lead investigator for the department and alleged harassment ringleader, resigned when he failed to provide a record that he'd received so much as a GED (general equivalency diploma), which rendered him unqualified to be part of the sheriff's office. In an article in the *Oklahoman* in 2000, Sheriff Vaughn was quoted as saying, "Cozart has worked in law enforcement in this state and the area for many years. . . . I never had any reason to question his eligibility." With Vaughn's arm being twisted by the Council on Law Enforcement Education and Training, Vaughn asked for Cozart's resignation with the hope that he could get Cozart a job in the jail, which "doesn't require state certification," he told the *Tulsa World*.

An investigative report from the *Joplin Globe* noted that "at least one drug case that Cozart had worked was dismissed because of his lack of certification."

"I was just shocked," Mark Hayes said to me, and described Cozart as being his best friend. In our interview, Mark smiled as he handed me photos of Cozart, the first ones I'd ever seen. He laughed. "Wanna know a secret?" he said. "I think it was his brother who turned him in." Mark was referring to Marvin Cozart, a violent criminal and neo-Nazi from Picher who had a history that included prison escape, assaults, burglary, and even murder. "I think Marvin was looking at some time and decided to turn on his brother" in an attempt to get a more lenient sentence when he was facing charges along with six others in beating a man to death with a pipe.

Marvin Cozart, who is in prison today, despite previous escapes, never responds to any of my letters.

The first time I speak to Mark Hayes on Facebook, he is tagged in a public photo with Charlie Cozart. In the comments, someone has written of Cozart: "He was my dealer, then he became a cop and busted me . . . not right." It is a sentiment I hear often.

"Charlie was loud, boisterous, and ignorant. Oh, yeah, he was a drug dealer," says now-retired CCSO lieutenant Jim Herman when we speak. Herman was a fellow deputy of Cozart and part of Vaughn's posse who was present at the crime scenes of both Shane and later Shane's parents. I'd personally speak to several people who supported the claim that CCSO investigator Cozart was a meth cook. "In Big Cabin, he was the only town cop, mechanic, and town drug dealer. . . . He sold dope like it was nothing," says Herman, who went into detail about instances when Cozart would pull over some "hoodlums" and take dope right out of his boot to plant it on the kids.

Jim Herman had always been described as a bit of a bumbling man, slow off the mark. But when I spoke with him for the first time, there wasn't a time, date, phone number he couldn't remember decades later; he has the kind of smarts my father has. He is an enthusiastic source who says that the Freemans believed that he, and not Cozart, was the one watching the trailer at all hours. "Our two cars looked eerily similar," admits Herman. "We [CCSO] all knew Cozart was heading west of Welch, toward the Freeman house. He was seeing if he'd see cars going in and out. Danny was a drug dealer on a far larger scale than Charlie." When I asked Jim Herman what it was like to work with Cozart, he said, "I didn't want to get in the car with him. I didn't want to be with him, uh . . . when he did something. I didn't want to be associated with him."

By the end of 2000, the men at the heart of the Craig County Sheriff's Office were more or less gone after Sheriff George Vaughn was voted out of office, his first loss since 1968. He lost his bid in November 2000 to Jimmie L. Sooter, who would take office in the new year. "Let's just say Sooter cleaned house," said Mark Hayes. It was known that the Bible-Freeman case was a significant factor in Vaughn being defeated by Sooter. Troy Messick, who'd delivered the news of the fire to Lorene Bible and was the first to respond when the Bibles found Danny the next day, was said to have left before the end of the year to go to the Vinita Police Department.

Cozart resigned in light of his falsified certification, eventually passing away in April 2003 of esophageal cancer.

Mark Hayes went on to Rogers County as a deputy.

David Hayes also went on to Rogers County as a deputy, where today he is captain of the Rogers County Sheriff's Office.

"Sheriff Sooter promised to solve the case," said Glen Freeman. In fact, this was something both the Freemans and the Bibles agreed on: that Sooter's assertions that he would solve this case were more than confident; they were sure. In the towns of Welch and Bluejacket alone (where Ashley and Lauria had gone to school, respectively), the residents "voted three to one not to reelect Vaughn."

"He worked it well in the beginning," said Lorene. "But not toward the end."

Looking back at the time, and at Shane's death, with the benefit of hindsight, the Freemans concede there does exist the possibility that the shooting of Shane was justified, that Shane made a wrong move with his hand and got himself in trouble. The fact remains that police behavior in the wake of the shooting was often suspect: the loss of documents, the harassment over the next year, the shocking deaths of Shane's parents and the disappearances of his sister and her best friend, then the resignation of Cozart.

But there is one missing piece of the puzzle that I know I need to understand before I can move on to look more closely at the theories of drugs, as provided by the Bibles. And that is DeAnna Dorsey, the friend of the Freemans who was best positioned to answer all the questions I had about the possible cover-up involving Shane Freeman, the anticipated law-suit, and the theory that the Freemans were killed so the police could keep a lid on Shane's death. In fact, in talking to the Freemans, I find that most of their anger comes to a head when their narratives land on DeAnna.

"If someone told you, 'If something happened to me, then look here,' wouldn't you listen?" said Dwayne, who also expressed over the years that Danny firmly believed that he wouldn't be alive a year after Shane died because of what he knew. "If police didn't kill my brother and his family, then they hired the people who did. And I think DeAnna's murder proved to us once and for all that this was police related."

15

THE MURDER OF DEANNA DORSEY

2001
Less Than Two Years After the Fire

I knew very little about forty-five-year-old DeAnna Dorsey when I first began to work on the case, and I'm afraid I know little more upon writing this. She was a heavyset woman with curly, short honey-colored hair and lively brown eyes, a good woman from Welch. In the few newspaper articles that exist about her, she is described as a God-fearing woman of "deep religious faith," a woman with a "strong work ethic." She'd worked at Craig County General Hospital since 1996, often going home with tears in her eyes for all the people she couldn't help, the sick and the unsaved.

It was during the late days of DeAnna's (née Bartell) adolescence, in Bernice on a particularly unforgiving hot day in August that the man who would be her husband first saw her. It was the mid-seventies, and he recalled her being "pretty cute," as she shoveled thirteen tons of sand from the back of her father's truck. Like many of the women I met in Oklahoma, from Lorene to Chris and others, she had that breakback strength, and a stoic, biblical approach to the world around her. Years later, people would jokingly refer to her as a drill sergeant. And back then, on that day in Bernice, she declined the boy's advances. "So I walked down to the store, bought bottles of Mountain Dew, and took one back to her," Dale Dorsey was quoted saying. And as luck would have it, it was DeAnna's favorite soda.

Five months later, they were married.

She was a woman who believed that God was constantly preparing her for His good work. As the secretary and treasurer of the local Assemblies of God church, she clung close to its Pentecostal doctrines: To passionately proclaim. To strategically invest. Vigorously plant. Skillfully resource. And to fervently pray.

"She was the closest thing to a saint that I ever knew," Dwayne Vancil said, citing that DeAnna worked for him at an automotive plant in the early nineties. Dwayne remembered that she had it rough, with her marriage starting out in poverty—the young couple lived in a home with walls and part of the roof gone—but stated that you had never met anyone "more committed to her family than her." While employed by Dwayne, DeAnna also went to nursing school, reportedly once working as a candy striper (though I never found proof of this), burning the midnight oil to see herself through school while raising her children and working on the assembly lines. At forty years old, she was the first in her family to earn her college degree, often having her family study with her at night. DeAnna persevered, and by all accounts, she was a successful woman who worked hard for the life she had, the life she was so proud of.

"She had such an air about her, such self-sufficiency," the charge nurse at Craig County General Hospital told local papers in 2001. "I wanted a piece of that."

In the aftermath of Shane's death, DeAnna was the person Kathy entrusted with all of the information pertaining to the shooting, delivered to her friend with the now familiar warning "If anything should happen to us . . ." And when the premonition came true on December 30, 1999, when DeAnna found herself at home with a daughter who, but for the grace of a last-minute grounding, would have been sleeping at the ill-fated

Freeman trailer the night before, she was ready to publicly speak out against the Craig County Sheriff's Office. DeAnna did not hesitate in pointing a finger at them for the deaths of Danny and Kathy and the abductions of Ashley and Lauria.

Entrusted with the documents pertaining to Shane (presumably his autopsy report, the police narratives of the men present, and any documents pertaining to the lawsuit), DeAnna kept them close to her chest in the months following the shocking deaths of the Freemans. She was rightfully devastated about what had happened, even saying that "Ashley was like another daughter" to her.

In September of 2001, DeAnna and her daughter, Katie, equipped with the papers left in her care, joined Lorene and Jay Bible, Dwayne Vancil, and CCSO lieutenant Jim Herman on a trip to Los Angeles, where they were going to be filmed for a series pilot for an upcoming show called "What Really Happened," hosted by Rolonda Watts.

Unable to find a distributor, the show never aired, but I manage to track down the original tape.

DeAnna and Katie sat in the audience. Dressed in a matching teal-colored blouse and pants, DeAnna had a small stack of papers in her hands. Rolonda Watts asked Katie to stand and recount how she was supposed to have been at the sleepover that night. When asked how this tragedy had affected her, the teary high school senior paused. "It's very difficult at school—you don't have anybody there," she said, her voice breaking. "Not the person you ate lunch with every day, not the one you spent every waking moment with." She was referring to Ashley.

When asked what she thought could have happened, DeAnna's daughter's voice sharply changed to anger. "I believe very, *very* strongly that the Craig County Sheriff's Department had everything to do with it." From the stage, Lorene and Jay watched Katie Dorsey speak. "Just because I know of instances that Ashley would tell me about. They [the CCSO] would watch their house. They'd park just, like, down the road in a barn.

And they would follow Danny into town and then follow him back home, park in that same barn, and just watch every moment they left the house." At her side, DeAnna nodded.

"So, then, Ashley did express fear for her family, because of the police shooting of her brother, and the fact that they stood up to the police officers?" the host asked.

"Yes," DeAnna's daughter answered matter-of-factly. "Yes."

Dwayne explained that on the day of the taping, DeAnna had a great deal to say about the situation, laying the blame at the door of the sheriff's office, as her daughter had. According to the families, at one point DeAnna stood up from her chair and yelled toward Lieutenant Jim Herman that the Freeman murders and the girls' disappearances were all their fault, that they'd lied about what they said while delivering the news of Shane's death when saying, "No gun visible." But by the time I finally come across the tape of the show, these parts have long ago been left on the cutting room floor, so I'm never able to see this confrontation firsthand. This said, there is a clear moment during the recording when a continuity error shows DeAnna taking her seat after Jim Herman scrambles to defend himself. This is where I can assume she scolded him. There are also parts where I see DeAnna standing, looking at the host as if she's waiting for her turn to speak, with those papers still in her hands.

During the show, when asked why no one searched for the girls, Jim Herman said it wasn't their job, that it was the job of the OSBI, whom they had turned the case over to. He would repeat this years later, as would Mark Hayes. It seemed they took the position that calling in the OSBI meant they were absolved of all responsibility. Lorene garnered applause when pointing out that each agency passed the job off to the other and that was the reason that parents, like herself and Jay, had to beat the bushes and ask the hard questions, and then be told that they were making trouble. "And I'm gonna keep on making trouble until I get my daughter home." As I'd come to expect, Lorene was the crusader, setting out her intentions to go to the ends of the earth and back to do whatever it took to find her daughter and her daughter's best friend, while Jay sat beside her, wrestling with his emotions.

What is particularly fascinating about this video for me is that it features the first public appearance of the OSBI that I've seen on record, as spokeswoman Kym Koch joined them via satellite and defended the bureau's actions. When first asked what the OSBI's investigation uncovered, she answered, "There were no rumors around town, really. It was real quiet, if you talk to Steve Nutter, our case agent. After that, the rumors started flying and—"

"I beg your pardon," Dwayne interrupted. "There were plenty of rumors flying around!"

At this point, Kym Koch confirmed that there *had* been rumors during the first few days—of Danny killing Kathy, then of the girls killing the parents, then of Danny dealing drugs out of the home, then of Mexican nationals, then of the girls being sold as sex slaves to truck drivers. But Koch was insistent that they had all been fruitless. "Nothing," she stated firmly. "We found nothing to corroborate or substantiate those rumors, including the one about the sheriff's office." It didn't look good for the spokesperson to have shifted so quickly from claiming no rumors to listing six right off the top of her head. She seemed smug, a little righteous in her power over these country folks. When asked what their most recent theory was, she stumbled and looked around for what to say. "Probably the most prominent one was the drug lead," she said, rolling her eyes, "that he [Danny] was involved in some sort of drug activity out of the house." The audience booed and heckled.

She would, however, admit that the OSBI had made a *mistake* and should have found Danny's body. When asked why the OSBI didn't notice Danny, how they couldn't feel his body under their feet, she simply shook her head: "I cannot explain that to you."

Listening to the tape, I can hear Dwayne's voice tremble as he comments on the fact that there are still two of their family members missing with nobody from the OSBI out there helping. "And *now* you tell us you made a mistake?"

Lorene and Jay, who did not comment on the accusations against the police at the time, later stated that they knew the show was trying to get the two families to fight with one another, but they refused to be baited, so they kept quiet about their instincts about the case on camera. The truth was, since the initial days of the fire, the Bibles had kept busy chasing the rampant rumors of drug debt that the OSBI seemingly refused to investigate while the Freemans firmly planted their feet in the notion of police corruption. The Bibles, since day one, had never publicly entertained the connection between Shane and the alleged cover-up of his death, and the murders of Kathy and Danny and the girls' possible abductions. The host returned to DeAnna's daughter, who was now standing, ready to defend the Freemans and directing her questions to the OSBI. "I just want to know, exactly, where she gets the proof that there were drugs involved. Where's the proof? We have yet to see any!"

"You asked for a theory, and I gave you a theory," Kym answered, once again to the audience's disapproval.

Dwayne Vancil never believed his stepbrother's marijuana use had had anything to do with the murders, and he defended his position well. "The cops had spent a year trying to get him on something, to lock him up," Dwayne pointed out. "If Danny was doing something illegal, they would have put him in the slammer."

At the end of the show, as the audience applauds, you can see host Rolonda Watts make her way over to shake her guests' hands, starting with DeAnna Dorsey.

DeAnna wore her white nurse's uniform with pride. Before the days when nurses of all levels wore scrubs, the esteemed white signified not just cleanliness, but the hard work entailed in training and braving the hue against the garden-variety stains of the profession. It was October 6, 2001, a

Saturday morning, and not an especially busy one, with only six patients on the wing. It was twelve days or less than a week (different articles cite different dates, and I am not able to find the exact date of filming) since DeAnna had traveled to Los Angeles and pointedly denounced the sheriff's office for their failures in her friend's case. That morning, she wore her watch, an old-fashioned nurse's honor. DeAnna had just changed the linens in room 100 and returned to the nurses' station to call her daughter, Katie. The call was never connected. A moment later, the phone still in her hand, a man wearing military-issue camouflage pants and a long army coat, with a red bandanna on his head, entered the hospital. Some locals have claimed that the man asked for DeAnna Dorsey by name, though I wasn't able to verify this. He shot at her six times, hitting her five times, in front of her coworkers and patients.

While I was never able to speak with DeAnna's children or husband, I called on a woman named Sydney Horton. Sydney was only ten years old on the day of the shooting, and she was there with her father, a doctor who worked at the hospital.

"He was making rounds," she said to me. "I was sitting at the other physician's [empty] desk, and I heard this noise and looked up."

Her father said he heard what he thought were lightbulbs popping.

"I saw DeAnna start to fall," Sydney continued, saying she was only ten to fifteen feet away from where DeAnna was gunned down. "And then my dad grabbed me and yanked me into the back room. There were some more loud noises. We just hid back there. Then once everything got quiet, my dad went out and checked if DeAnna was OK, which obviously she was not. Then he came back to me and made sure everything was fine. He told me to close my eyes when he walked me out." When I asked her if she knew what had happened, she said she didn't until seeing her father's face and realizing the severity of the situation.

Sydney was unsure if she ever actually saw the killer, or if the memory emerged from everything she read about the day over the years.

Five bullets pierced DeAnna Dorsey that day when the killer emptied a gun into her, missing once. The first one went through her left eyebrow, entering her brain and lodging there. The second went through the base of the front side of her neck, exiting through her upper back. The third entered right behind her left ear, through the bottom of her skull, dislodging a molar on the opposite side and exiting the right cheek. The fourth and fifth bullets went into the back of the head on the left side, behind the ear, exiting out of her forehead. She died instantly at 9:50 a.m.

Moments later, forty-seven-year-old Ricky Martin attempted to reload his semiautomatic pistol out in the parking lot. Officers responding to the scene, part of the Vinita Police Department, found Martin standing on top of a car there at the hospital. Martin cursed at them as the two officers drew their weapons, demanding that Martin drop his gun. When Martin pointed his now-loaded gun at the officers, they each shot their gun once, one being a shotgun and the other a .40 caliber pistol. According to his autopsy, Martin died only minutes later, with five large shotgun pellets hitting his lungs, heart, liver, and "other soft and bony tissues." He died only ten minutes after witnesses watched him gun down DeAnna Dorsey.

It was later reported that Ricky Martin was a paranoid schizophrenic who had had zero affiliation with DeAnna. The local police could never explain why he sought DeAnna out, admitting, "For some reason, he just picked her." According to reports, there were no drugs or alcohol found in his system.

Prior to the murder, Ricky was often seen wandering around the streets of Vinita, wearing his fatigues and long army coat, a vagabond who seemed to have fallen from the grace of one of those all-American youths many people dream of: the football scholarship, the good looks, the wholesome family, all of which he apparently had while being raised in Ada, Oklahoma, a three-hour drive from Vinita. But the symptoms of schizophrenia reared their ugly head shortly after high school, and Ricky Martin soon found himself traveling from town to town, where people often found him sleeping in alleyways or by the train tracks behind the virtuousness of Vinita's Route 66, intermittently trying to find somewhere to level out his medications. One family member reported that Ricky's issues first came to light after a car accident, in which he was ejected from the vehicle, causing lasting brain damage.

Before DeAnna's murder, in January of 2000, the Eastern State Hospital for the Insane in Vinita began to close its doors, a process that seemed to take months, from state-implemented downsizing to fading from existence altogether, creating an exodus for hundreds of mentally ill patients to relocate to the overcrowded asylums in Tulsa and several smaller and ill-equipped community-based hospitals and residential care facilities. The latter centers fell under contract with the Oklahoma Department of Mental Health and Substance Abuse Services (ODMHSAS), and some of the buildings on the hospital grounds in Vinita were converted into a facility for the Oklahoma Department of Corrections (it was already the official treatment center for all ODOC inmates in need of court-ordered evaluations and observations since 1979), where prisoners found not guilty by reason of insanity were stationed; the last of its patients seeking mental health care were all moved out of the original houses by 2008.

Patients, many spending years at Eastern State, had once kept busy in work programs, making the hospital one of the biggest employers in Craig County (their Holstein cows were prizewinners). The grounds were equipped with barns, greenhouses, and canning plants, and even military barracks during World War Two. It grew more in America's ending of segregation, adopting patients from the Taft State Hospital for the Negro Insane in the sixties. Today, thousands of patients are still buried there, though only a few hundred markers remain due to vandalism and teenage hijinks and a lack of record keeping in the now-abandoned premises that looks more like a haunted attraction than a once-working hospital. The yellow signs reading HITCHHIKERS MAY BE ESCAPING INMATES still stand erect, though go mostly unnoticed by locals. For years, the hospital in Vinita was a home base for Ricky, where he'd frequently admit himself to have his medications readjusted. When the hospital went under, Ricky reportedly became aimless, wandering without knowing where to turn to receive the help he was so accustomed to. One week before the shooting, Ricky was in Tulsa getting help, but for what were assumed to be budgeting reasons on behalf of the hospital and state, Ricky was turned away, and he returned to Vinita, where he hoped help was calling him.

Locals agree that DeAnna's murder was a senseless act committed by an unstable man with mental illness who had either run out of or stopped taking his antipsychotic meds. There was no concrete reason outside of Ricky's ill mind to kill the woman.

The Freemans disagree. "He was impressionable," they claim. "DeAnna stood up to the Craig County Sheriff's Office just days before." The Freemans have long believed that DeAnna's murder could be the connecting link to the murders of Danny and Kathy and the abductions of Ashley and Lauria. They stand firm in the belief that law enforcement hired Ricky Martin to shut DeAnna up. They also believe that this was the case for the murders of Danny and Kathy, as they were in the process of filing a wrongful-death suit against the county.

The deaths of DeAnna Dorsey and Ricky Martin were handed off to the OSBI, as Martin's was a police-related shooting. It unexpectedly shone a light on a mental health crisis that was sweeping over the state as swiftly as the methamphetamine epidemic, and calls emerged for the governor and the state commissioner for mental health to conduct a full-scale review of the incident. They, along with State Representative Joe Eddins, acknowledged that with the "downsizing of Eastern State and more emphasis on community-based treatment, the mentally ill are ending up in prisons." The results of the inquiry were turned over to Governor Frank Keating and not released to the public. However, Commissioner Terry Cline of the ODMHSAS sent a letter to the governor, acknowledging that the ODMHSAS's Consumer Advocacy Division's investigation found that neither their own department nor local mental health providers were at fault.

In December of 2001, widower Dale Dorsey expressed his anger, accusing Governor Keating of not taking his wife's murder seriously and "turning a deaf ear" to the reality that his decisions for downsizing would inevitably cause something like this to happen in their community.

"I would like to have the opportunity to pass pictures of my wife in the body bag out to state legislators and the governor," Dale told the *Tulsa World*.

"The downsizing has already occurred, it's over," said the mental health commissioner in the same article.

The case of DeAnna Dorsey dwindled to only a few sentences in print at the back of local papers, a case that was never really fleshed out into something as locally momentous and tangible as the Bible-Freeman case. Her family kindly rejects my requests to speak with them. All I have on DeAnna today is a grainy still shot of the woman in her matching teal trousers and blouse, sitting in the audience of a talk show that never aired.

Today, the people of Craig County are split as to DeAnna's murder being a senseless act of violence versus the conjecture that her murder was fundamentally connected to the Freeman murders and the prior death of Shane, with her brave decision to speak out against the CCSO positioning her in the firing line.

Authorities never discovered a connection between the Dorsey and Freeman murders. Likewise, the Bibles, while acknowledging that it was a shocking coincidence worth looking into, do not agree that DeAnna's death was connected to the Freeman murders or the disappearance of their daughter. Yet again, the two families found themselves on opposite sides of a growing rift, where the Freemans stood firm in their belief that Shane's death and police corruption were at the core of the murders while the Bibles still alluded to drugs, a theory I'd soon examine.

While I look into the Freeman family's side of this significant story, it is just as important that I inspect the drug rumors they dismissed in favor of police corruption and cover-up. This drug angle, supported by the Bible family, carries me to the neighboring county of Ottawa, the northeasternmost corner of the state, punctuated with ghost towns and meth communities and the no-name terrains even some locals won't drive through colloquially known as the Outlaw Lands.

But despite their differences of opinion, the Freemans and the Bibles agreed on one thing: that no matter the reason, their loved ones' case was not being investigated, leaving them to hire their own private investigators and to do the work themselves.

SECTION 3

DRUGS

16

THE MOST TOXIC PLACE IN AMERICA

Oklahoma is breathtaking in more than one way; I can become spell-bound by its beauty or smothered by its desolation. It's important that I listen to the prairie, but just as important that I connect with its cancer. I have a difficult time thinking up a place like Picher, just a half-hour drive northeast from Welch, an environmental disaster that few outside the area have heard of, myself included before this investigation. It is a place that sounds like the nightmares of an apocalyptic wasteland, and back in the first weeks of 2000, private investigators Tom Pryor and Joe Dugan landed there after following up on the insurance card found at the Freeman property. After failing to grab OSBI agent Steve Nutter's attention, they took it upon themselves to follow up on it.

The Picher I come to acquaint myself with and the Picher of old are different worlds; to familiarize myself with the case, I must familiarize myself with this place, understand it in context. More than once, I ignore the government warning signs that decorate the white mountains of this ghost town just 1.75 miles south of the Kansas border. I wrap my arms tightly around the waist of a former local who describes himself as half white and half Quapaw, fearing the four-wheeler will tip over on the bone-colored gravel that makes up what are called "chat piles." Hills of dolomite and limestone deposits long separated by way of ore processing during the country's lead and zinc mining boom now dominate a once-thriving town, a town formerly referred to as the buckle in America's Lead Belt. They glare from the majestic crow poison and dayflower fields like a string of pearls hanging from the Kansas border, now contaminated and toxic. Once silver and gold, the carcass of Picher is a cavity-riddled mouth that swallowed its homes and roads in its sinkholes and undermining hazards created when too much mining and hollowing out of the ground below weakened the land above.

It is here that the prairie stops singing.

The muscles in my eyes are tired, working hard against the white mountains that I stand on, causing gray shapes to move in and out of the abandoned homes below. This investigation turns the shadows of my fatigued psyche into killers always ready to meet me, swimming in paranoia and swift hallucinations.

"Oklahoma's Death Valley," says seventy-five-year-old private investigator Tom Pryor. Today, he is retired and struggling with chronic obstructive pulmonary disease (COPD), because of which our conversations are punctuated with coughing fits. "There's no telling how many bodies are down there." The breeze picks up, and I'm afraid to breathe in the air of this ghost town, but no one around me seems to mind. "All those mines and pits."

I assumed that the bright memories of Picher's recent history wouldn't be so faded in people's minds. Some who've been scattered in the surrounding towns, like Miami (the pronunciation of which—"My-yam-uh"—I'll forever be corrected on), Cardin, and Commerce, still proudly refer to themselves as Chat Rats, after all. (A couple thousand former Picher residents still gather at Christmastime to form a parade through the abandoned streets and past the rubble of old buildings.) But others want to keep this place as far from their thoughts as possible. Bitterness, as acrid as the chicory that weeds over at the town's edges, lingers both in the air and in their souls. Today, the town is the Tar Creek Superfund site—a beneficiary of a government-implemented program designed to safely remove hazardous waste in accordance with the Environmental Protection Agency (EPA). The EPA chief once referred to Picher as "the most toxic place in America." The name sticks.

A decrepit sign at the town limits today welcomes me to Native America.

But it wasn't always this way. In its heyday, Picher was the heart of the Tri-State Mining District, an area of about twenty-five hundred square miles across northeastern Oklahoma, southeastern Kansas, and southwestern Missouri that produced nearly 75 percent of the bullets and bombshells used in World Wars One and Two. At its thirty-year peak, between the 1920s and the 1950s, Picher produced the equivalent of $290 billion worth of ore, making it the largest exporter of lead and zinc in the world. Patriotism was alight and the booming industry brought with it a strong sense of community. The miners came and went underground, blanketed in a healthy dose of black and silver dust with their daily bread, and ever grateful was the Oklahoman who didn't have to travel far for honest work. Picher: a steady population of fifteen thousand and a total of fourteen thousand mines.

Today, the thousands of square miles of tunnels and mines, many once acting as underground interstates, have largely collapsed and filled with poisonous water. Despite this, the old-timers, the stubborn men who refused to ever admit that the land they so loved had betrayed them, still laugh when reminiscing about their childhoods and shake their heads at the later generations who never set foot in the mines or knew the town when it flaunted six movie theaters and two dozen saloons.

This postcard picture of Picher is impossible to imagine today.

Over time the ventures of thousands of Midwestern men enticed by the luster of two hundred fifty mining mills began to dwindle. The toxic chat piles were growing too big, and the demand was lessening. The lead and zinc started to turn into common dolomite and limestone the farther they dug, no matter which direction the miners mined. You could say that it was too much of a good thing for people long used to suffering before the mines changed their fortunes. Abundance, in those days, was something otherwise foreign to Oklahomans, whose overzealous mining would hollow out the ground below, forming sinkholes and collapses in smaller surrounding ghost towns like Zincville (St. Louis) and Hockerville, in the shadows of adjacent and foreboding Picher.

For years, citizens took all the stone they wanted from the chat piles, using it to fill their playgrounds or for school track meets.

What's left today is the disembowelment of a promised land: fourteen thousand abandoned mines. Seventy million tons of chat that still today sit piled up to two hundred feet tall and two hundred yards wide, the width of four football fields. And thirty-six million tons of toxic waste that would go on to contaminate the waters. For every ounce of lead extracted from the earth, there were ten pounds of unusable mineral, thus the chat piles.

Before the exodus, children played in the man-made ponds brought to them by rainfall and the natural water below, along with the tailing ponds created to dispose of the fine powders of lead-zinc ore processing. They cried of sunburn after playing in the red swimming holes that smelled like vinegar, but they always seemed willing to overlook such annoyances, so long as the waters were cool enough to offer relief in the brutal summers. The pools were red like rust, and they gradually realized it couldn't be sunburn permanently dyeing their hair orange. It later transpired that the sunburns were chemical burns from cadmium- and arsenic-laden waters that had been flushed out from the mines, but the residents wouldn't understand the extent of the damage until scientists came to test the waters in the 1990s. Over the years, the same groundwater broke free of the swimming holes and began to fill the abandoned mines.

Up until then, no one knew of the dangers that Picher's most precious resource posed to its people, and this obliviousness made its way down through the generations. They spent their lives reveling in the dust, damn well proud of it, and drinking and swimming in the contaminated water.

After high school test scores began to plummet and sickness made its way into nearly every home, a study in 1996 showed that 46 percent of the children in Picher between the ages of one and five had high concentrations of lead in their blood (more than eleven times higher than in the rest of the country). The miscarriage rate of its mothers was more than double the national average, and chronic lung disease was 2,000 percent higher. And it wasn't just lead and zinc in the air and in their water; iron, manganese, and cadmium also played a part in slowing neurodevelopment in children. Because the absorption of lead causes irreversible damage in the brain, organs, blood, and nerves, most of those affected would suffer the symptoms of poisoning for the remainder of their lives.

At first, many of the complaints were dismissed as your garden-variety homemaker's "nerves": insomnia, hallucinations, memory loss, aggressive tendencies. Women were moodier and harder of hearing, and the men couldn't perform in bed. But then blue-and-black lines started forming on their gums (known as the Burton line), and their speech became slurred. Headaches, loss of coordination, gastrointestinal disorders, depression, numbness in the extremities, decreased urine, brain damage. Neurologically, the children of Picher were affected far more, with spiking rates in severe intellectual disabilities. They lost their sense of smell; their bones lacked density to such an extent that their own body weight would cause fractures. At suppertime, after grace, their noses and mouths would bleed at the table. Liver, lung, and kidney diseases would claim many lives but remain undocumented among a stubbornly proud population that refused to admit the land they were raised on could have turned on them this way. The trains stopped coming, and the welcome signs began to disintegrate.

Today, the overwhelming pride still carried by those who grew up here feels like stubbornness and denial, especially by people who evaded illness.

While several government-funded health studies were carried out on children after the area was declared a superfund site, there appear to be no public reports that show how many teens, adults, and elderly became sick and how many died from metal toxicity. With so many people sick and in pain, the blinding platinum memories of Picher's former glory were rusting over, and all that was left was despair.

In 1999, there were just over sixteen hundred people remaining in Picher. Many of those who stayed were men who refused to submit to *the man*. But others, blood long poisoned, took a more pragmatic approach: the town's poverty level at the time was twice the national average, and into that desperate climate came a wave of methamphetamine production and addiction. The mines, once a symbol of Picher's prosperity, presented the perfect opportunity to easily ensure that evidence of meth cooks and laboratory equipment disappeared forever. The local houses, formerly adorned with cherry pies on windowsills and the singing of Johnny Cash on record players, became hubs for meth makers to cook and go, never staying in one abandoned home for too long.

One such man was a Kansan named Warren "Phil" Welch II, who lived within a twenty-minute ride of Picher for a good portion of his life. While it's not clear exactly how long he lived in the town itself, it is known that he was an inhabitant at least from October 1999 to April 2000, according to receipts obtained by private investigator Tom Pryor.

Depression spread as fast as the metal toxicity, and Picher never would see enough money to pay for cleanup. It was a religious town in the Bible Belt, but the God the locals loved was nowhere close for some, and to bridge the gap many searched for new crutches. In the late nineties, meth was their master, opening its arms to the weary and burdened and then unemployed and removed. Within a fifty-mile radius, it was the epicenter for the disease. Like many others, Phil Welch took his trailer where no one would care to bother him, and he settled at 412 South College Street, folded neatly against the backdrop of poison.

While rumors related to Picher were some of the earliest in the case of the missing girls and the murdered couple, they never gained traction in the way some of the other theories did.

"The private investigators' updates comprised of vague facts," said Lorene Bible, something the Freemans agreed with. "They said they'd heard stuff, but then they wouldn't be clear about what they heard. Or they'd tell us about a piece of evidence, but then wouldn't tell us where to find it."

"Everyone was talking about Phil Welch," PI Pryor tells me. After discovering the insurance card on the Freeman property, Pryor and Dugan traced it back to a woman in a town called Chetopa, Kansas (just north of Welch and about seventeen miles from Picher). The woman, known as E.B., pointed investigators in the direction of her boyfriend, Phil Welch.

In January of 2000, about two weeks after the bodies of Kathy and Danny were discovered, fifty-four-year-old Phil Welch wandered around the crumbling remains of Picher, the chat piles at his back. He wore a Western shirt with pearl snap buttons, and he walked up and down the prairie that surrounded the town. In the early afternoon, he scanned the silver horizon, taken by the beauty of the frost and the weight of the clouds. With tears running down his face, he sang "Nothing but the Blood" without having to look at the hymnal in his hands. And when the fields failed to sing back, he was struck by a pang of emptiness. It was a void that could only be filled with poison.

Despite his religious convictions, most people I speak to about Phil Welch refer to him as the devil himself. He was a well-known meth addict and manufacturer who moved frequently, though never far. When I ask around, the most common word associated with him is "terrifying." And when I reach out to one of his stepchildren for the first time, the initial response is a short one: "Phil Welch is a horrible man."

Phil Welch had two homes, one in Picher, where he cooked meth, and one in Chetopa, where his wife and her children lived. "She was only married to him because she was scared he was going to kill her," his stepchild tells me. "He was a horrible man who would beat her and her children. He did a lot of bad things."

On the icy outskirts of Picher in January 2000, a couple weeks after the murders of Danny and Kathy, Phil continued to survey the land, perhaps consecrating it with one of the religious ramblings he was so known for (they went on for days, I'd hear). The machinery of the mines behind him was cold, and the sickness that had taken grip in those shafts never had worked its way out of Picher's system—or out of his. He looked down at his hands, which were becoming less and less coordinated by the day. He cursed those hands, unaware that their clumsiness was the beginning of a sickness he swore was his punishment from God.

"We weren't allowed to be sick," another relative tells me. "He'd think it was God's punishment coming upon the house." Family members would often cough into their pillows to avoid him or stifle their sneezing. I wondered what his thoughts were when he started to lose the strength in his hands.

In the distance, a familiar streamer of dust signaled an approaching car. This time a blue Ford pickup with two men inside, both wearing ten-gallon hats that bobbed in unison and created shadows against the illuminated back window.

The two men in the truck were private investigators Tom Pryor and Joe Dugan. Today, Pryor still sports that ten-gallon hat.

"We found him walking down the road," he remembers. "I asked Joe if that was Phil Welch, and he said, 'I think so.'"

Phil Welch watched the car slow as it approached him; then the men pulled over. Like him, they were coming from the direction of Chetopa, Kansas. Tom recalls, "We didn't tell him who we was or anything."

Phil had a habit of thinking that most everything was a sign, and this day was no different. God was leading him somewhere, or putting someone in his path, for a reason. Phil held his head up proud. "Hey, fella, you need a ride?" asked Pryor. Phil shot them a hard sideways glance, reading them for a moment. But he didn't have anywhere in particular to go, and from nowhere in particular was he coming. He was restless, and the sky overhead wasn't moving fast enough for him anyway. "Well, I guess."

Pryor climbed out from the passenger's side and let Phil sit in the middle of the bench seat.

"The first impression you get," Pryor tells me, "was Charles Manson. He's that type."

Crammed between the pair, Phil hummed the remnants of the hymn that wound through his head. He faced forward, his eyes distant and empty, like he wasn't there at all. In this way, he had a dreadful intensity to him, one that made those around him stand on edge. "Where you going?" Pryor asked.

"Picher, I suppose." The tips of his fingers were burned, nails black and amber and exceedingly brittle as he tapped on the leather-bound songbook. He also had a habit of constantly smacking his tongue against his teeth, an obsessive behavior when he was high, which was at most any given time.

"Joe, you wanna stop for a hamburger?" Pryor asked before glancing at Phil, who never took his eyes from the road. "You want a hamburger?"

Pryor describes him as "really weird," and says, "He could be talking and he'd break into religious mode, start preachin' about anything. I think he knew every page of the Bible. His daddy was a preacher. I think he punished him by beating him with it." But I am not able to verify this, and what family does exist out there seems to have put a great deal of distance between themselves and Phil over the years.

The three men headed to the drive-through of the Gorilla Cage, a now-extinct burger joint that sported a large gorilla out front (it was the mascot for Picher). They parked in front of the small building, which resembled a shoebox with bright red and white stripes painted on its metal fringes. Brightly lit roadside signs and arrows pointed to the building from either side, a compact version of a neon-lit eatery you'd find on the nearby Route 66, begging passersby to try their famous calf fries, a beguiling term for the locally popular fried cow testicles. From the small restaurant's loudspeakers, Tammy Wynette's "Stand by Your Man" played, as if the locals were desperately hanging on to a past Picher still longed for. Pryor knew who Phil was, and several times he tried to get Phil's eyes to meet his. There were sunken moments of silence, filled with the electricity of an impending storm crawling overhead.

Phil pointed to the poisonous hills around them. "See this place?" Phil remarked. "God's damnation. Wicked people. There's no saving anyone here." Phil watched the private investigators closely, then returned to his burger, adjusting to the silence from the two men at his side. "Like Sodom." Pryor and Dugan agreed, nodding. Phil inspected each one of the chat piles looming in front of the truck. "Man, I can't keep count of the transgressions. The whites took this earth and raped it to death before giving it back. And you wonder why God got angry. One day, God's gonna just cut this place down, give it the natural disaster it so deserves."

I know today that this would be an accurate prophecy, as the coup de grace for Picher was an EF4 tornado in 2008 that killed seven and destroyed a hundred fifty homes.

Residents with obvious signs of meth addiction came in and out of view. Their lips scabbed over, the emaciated characters wore the loose cowboy gear of their forefathers. Enveloped in the toxic wind, they were a stark contrast to those still hanging on to the dreams of the old town, smiles twisted tight as they pretended the junkies overrunning the place weren't there.

"After a while," Pryor remembers, "I asked him, 'Say, you hear about those girls in Welch?'" in an effort to divert Phil's attention from fire and brimstone.

"Yeah," answered Phil, angry and jittery in equal measure, "I heard about them two little bitches."

Pryor tilted his head back fractionally to gauge his partner's reaction. "I wanted to grab his throat right then," says Pryor. "But I kept my cool."

"Where you say you from?" Joe Dugan asked Phil.

"Chetopa, but I do missions around here too."

"You know, I used to live in Chetopa," Pryor told Phil. Not only had he lived there, but Pryor was the chief of police there long before he launched his own private investigation business.

"These girls I was talking to up there said that a guy by the name of Phil Welch killed those girls. I don't suppose you know Phil Welch, hmm?" Phil stopped chewing his food, stored what there was in his cheek.

"Yes, I'm Phil Welch." Phil began to stutter, answers half-coherent, half-ecclesiastical, the religious rambling he was so known for amplifying with his anxious outward demeanor. The two men sitting on either side of him caught just fragments of sense from Phil Welch. "I hear they're somewhere in the mine shafts." Pryor saw the emptiness of his glare and says that he knew right then that he was sitting with a murderer. "Those two little bitches."

Phil started to jerk around, scratching at his arms, babbling barely comprehensible lines from sermons and Bible verses. Pryor and Dugan felt confident that this man had heard something about Lauria and Ashley in the weeks after their disappearance.

Pryor feared that if he didn't let Phil out of the truck, he might become violent. Phil nearly climbed over Pryor to escape what was too quickly becoming an interrogation. He landed on the chat-filled pavement of the burger joint, then walked away as fast as he could with high shoulders, inflated with a rage that always lurked just beneath the surface. *Righteous anger,* he'd tell himself over the years. Pryor and Dugan silently watched Phil march off and disappear back in the deteriorating lands of Picher. Even after he was out of sight, they could still hear the scripture emanating from Phil's lungs.

Later that evening, Phil retreated to his Picher trailer. It was a ramshackle home used to cook meth, littered and filthy. There was no running water, and electricity was tentative; the place felt damp, cold. Porn rags and cigarette butts covered the floor, and stray cats and rats came in and out as they pleased. Phil's hands weren't working right when he tried to turn the knob of the front door, and it took him some time to regain his grip. He cursed those hands once more, confounded by spells of paralysis that would only get worse with time. He became gripped by the idea that God was telling him not to go inside. But when he turned around, the storm clouds were bruised and inflamed, surely a sign that his capricious God intended him to seek shelter in the trailer. After nearly a half hour of trying to get in, when God released him from His discipline, Phil Welch finally stumbled across the threshold.

Already inside was a small group of people—associates, lovers, wheelers and dealers. They included one of his girlfriends, a sex worker or two, and two men as thick as thieves named David Pennington and Ronnie Busick—men who'd spent most of their adult lives in the throes of meth addiction, and more recently, under the dominance of Phil Welch.

"Everyone was scared to death of Phil Welch, because they all knew what he was capable of," says a source of mine. Bruce, a hard-core biker and meth user out of Picher, a man who would have never struck me as a man scared of anything, tells me of a time when Phil Welch nearly strangled him to death. "If you want to know what pure evil was, it was Phil." Evil, I keep hearing, had a home in Phil's eyes.

"Have you ever seen the devil?" one source asks me while he's getting high. "I mean it, Jax. I'm asking. Have you ever seen the devil? Because I have, and it was Phil Welch."

In those days and weeks surrounding the date of the Freeman murders, David Pennington and Ronnie Busick followed Phil Welch closer than ever, higher than ever. The men, both bread-and-buttered in Chetopa, Kansas, were boys of poverty and products of meth. And as they looked up to Phil's finally returning, the gospel music that Phil demanded be played in his presence revved back up to life—an old, rugged country hymn you might have found in the days of the dust bowl.

The three men continued to get high, with Phil Welch briefly stopping to look over at the dirty wall where a clean piece of paper hung. . . .

It was one of the missing flyers that Lorene Bible had drawn up days before, with the faces of Lauria and Ashley smiling back at Phil Welch.

17

THE OUTLAW LANDS

2001
Less Than Two Years After the Fire

I drive for days. Ice has turned each and every square inch and bare twig to crystal, weighing them down so it feels like winter closes in on me. It's a wonderland like something on the front of a Christmas card. I think I'm going to freeze to death in the Arkansas Ozarks, trapped by ice and desolation, car-rocking gusts, and the darkness of the razorbacks. I pull over, left with a paranoia that welcomes me to the Midwest every time I drive here from the East Coast. I like the mindless hours, the changing terrain as it races by, and the wide-open sky; I like the snow in my sleep. When I wake, it's to a spectacular, blinding beauty—milk white and opalescent hues. But I need to get warm—I need to wash myself of the scent of truck exhaust and Krispy Kreme glaze and get back to work; I plan to investigate the drug theories that have plagued the Welch murders and the girls' disappearances since day one.

To me, it has always seemed that the Freemans focus on the "whys" of the crimes against their family while the Bibles choose to focus on the "wheres." The former look for answers in the patchwork leading up to the murders while the latter remain grounded in the present. There is no right answer, and here there are no answers at all. "What do I have to do next to find my child?" Lorene always asks me rhetorically. To her, what is in the past is unchangeable; it doesn't matter. She never shows the desire to *dwell*, as she puts it, just a rigid determination to track down her daughter.

It is a late night in early January, and I curl up on the couch of Ottawa County sheriff Jeremy Floyd. The fire keeps us warm, the sheriff in his pajamas with a flannel blanket over his legs. His wife entertains a couple of Yorkies; our stomachs are full from a wild hog the sheriff killed and prepared himself. The Floyds are gracious in letting me sleep there and work from their dining room table. Jeremy is a soft-spoken man, once a boy from Commerce, Oklahoma, just a few miles up Route 66. I try to impress him by pointing out how he was raised in the same town where the infamous Bonnie and Clyde killed Constable Cal Campbell for their thirteenth and final murder in 1934 (marking Ottawa County's first lawman to die in the line of duty) and abducted Chief of Police Percy Boyd, who was shot, taken hostage, then let go about seventy miles north in Kansas.

Today, you'll find a black-and-white photo of Floyd's great-grandparents on the wall behind his desk in his office. "My great-grandpa Smith was plowing mules on his ranch, just west of Commerce," Jeremy starts. "Some young, well-dressed man walked up and pulled a gun on him. He made my grandpa take his horses to where the young guy had his car stuck in a ditch on the county road. And back then, having a car was a big deal. As the story goes, there was a woman in the car, and Grandpa Smith was convinced that as soon as he used his horses to pull the car out, this man was going to kill him. But, instead, the man gave him some money, and they were on their way. Soon after, they killed that lawman in town."

Sheriff Floyd is also a direct descendant of infamous gangster, once public enemy number one, Charles Arthur "Pretty Boy" Floyd, and he tells a hand-me-down family tale of Jesse James: "Jesse James showed up shot in Commerce, but my great-aunt, being the Christian woman that she was, wouldn't let outlaws in her house. She let him heal up in the barn outside. After some time, when Jesse James was ready to head on out, he left a jar of money for the woman." Sheriff Floyd goes on to explain that the rumor was that she'd buried it, much to the entertainment of later generations, who dug holes in the gardens. "Ottawa County has a rich history," Jeremy continues. "Every outlaw you could imagine had ties here. It's always been outlaw country." Like his forefathers, Jeremy Floyd is no stranger to crime, but he carries with him a sense of rightness that seems to have eluded so many of the Ottawa lawmen before him. Floyd is reserved, gentle, with jet-black eyes and a childlike smile that always feels unexpected when quickly flashed, even as we sit near the dying fire. Only weeks after being elected sheriff in 2016, he earned himself a reputation around town as a force to be reckoned with when he shot and killed a forty-two-year-old criminal in an indisputable case of self-defense. Beneath his unassuming demeanor is a power he can wield swiftly, one you'd hate to be on the wrong end of, and a voice so quiet that I can't press one ear to the couch.

"The sheriff's office was so behind the times, I guess you can say," says Floyd. "It was important to me when I became sheriff to pull us out of that rough patch."

The next evening, we eat at a steak restaurant, where the sheriff, dressed in a tee and sweats, keeps his head low under a baseball cap to avoid being interrupted by locals. Before us, the bright lights of Route 66 flash on our skin, sweet potatoes and butter warm on our forks. In thought, he looks out to the very town, the very county he is sworn to protect. His eyes don't necessarily land on anything; he knows what's out there. "It's something of a haunting place," he says. "Once you're part of it, you can't ever leave." So I have noticed.

I don't need to venture far into the backcountry to see the grip that meth has on his county, an epidemic like a slippery bar of soap in the sheriff's hands. "Meth came in like a tidal wave," he explains, discussing the modern-day outlaws who arose in the investigation into Lauria Bible and Ashley Freeman's disappearance. "Meth was the biggest monster to this area and still is." And it was safe to say that it made its grand entrance in the 1990s, not long before the murders of Kathy and Danny Freeman. Back then, drug-related murders were rampant, as drug enforcement agencies scrambled to keep up with the influx of meth in Oklahoma.

Tomorrow, I will head to Wyandotte, where the first two official searches for Ashley and Lauria took place weeks apart, only a cigarette toss away from each other in the summer of 2001.

Wyandotte, home to the federally recognized Wyandotte Nation American Indian tribe, sits anatomically in the stomach of Ottawa County. A town of only about three hundred people, it is here where investigators on the Freeman-Bible case lingered for most of 2001, just twenty-seven miles east of Welch. Northwest of Wyandotte is Twin Bridges State Park (most locals refer to the 2001 searches for Ashley and Lauria as taking place in Twin Bridges, though the searches never occurred on the park grounds themselves, but nearby). Maps show its rivers tangled in knots and gangs of unspoiled forestry, a mecca for snagging spoonbills (paddlefish) and catfish and other bottom feeders, human and not.

For summers, I saw it alight with handheld sparklers and smelled burning charcoal. American flags were vibrant against clear sky and pontoons skimmed across the shimmer of the Neosho River. For falls, the white pelicans came in droves, honking against a multicolored backdrop of leaves falling onto the water. As winter creeps in like sickness, I watch the gaunt frame of a meth head come out of his house at one in the morning to mow his dead lawn by the light of the moon. Looking down the river, I might make out the glow of the bonfires on top of a hill where the river begins to bottleneck and bend into what's named Lost Creek. At the time of the Welch murders, a documented meth cook named Chester Leroy Shadwick II lived here, and in 2001, it was where authorities conducted their very first search for the girls. However, it's hard to deny, based on the records at hand, that the girls were only an afterthought in the execution of meth house raids and pursuit of other drug charges, with Lauria's and Ashley's names being brought up only when addicts were looking down the barrel of jail time. It was never a matter of authorities looking for the girls that led them here, rather authorities coming here and the meth heads bringing up the girls.

It bears repeating that many of the names throughout this book, especially in this chapter, have been changed.

"Wild and fun." Amber Powell laughs when I ask her what the parties out in Wyandotte were like. "I mean, for back then." We sit at one of those classic American diners closer to Tulsa, the kind that desperately cling to time-honored values. Our interview is chaperoned by posters of Marilyn and Sinatra over fried pickles and ranch and a jukebox full of the oldies. Amber Powell: meth addict, reformed, long familiar with the underbelly of Ottawa. She is thin, and she surely would have been beautiful in her heyday, now left with a crooked smile where parts of her teeth were knocked out of her skull from one domestic incident or another. She has with her an air of hard times and menthol. But most important, she is one of the many people mentioned by name in a 2001 affidavit for a search warrant.

I wear the twenty-one pages of the affidavit out until they are soggy after years under the oil and sugar of my fingers. The document was created and sworn by then OCSO detective Mike Eason. Today, Eason is the district attorney's investigator for Delaware County, just south of Ottawa and bordering Arkansas. While never assigned to investigate the Freeman-Bible case, he was once the director of the District 13 Drug and Violent Crimes Task Force, which made him well acquainted with the miscreants of the ever-growing methamphetamine scene here in Ottawa County. Eason wasn't looking for the girls when "[f]rom July 2000 through November 2000, Affiant [Eason] received information from different sources which were either CI's [confidential informants / cooperating individuals] or sources who were incarcerated in the Ottawa County Jail." While Detective Eason was the affiant named in the affidavit, it is standard practice that reports are written in the third person.

"We had a lot of guys start talking about those girls," Eason told me. "But that was a long time ago."

As I pore over the affidavit, it tells of several sources who lived in and/or frequented the seedy areas of Wyandotte, namely around the home of established meth cook Chester Shadwick. On January 5, 2001, just over a year after the fire, Detective Eason spoke to an Ottawa County Jail inmate by the name of Donovan Maxwell, a thirty-one-year-old white man with a shaved head and scarred chest in prison for attempting to manufacture methamphetamine.

Maxwell stated that in the last part of November 2000, he received a "videotape from a Shannon Burleson [a criminal with a litany of drug charges, burglaries, and assault on his record] that showed Amber Powell having sex with James Payne." Amber, the same Amber I'm sitting with in the diner, is the mother of James Payne's mentally disabled son. She tells me of a time when James Payne, a boxer and rumored meth cook from Wyandotte, was charged with assault and battery with the intent to kill after beating Amber with his bare fists until her heart stopped. As it goes, it was Detective Eason who performed CPR on her bloodied, broken body until the Life Flight helicopter arrived and plucked her lifeless eighty-pound body from the black hills of Wyandotte. Eason confirms all of this when we speak.

Beyond the claims from the affidavit, I can get no actual details of how this videotape exchanged hands, nor can I gather how inmate Maxwell first gained Detective Eason's attention from jail. But Amber admits to me with a laugh that she and James Payne often made sex tapes. "Back then, I was so skinny that I'd make my shirts by tying a bandanna around my body." She looks longing, and I ask if she misses those days. "Just the crash," she admits as she relives it in her mind. "I just miss that sleep."

According to inmate Maxwell's statement to Eason, the recording of Amber and James having sex ended, but the tape went on, leading to a previously recorded scene in which Maxwell watched a "young, dirty-blond-headed girl tied up by the wrists, on her knees, and a James Payne

W/M [white male] 28-years having sex with this girl." Maxwell described that the room had a "rock wall in the background."

"It was the girl I saw on the news," Maxwell told Eason, referring to one of the missing girls.

Amber denies having any knowledge about the alleged video on which her son's father and the man who left her to die was recorded raping one or both of the missing teenagers.

After seeing the video, inmate Donovan Maxwell claimed, he gave the tape back to Shannon Burleson.

Detective Mike Eason tracked down Shannon Burleson. Shannon Burleson claimed that he had borrowed it from a man named Logan Sherry. Giving a statement nearly identical to the one made by Maxwell in jail, Shannon said that on the tape was a young girl "tied up by the hands on a bed and that James Payne was performing sex with this young girl." Again, like Maxwell, the one distinguishing factor he described was a rock wall in the background. Shannon Burleson didn't know which of the two girls it was by name but he did admit that it was the one "with the sandy blond hair," which could have described either one of them. Shannon Burleson claimed that he later returned the tape to Logan Sherry in December of 2000, and he believed Sherry still had it.

I reach out to Shannon Burleson on Facebook, but he denies being the same man featured in the affidavit (although it's easy to establish that he is, by comparing all his public photos with his mug shots on file, and verifying birth date, et cetera). But I'm not out to trap anyone, and I accept his lie. He wishes me luck and I go on my way. But after months of no correspondence, he sends me a "Happy New Year" GIF before blocking me from writing back.

Nine months later, Shannon Burleson will die in a motorcycle accident.

I later try to reach out to Logan Sherry, who was the last person said to be in possession of the sex tape. It was reported that Logan has since cleaned up and become the owner of an auto repair shop in Ottawa County. But when I go to ask him about the affidavit, his wife makes a scene at their place of business, marching up toward me and screaming in my face. Even though I feel her breath, I can still watch Logan stare off with a blank expression on his face, lost in some other world where not even his wife's screaming is enough to break his attention. She also threatens to involve Eason, as though he were some pit bull she kept locked up in her yard. And though I go on to meet several suspects, seeing Logan Sherry drift off is the only instance in all my time in Oklahoma that I get the chills from a man. I'll forever wonder where he went in those blank-stare moments, and wonder if the girls were there.

On February 16, 2001, Detective Eason obtained a warrant to search Sherry's property for the videotape. No tape matching the description given by Burleson and Maxwell was found, though Sherry, along with two other cooks who were present, was arrested for attempting to manufacture methamphetamine. According to the affidavit, "Sherry said that he heard a rumor that the tape existed but has never seen it."

In June 2001, a "cooperating individual" known as CI#99 (often the initials for a confidential informant) said that Logan Sherry told CI#99 that he did see the tape, which showed "the two Welch girls" being molested. According to CI#99, Sherry said that Chester Shadwick, the popular Wyandotte meth cook who threw the wildest parties in the hills overlooking the Neosho River, was angry with Sherry for showing the tape to Shannon Burleson and "another person," and that Shadwick wanted the tape back. Sherry claimed that Shadwick came to pick up the tape prior to February 16, 2001, and that Shadwick told Sherry that he had subsequently "got rid" of the tape.

CI#99, who had at one point lived on the Shadwick property, went on to describe, in great detail, Chester Shadwick's tricks of the trade: where Shadwick would bury the cookware and chemistry equipment for meth production by a tree line in the backyard, how Shadwick opted to cook in the garage as opposed to the main living quarters. He gave precise measurements on how to divvy up the red phosphorus, warnings of violent chemical reactions. CI#99 claimed that Shadwick threatened to bury

CI#99 "with the rest of them" should Shadwick's name be raised in any drug investigation. As stated in the affidavit, and as confirmed by a relative of Shadwick's when I speak to them, Shadwick was known to bury barrels and boxes of incriminating evidence by that tree line, with "numerous" rifles and long guns, not far from one of the several campers on the Shadwick property.

Shadwick's property consisted of two acres, only accessible through a red cattle gate at the end of a dirt dead end that ran uphill from US Route 60. Beyond the gate, there was the main residence, a tan single-wide mobile home with brown trim. Another dwelling consisted of a gray single-wide mobile home with maroon trim, as well as a white camper and several outbuildings, junk cars, and other curtilage and appurtenances. Surrounding the two acres belonging to Shadwick was dense and weedy land owned by the Grand River Dam Authority.

Six months before the submission of this affidavit, which was created by Eason to ultimately search for the girls' bodies in light of all the rumors, CI#99 said that he was with Shadwick by the camper on the property and that "there was a hole dug by the camper and there was also a 55 gallon drum." According to the informant, the drum contained what he described as "a leg bone with a foot bone connected to it."

At night, the tweakers drove up the hill to the Shadwick house, pairs of headlights dancing above the Neosho where the echoes of heavy metal music hollered downstream and over Lost Creek. The bonfires were lit and the ripples of the black river lit with amber like nerves. The property seemed to float over dense vegetation and swampy ground where the trees were bare by winter, as skinny as the guests around them. The windproof torch lighters stayed hot under blackened thumbs, contouring lean, hard faces. Because of the increased sex drive and reduced inhibitions brought on by methamphetamine highs, you'd sometimes catch a flash of thumping flesh from the shadows.

By day, they slept, having blacked out the windows with shoe polish and soggy newspaper, unable to let their eyes adjust to the light outside.

Today, these partygoers are older, and the india ink on their skinny arms has faded to a sickly green. But that generation of vampiric lost boys is still feared today. I am repeatedly warned to steer clear of the outlaws, told that they'd skin me alive without much thought and that they have the police deep enough in their pockets that it wouldn't cause too much of a blip on the radar of law enforcement. Just like in Craig County, the plethora of documented scandals and the extent of police corruption run deep in Ottawa.

"I'd heard through the grapevine that some of the local law enforcement were confiscating drugs for their own use," says current sheriff Jeremy Floyd. But I sense he doesn't want to discuss the subject much further than this.

At the time the affidavit was created in 2001, Chester Shadwick was serving part of a three-year sentence for charges related to possession of meth, firearms, and a police radio, the latter being a popular charge leveled against the outlaws for alerting and being alerted by dirty cops to approaching danger. This corruption was raised at every corner, in fact, and extended as far as a former sheriff who was implicated in the executions of minors. And another sheriff who was stabbed to death only days before the Freeman murders. Even during my own visits to Oklahoma, I'd see a former assistant district attorney arrested for the solicitation of murder and pandering for prostitution (among other charges). I'd also see a state representative who felt the need to publicly defend himself on Facebook by asserting, "No, I have not murdered anyone, and no, I am not a child molester." While this is a permanent backdrop to my investigation, it's something I have to put on the back burner.

"We can't lose focus," Lorene Bible tells me time and time again. She consistently says that she'll have her day to come back and get angry at authorities and law enforcement who botched the case or saw to it that certain crucial people were not adequately interrogated. "You see it all the time, and you know what happens? It becomes about them, and not about the girls." Even though I uncover more than a dozen murders and missing-persons cases throughout northeastern Oklahoma in which families cry police corruption, I have to put them on the back burner. There has been a series of shocking misdeeds at every level of law enforcement, but I am here to find out what happened to Lauria and Ashley, and no one can afford to get distracted.

As authorities readied for a search, and with Chester Shadwick in a Missouri prison, Shadwick's residence was being watched over by a man named Nick Joseph, who was staying there temporarily to keep an eye on things. After conferring with the local drug task force, Detective Eason learned that Joseph was a career meth cook and was "in possession of a machine gun and a .50 caliber." On June 8, 2001, the same day that the affidavit was written and signed by Eason, he sought the help of a CI who went by CI#98, an informant whose information had led to meth-related arrests and the confiscation of a meth lab in the past. CI#98 advised Eason that while they had been to the Shadwick property before, they were "scared to go out there because people get shot at," and stated that they "heard that there are people buried out there at the residence." Eason opted to fly a plane over the property, which isn't an uncommon practice for law enforcement—the county has its own municipal aircraft available out of Grove, Oklahoma. Eason noted each of the two mobile homes on the property, a tin garage, a camper, and what appeared to be disturbed dirt near the camper, all coinciding with what CI#99 had previously mapped out. The places near the camper where the loose dirt was were "where CI#99 saw a barrel buried that had human bones in it."

The cover sheet of the search warrant describes how Eason found probable cause to believe that "murder, kidnapping, lewd molestation, manufacturing methamphetamine, possession of automatic weapons, illegal proceeds of drug sales . . . are being or have been committed" at the Shadwick property. The search, as listed, was planned for fifty-five-gallon barrels, human bones or human remains, videotapes, firearms, and items related to the manufacturing or selling of meth, and paperwork and records documenting meth-related business and traffic.

On June 14, 2001, four Ottawa County detectives, including Eason, and nine deputies stormed in at sunrise and seized five VHS tapes and one roll of film.

It was not specified whether or not the sections of disturbed dirt were ever explored, and this question remains today.

In the end, they found nothing to corroborate the statements of the CIs. No one was charged with any crime relating to the murders of Danny and Kathy Freeman or the girls' disappearance.

Though the affidavit and search were executed in June of 2001, it wasn't filed with the state until the year 2004. While no one would, or could, comment on why it took authorities years to file the documents, Lorene Bible believes it might have been to keep her from knowing about the search, as authorities felt she was "too involved." It was no surprise that Lorene felt left in the dark still, rightfully angry when she was the one doing all the investigating. She explains that she would have been at the Shadwick search, had someone told her about it. "The OSBI, the sheriff's office, not one single person kept us posted about what was going on."

"We'd have to chase them down and say, 'Hey, what's going on?'" says Jay Bible. "It was like pulling teeth."

"We didn't even know about the Shadwick searches until we heard about them at the Glover searches a month later," says Lorene. "Nutter didn't tell us anything. In fact, we didn't even know they were looking in Wyandotte until then."

18

THE OUTLAW LANDS (CONTINUED)

2001
Less Than Two Years After the Fire

Wyandotte is about a half-hour drive east from Welch and only ten miles from Missouri's southwest corner. One particular trip finds the roads littered with dead turtles after historic flooding. The snapping turtle, the symbol of the Wyandotte Nation, and of the ancient American Indian belief that life started on its shell, crushed on the shoulders of US Route 60. The mornings are rosy and have no resemblance to the nights and the men who inhabit the Outlaw Lands. Wyandotte feels like a graveyard where you hold your breath upon driving by to avoid drawing up restless spirits. Streetlights dwindle to blackness, and my imagination stirs the darkness into the silhouettes of men leaning on the shadows of broken-down signs and long-out-of-order stores. My headlights reflect off the animals' eyes that now belong to the shadows of imagined killers. Anxiety is a red-hot flash up my breastbone, like the devil licks my sternum. I shut off the music and roll down the car windows to listen to the hot wind outside and never take my eyes off the road the many times I have to drive past the meth houses.

My heartbeat is but a demon on my shoulder, tapping the backs of his heels against my ribs. But I fashion my past into a shield so that I meet the addicts where they're at. I speak their language; I know their pain. Unlike the missing girls, these are the ones that I understand.

In the spring of 2001, shortly before the Shadwick searches, a twenty-six-year-old up-and-coming meth cook from Miami, Oklahoma, named Johnny Rose was hired to help transport berries from the fruit farms of Oklahoma and Colorado. While on one such trip, Rose divulged to the driver that he knew who'd taken Lauria and Ashley. Perhaps the cattiness of meth drove Rose to tell the driver what he'd seen and heard of the girls. Perhaps guilt pressed his impulse control. Perhaps it was to make room at the top of the food chain when Rose told the driver that the crimes landed with the Glovers of Wyandotte, a father-son duo who helped control the local world of methamphetamine.

When the driver provided the girls' families with this new information, they sent over one of several private investigators they had hired to speak with Johnny Rose, who'd grow into one of Wyandotte's more notorious violent criminals over the next few years. "Johnny Rose started talking about the Glovers, but we hadn't heard of them before," Lorene says as we drive through Wyandotte. She and I have driven this way before, a terrifying thing in and of itself if you're familiar with Lorene's notorious lead foot. "We'd heard a lot of stuff coming from the Wyandotte area." So Lorene and company took it upon themselves to shake the trees, hoping for fruit to fall. Still, no one was searching for the girls outside the relatives and those they hired.

One of the more interesting aspects of the families' investigations was the numerous mentions of a New Year's Eve party, about forty people in total having brought it up at that time, according to relatives. While still talked about today, the party has never been officially or publicly addressed by authorities (even though most of my Wyandotte sources, in and out of law enforcement, will not disagree that the probability of this party having taken place is quite high). It was not made known whether or not Rose attended this party, which was thought to have a figurative revolving door for criminals coming and going. Several meth heads allegedly partook in the rape, torture, and ultimate murder of Ashley and Lauria, who were held at the party against their will.

I am reminded of Shannon Burleson's New Year's GIF to me prior to his blocking me shortly before his death.

"We heard about the New Year's Eve party since the first whispers from Wyandotte," Lorene tells me, and retells rumors laced with mentions of gang rape, sodomy, drugging up, tying up, murder, and dismemberment, all things that no mother should ever have to hear about. "The party took place somewhere there [in Wyandotte]. The problem is we don't know where. Could have been the Shadwick property. Could have been the Glovers'. All of those drug guys, they're connected in one way or another. Anyway, that's how we first caught wind of the Glovers."

The Glover property is situated just three miles upstream from Chester Shadwick and once housed a hard-eyed father-and-son duo of stocky stature: Paul Glover Sr. and Paul Glover Jr. Rumors of how dangerous they were were brought up nearly every time I mentioned their names. Today, the Glover residence is a run-down brick house that sits on a tall-grass corner of an eleven-acre property just across the street from a church whose crows outnumber its parishioners. The yard is littered with junk cars and old water tanks.

"They had a very bad reputation in the drug world," Lorene explains. "You cross 'em, you pay for it."

"Well, if they start shooting at you, at least you know you're in the right direction," says Jay Bible.

Back in July 2001, Paul Glover Sr. and his son, Paul Glover Jr., were serving time for the manufacturing of methamphetamine and running a chop shop in which stolen automobiles and motorcycles were disassembled and sold. Like Chester Shadwick, the Glovers catered to an ever-growing community of meth addicts nearby, cooking more product than their neighbors across Twin Bridges. "The Shadwicks were where you partied," says one source. "But the Glovers was business, and you don't fuck with business."

"The Glover family involvement with this homicide was the result of a jailhouse rumor," said OSBI agent Nutter in our previous interview. "I was able to get enough evidence to get a search warrant of the area that they had been living in at the time." I wasn't sure which was correct: the Bible family's assertions that young meth cook Johnny Rose had opened his mouth to a driver and talked about the Glovers' involvement, or the OSBI's response that the tip came from jail.

To learn what the official record was, I went and tried to obtain a copy of the 2001 Glover affidavit, drawn up by OSBI agent Nutter himself. It should have been easy enough to do: a quick call to the county clerk's office, being as the affidavit fell under the statutes of public record. But upon several searches by the office's personnel, the Glover affidavit was found to be missing.

When I mentioned the mix-up to Lorene, she called everyone that she had to call, finally locating the Glover affidavit in Tulsa with the OSBI. Though Nutter had drawn it up back in 2001, it was never filed with the district court. Because it had not been filed, there existed the implication that should anything have been found on the property during this search—and there was—it would have likely been inadmissible in a court of law, or grounds for a mistrial. Essentially, if anything was found during the course of this search, it'd all go south.

Seventeen years later, the Glover affidavit was finally filed by the clerk's office after current OSBI agent Tammy Ferrari submitted it. However, reading the affidavit doesn't make clear how authorities came to the Glovers.

According to the affidavit, which is considerably thinner at five pages than the twenty-one-page version belonging to Shadwick, Agent Nutter focused the search on "human remains, fingerprints, blood, hairs, fibers, and other microscopic and physical evidence" related to the cases of Danny, Kathy, Ashley, and Lauria. Most of the information provided in the affidavit seemed to come from Johnny Rose.

As stated in the 2001 affidavit, Rose told the OSBI that back in 2000, shortly after the deaths of the Freemans, he witnessed Lauria and Ashley inside the Glover residence "shooting pool and not acting normal." Rose said he was sure that he recognized the girls from missing posters being circulated in the area. He claimed this was the only time he ever saw them.

However, a few days after seeing the girls, Rose said, he saw Nick Joseph "driving a backhoe he had rented from Big D Rentals and Sales, Miami, Oklahoma." Rose stated that Joseph was doing some "dirt work," and that he personally witnessed Joseph with a large roll of cash for his work soon after. Agent Nutter determined that Joseph had in fact rented a backhoe on February 12, 2000. According to the affidavit, "ROSE reported JOSEPH began having nightmares about the time ROSE had seen the girls. On one occasion, exact date unknown, JOSEPH told ROSE he was as deeply involved in what was going on as the rest of them, although he was never clear about what he meant about the comment."

"Come on, of course I know about the New Year's Eve party," said one of my Wyandotte sources as we sit by a home where he used to cook meth. "Everyone knew about the New Year's Eve party. But am I going to tell you about it? Nope."

"Why not?" I ask.

"Because I like living."

I was sure Ashley and Lauria did too.

Lorene tells me of a time she went to visit Johnny Rose in a Tulsa jail, at a later point in time when he claimed to have been saved. "He [Rose] went to leave. But then he came back with a pencil and paper. He wrote a name and said, 'This is my alibi.' Then he swallowed the piece of paper right in front of me." Lorene believes it was an act of nervousness, as cameras above monitored the pair. I would learn the name written on that piece of paper, but have never heard it again, though it's reported to belong to one of the several people at the New Year's Eve party.

When I reach out to Johnny Rose, he is serving time in a federal prison for drug-related charges. He will, however, be released before I finish this book, a man whose body has been made rock-hard by prison walls and who has a rap sheet saturated with assaults and meth manufacturing. The look of him scares me. And he never responds.

The Glover affidavit continues.

On top of Rose's claims that he'd seen Ashley and Lauria held against their will at the Glover house, and his suspicions that Joseph had later been involved with burying the girls, the affidavit mentions a damning OSBI interview with a man named Jesse Black, another known meth addict and violent criminal, from Galena, Kansas. Jesse Black insisted that at about the same time Rose claimed to have seen the girls at the property, Jesse had "observed two [American] Indian males come into the [Glover] residence . . . and go into a bedroom with Glover." Despite the information in the affidavit, Nutter wasn't clear as to whether or not Jesse was referring to Glover Jr. or Sr. Nutter also went on to write that "He [Jesse Black] heard two gunshots and another man walked into the bedroom with a saw. He heard the noise of the saw. The two Indian males never came out of the bedroom."

These were the new outlaws of Oklahoma. These were the names whispered from the scabbed-over lips of the junkies who replaced the tommy guns and bootleggers. And in 2001, they were the biggest leads the families had to date.

On the early morning of July 26, 2001, three members of the Ottawa County Sheriff's Office, including Mike Eason (who led the Shadwick search), and lead agent Nutter and Ben Rosser of the OSBI, a member of the FBI, two members of the DA's office, and dozens of both Bible and Freeman relatives met at Twin Bridges State Park. There, they exchanged plans before flocking over to the Glover property, where relatives waited on the sidelines, something that wasn't afforded to them for the Shadwick search. Hearts thumped and stomachs sank at the idea of finally, after a long year and a half, finding the remains of Ashley and Lauria. Before the sun had breached the horizon, five search dogs lined the ditch by the temporarily empty Glover home.

"You learn not to get your hopes up," says Lorene. I'm not sure why this single line, which she'll repeat over time, makes my spirit cringe with grief.

As authorities combed the Glover property that summer morning, and news cameras followed, the community waited with bated breath. The new sun on the rows of abandoned cars blinded bystanders, the tall grass attracting bugs from nearby swamps and black pools of old rainwater. The community had long known that both the Freemans and the Bibles took issue with how authorities had been handling the case, and this was the biggest break the OSBI had managed so far. Celesta Chandler, Kathy's mother, continued to share her frustrations. "They got there and were gone in two hours. They said they definitely covered everything, but who knows?"

According to OSBI spokeswoman Kym Koch, they used "equipment similar to a metal detector" to locate two spots on the property where the ground had been recently disturbed. The families say authorities didn't dig, but that Danny's stepbrother, Dwayne Vancil, returned with a backhoe after authorities left the Glover scene. The biggest revelation of the day, however, came when Nutter emerged from the house and made his way over to the families, who were waiting outside at the weedy border of the property. I wonder if it brought their minds back to the days of the fire in 1999, when they had been waiting at the edge of a crime scene and made to keep away a certain distance.

"We got something here," Nutter said.

In the search warrant return, an official list of what was confiscated during the search at the "Residence of Paul F. Glover Jr.," Agent Nutter wrote the following:

> On July 26 2001, a search of the residence identified above was completed by law enforcement officials from the Oklahoma State Bureau of Investigation, Federal Bureau of Investigation, Ottawa County Sheriff's Office, and Ottawa County District Attorney's Office.

As a result of that search, one suspected bloodstained piece of carpet, approximately 12 inches by 12 inches in size, was obtained as evidence and retained by the Oklahoma State Bureau of Investigation.

It is a winter's night in Missouri, a wintry mix falling outside as Paul Glover Jr. and I sit in front of a restaurant's large window. It is the first time he speaks publicly. I am down twenty pounds, and it shows in my face, my appetite held hostage by anxiety; my eely stomach can't handle much more than water, which is what I order. My previous visions of some bumbling, scrawny tweaker are replaced by a muscular man in a tracksuit with the most intense and fastened stare I've ever seen. He is well-spoken, polite, and fixed on the subject. "I was in Oklahoma City, in the jail being held," he explains when I ask about when he first became a suspect. "I was watching the news and see my mug shot come on."

We discuss the events leading up to the search on his property. He makes note of someone not listed in the affidavit: Johnny Rose's then girl-friend pointed authorities there with testimony of seeing the girls playing pool and acting like they were there against their will. "She told them that her and her boyfriend were driving down the road in front of my house, pulled into my house, went up, knocked on the door. So they went through the kitchen window and looked in there and saw the two girls playing pool and drinking beer." Paul Glover Jr.'s eyes never leave mine. "She didn't know if it was a dream or not because she was really high at that time." It's his opinion that because he and his father were already locked up, the OSBI wanted to seal the case and hang it up as fast as they could; the Glovers were all easy pickin's on account of their active role in the local meth scene.

Paul Jr., sober today, distances himself from his father, who still lives in the same house out in Wyandotte. He denies knowing many of the names I bring up from the affidavit and elsewhere, and he also vehemently denies involvement in abducting, abusing, or killing Ashley and/or Lauria.

Ashley Freeman *(left)*,
Lauria Bible *(right)*
Courtesy of Lorene Bible

Lorene Bible
Tiffany Alaniz, Fox23 News

Missing-persons flyer
Courtesy of Lorene Bible

STATE OF OKLAHOMA
COUNCIL ON LAW ENFORCEMENT EDUCATION AND TRAINING
Armed Private Investigator
TOM D PRYOR
00API22717 Expires 4/28/02
This license is issued based upon the provisions outlined in O.S. Title 59, Section 1750.1 et seq. and entitles the licensee to provide such services for the type of license issued in the State of Oklahoma.
Director of CLEET

PI License for Tom Pryor
Courtesy of Tom Pryor

Jay and Lorene Bible, 2018
Tiffany Alaniz, Fox23 News

Classroom photo with Lauria *(top, second from left)* and Ashley *(top, center)*
Courtesy of Lorene Bible

Ashley and Shane Freeman
Courtesy of Lonny Freeman

Lorene and Lauria Bible, 1994
Courtesy of Lorene Bible

Ashley Freeman
Courtesy of Lorene Bible

Birthday party with Ashley
(second from left) and Lauria
(second from right, center row)
Courtesy of Lorene Bible

Craig County Sheriff's Office *(bottom row, from left to right)*: Deputy Troy Messick, Investigator Charlie Cozart, Undersheriff Mark Hayes, Sheriff George Vaughn, Lieutenant Jim Herman, around 1999
Courtesy of Mark Hayes

Craig County Sheriff's Office: Lieutenant Jim Herman *(far left)*, Deputy David Hayes *(second from left)*, Undersheriff Mark Hayes *(bottom left)*, Sheriff George Vaughn *(bottom right)*, Deputy Troy Messick *(standing in center)*, Investigator Charlie Cozart *(far right)*, around 2000
Courtesy of Mark Hayes

CCSO Investigator Charlie Cozart and Undersheriff Mark Hayes
Courtesy of Mark Hayes

CCSO Investigator Charlie Cozart
Courtesy of Mark Hayes

Wedding photo of Jay and Lorene Bible, 1978
Courtesy of Lorene Bible

Danny and Kathy Freeman
Courtesy of Dwayne Vancil

CCSO Sheriff George Vaughn
Courtesy of Mark Hayes

CCSO Lieutenant Jim Herman
Courtesy of Mark Hayes

Suspected killer David Pennington
Photos courtesy of Jerri Shelton

The 2001 search at the Glover property in Wyandotte, Oklahoma
Lonnie Leforce

Murder victim Judith Shrum
Courtesy of Karen Cook

Justin Green *(left)* and
Shane Freeman *(right)*
Courtesy of Justin Green

Suspected killer Phil Welch
Courtesy of Anonymous

Phil Welch at a dog auction in Kansas
Courtesy of Anonymous

Jax Miller with Glen Freeman
Courtesy of Jax Miller

Jax Miller with Glen Freeman *(standing)* and Celesta and Bill Chandler
Courtesy of Jax Miller

Former CCSO Sheriff
Jimmie L. Sooter
Jax Miller

Jeremy Hurst
Jax Miller

The Bible family,
Christmas Eve 1996
Courtesy of Lorene Bible

Bible family, 1999
Courtesy of Lorene Bible

Lauria Bible, 1999
Courtesy of Lorene Bible

Lauria Bible
Courtesy of Lorene Bible

Lauria Bible, age seven
Courtesy of Lorene Bible

Lauria, age nine
Courtesy of Lorene Bible

Ashley Freeman, age fifteen
Courtesy of Lorene Bible

Lauria Bible, age sixteen
Courtesy of Lorene Bible

Lauria and Brad Bible
Courtesy of Lorene Bible

Singed photo recovered from the fire:
Danny, Kathy, and Ashley Freeman
on Ashley's fifteenth birthday
Courtesy of Lorene Bible

Lauria Bible at the "crick"
behind the Freeman home.
This is the only known photo
of the Freeman trailer.
Courtesy of Lorene Bible

Photo of Ashley Freeman
recovered from the fire
Courtesy of Dwayne Vancil

Lauria and her brother, Brad
Courtesy of Lorene Bible

Lauria Bible, age five
Courtesy of Lorene Bible

Ashley Freeman
Courtesy of Dwayne Vancil

Kathy and Danny Freeman
Courtesy of Dwayne Vancil

The crime scene: the ruins
of the Freeman trailer
Courtesy of Lorene Bible

The Freeman
driveway
Jax Miller

A local sign
Jax Miller

The Freeman tombstone
Jax Miller

Jax Miller with Charles Krider
Courtesy of Jax Miller

Jeremy Jones with a
former girlfriend, 1999
Courtesy of Jeremy Jones

Jax and Randy "Cowboy" Madewell
at the Serenity Inn, formerly the
Frontier Motel, 2018
Courtesy of Jax Miller

The arrest of Ronnie Busick with
CCSO Sheriff Heath Winfrey *(left)* and
DA investigator Gary Stansill *(right)*
Lisa Bible-Brodrick

"I don't know those girls. I don't know their families. I don't know anyone that knows them," Glover starts. "Never had any dealings with them and nobody ever told me anything in the drug world while I was out there or in jail or anywhere else." Glover also expresses his disappointment in authorities who plastered his face all over the news in relation to the Welch crimes. "Everything I know is from the TV and media. So knowing that, I thought, why are these people pushing me so hard? Why are they on my place out there?"

While Glover hasn't been back home in years and has settled into a new Missourian life after not using in eighteen years, the reputation sticks. Today, only weeks after Johnny Rose's release from federal prison, where he served fourteen years of a twenty-two-plus-year sentence, Glover has begun helping Rose get some work in Missouri.

"I guess I was one of the bigger names around in the drug scene at that time, so."

After Nutter and company took the carpet sample from the 2001 search and submitted it as evidence, there was only radio silence. Despite consistent pressure from the families, every response from the OSBI was that there was a backlog, and when the results were finally obtained, four years later, they were arguable and disclosed only by word of mouth.

Agent Nutter told Lorene Bible that the sample collected was an "oily red substance," like chain saw oil.

Agent Nutter told Dwayne Vancil that it was animal blood.

No family member related to this case has ever seen an official report, so no one can be sure what the actual results were.

"We found numerous buried drug labs all over the property, but found no bodies," Agent Nutter told me. "There was a bloodstain found in the Glover house. I don't recall it being animal blood, but I recall it wasn't human blood. I think it may have been something else, but I'm not sure." This was the closest I could get to the official results of the stained carpet.

Despite this, ultimately nothing came from either the Shadwick or the Glover property searches, and once again, everyone was back to square one.

That winter's night in Joplin, I watch Glover Jr. leave and I focus more on my rearview mirror than on the road ahead. In winters identical to the one I drive in, and the lights of the city bright with Christmas's greens and reds, I remember that this was Lauria's favorite time of year. And on the drive back, I contemplate the numerous anniversaries and Christmases that have come and gone.

For years following the empty searches, the festive carols felt like dirges, and the snow went from soft and delicate to hard and embittered. In the Bible house, what stood as a symbol of hope for the family was the Christmas tree that Lauria had erected herself in 1999. Lorene kept that tree up in the living room all year round, a reminder of a time when Lauria still lit up her life. It stayed permanently adorned with tinsel and angels and twinkling lights. But it was around 2005 that it finally disintegrated, marking one of the very few times anyone close to Lorene saw her physically grieve for Lauria.

Lauria's cousin Lisa remembers that Lorene packed those emotions back down as quickly as they came. "We had work to do," she says, "and that was to find the girls."

The winters continued without the girls.

So did the springs, summers, and falls.

The three-and-a-half years after the Glover searches didn't feel very long for investigators, but they dragged like a dull knife across the skin of the families of the missing girls, families left in the dark.

It was about this time that a thirty-one-year-old called "Oklahoma" came forward to claim responsibility for the deaths of Danny, Kathy, Ashley, and Lauria. And though I'd heard about him long before I came to the Midwest, I had to understand his confessions in context, taking me back to 1999 and the morning of the fire, just east of Welch, to a man named Jeremy Jones.

19

EAST OF WELCH

December 30, 1999
The Morning of the Fire

From Welch, along the dust roads, through the vast swaths of buffalo grass, the land will open up to reveal an underbelly glistening with crystal meth. This land—these blighted lengths of the prairie—robs virtue, takes teeth, carves notches on the crooked bedposts of the area where Oklahoma, Kansas, Missouri, and Arkansas almost meet, counting the lovers she takes and leaves. Crystal meth sweeps the plains like a thief in the night, turning meadow into abscessed wound. Its victims emerge at sundown, skinnier than the day before.

At night their anxiety is contagious. I relate.

Jeremy Jones (not to be confused with the other Jeremys I've met so far) was by all accounts a handsome man: a scamp sculpted by the gods of straw and sun mixed with a touch of trailer trash mischief. "Hey, I never lived in no trailer, OK?" he corrected me over the phone. He struck a match and lit a Maverick, only smoking because he had a few beers in him. He was reared to have a permanent smirk on his face, no matter what his mood, like he always kept a secret in his pocket for emergencies. He perched himself atop the rusted-over shell of a Ford Model T Roadster from the 1920s, reminiscent of times as a boy when he would pretend to be one of the many "Public Enemy"–era outlaws who had once governed this land. He ran his hands through his dark, wavy hair and looked out to the fields where imaginary shadows moved, conjuring up the ghosts of Ma Barker and her sons, who were buried over in Welch. Or Bonnie Parker and Clyde Barrow, their famous hideout just over in Joplin. Jesse James, even, whose gold was buried somewhere in the state. Give Jeremy a twenty, and he'd show you where.

Jeremy's nerves were jangling as he started to come down off his last high. The puncture wounds in the crook of his arm were scabbed over, growing sorer by the minute. A light sweat germinated on his skin, almost steaming in the cold air of Dotyville, Oklahoma, about fourteen miles east of Welch in Ottawa County.

It would be two hours before the Bells would find the Freeman trailer burning . . . or it was ten minutes after the fire was discovered, depending on which version of the official record I'll choose to believe.

Today, Dotyville juts into the famous Route 66 for half a block, just long enough to check your gas gauge at fifty-five miles per hour before putting your eyes back on the long road ahead. It's a town that never crosses my mind, even as I drive through it daily. In comparison with Welch, it's but a lump of coal, a town with a population of only seventeen people back in 1999. Less than a square mile of land area, it consists mostly of a junkyard that has no confines, where the town spills the corroded remains of Route 66's classic-car shows: Buicks and Chevrolets in decay, abandoned school buses, junk cars that outnumber Dotyville's people by the hundreds. The town feels like it is in mourning for the "could have beens"; it brings to mind tetanus and the rusty recollections of the heartland.

Dotyville can't be found on most local maps, and there's no sign, complete with some spurious claim to fame or a wholesome homemaker's smile painted on wood, to welcome me or see me off. Today, only locals know Dotyville by its Christian name, since it later became part of the larger

Miami area. It is a dark town without any streetlights, but at night it glows a sickly yellow. A small convenience store with bloodstains at the gas pump, sprinkled with kitty litter. A family-owned butcher that has done well since 1969. Other than this, there is just one business operating, and locals know not to go there past sundown.

The Frontier Motel.

It's hard to imagine back to when it attracted family-friendly crowds in the fifties and sixties, when it had a pool, which now serves as the butcher's pond, where the carcass heads of cattle are tied to ropes, thrown in so the snapping turtles can rip the meat off with their beaks, then returned with just the bones. In its day, beautiful cars lined the front of the motel. I speak to many who hold to the delicate memories of the motel, an older generation remarking that *those were the best summers of my life.*

In 1999, the Frontier Motel came alive at night, two ramshackle rows of one-story rooms on either side that were available by the hour and by the month only. The motel was guarded by BB, a fat man with a handlebar mustache and everlasting sweat stains whom people once knew as one of the best rodeo bull riders in town. But in a town of seventeen, that wasn't saying much at all. "He was like Patrick Swayze in the day, before he let himself go," Jeremy Jones tells me. On the dark early morning of December 30, BB leaned against the window that faced the highway, using a pocketknife to strip some copper phone cord in the small motel's front office, which was only the corner room closest to the street. As Jeremy Jones passed by for the sixth time that morning, BB used the tip of his knife to tap on the glass. He tilted his Stetson just high enough that he could lock eyes with Jeremy. "Yer tap-dancing on my nerves, boy."

Jeremy never stopped, only turning and walking backward to salute the manager. "Aye, aye, Cap'n."

BB went back to his copper.

Jeremy was a frequent visitor at the Frontier, where he'd find fellowship with the like-minded people there. He'd sometimes clean rooms in lieu of rent, thinking it'd help him pocket the odd watch or coin, but to his disappointment, valuables were never kept long enough in the kind of company you'd find there.

One couldn't park at the Frontier, since the pavement had been washed out by flooding, leaving the few guests who owned cars to park with the engineless clunkers that surrounded the motel and hope someone didn't mistake their vehicles for scrap. If anyone owed BB a dime, then it was in one of those old rust buckets they slept: a graveyard of cars and trucks that whined when the wind turned the wrong way. From the tall grass, those junkies still in the black emerged at dusk, snaking in from the wildflowers and wheat. The same still goes today.

The northern side of the building was reserved for the drug fiends, while the south was known for those seeking companionship of an illegal nature. An emaciated mother looked out for a suitor for her ten-year-old daughter, selling her cheap at half price if it got her the next fix. Another room had a police show blaring so loud that it made guests even more paranoid. A man crashing from the highs of meth hadn't been conscious since the previous morning, though no one cared to check if he was alive after almost twenty-four hours.

It takes me two years to locate a man by the name of Randy Madewell, also known as Cowboy, who can tell me firsthand what happened that night at the Frontier Motel. When I find him seventeen years after the Welch murders, he's recovering from a punctured lung and sepsis after being stabbed weeks prior. He is sober, but meth has already taken what it wanted out of him, including some of his real teeth. He discusses what it takes to cook meth, which is exactly what he was doing at the Frontier Motel that night. "I ain't in that game, not no more," he tells me several times.

Right before the publication of this book, Cowboy was murdered in his home west of Tulsa. With OSBI agents leading the case, it remains unsolved.

"You drop the iodine crystals and the red phosphorus, and that's the devil's breath." At the risk of turning this book into an instruction manual on the best way to cook methamphetamine, I skip writing the lengthy details. But I let him talk. That's something he likes to do: talk about meth. "If anyone asks, I only saw this on YouTube. But I was rolling back then. Two short swords on my back. That was my calling card. And Jeremy Jones? Well . . ."

That morning, sometime near to when Kathy and Danny Freeman were shot to death, Cowboy was cooking away in one of the rooms of the motel, hot plates turned up high and chiming with beakers. With him was one of his ex-girlfriends. "And this bitch, she was talking about race wars and God knows what else. Couldn't get her to shut up." The room would have been sticky and hot, his veins like razor blades. "Jeremy was a rat, and he kept knocking on the fucking door. Excuse my French. I couldn't stand that prick."

Back then Cowboy had long dirty blond hair he'd tuck behind his ears. He turned the electric hot plates down and moved the red phosphorus around, the brick red that exactly matched the iron-rich roads that led there. It was the same chemical element used in matches—Oklahoma was the striking surface of a burning fatherland. He was a local celebrity in that world, cooking some of the finest product and traveling often, moving labs to avoid getting caught and to tailor to a wider clientele. That night, he wore only a pair of boxers and stockman cowboy boots, his flesh stamped with skulls and crosses, prison dots and knives of greening india ink. Sometimes he'd see the ink crawl under the skin, slithers of methamphetamine carnality keeping him restive at the edge of sanity's hold. On his right arm, the words "Death Before Dishonor."

A knock on the door.

"I was going to beat his ass," Cowboy says. For the third time that night, it was Jeremy Jones. He was shirtless, not minding winter, not since his by-the-hour girlfriend waited for him across the driveway at the south side of the motel. Her name was Stacy, and she was a Texan who would recall this specific night because it was when Jeremy Jones gave her crabs, of which she publicly told the *Miami News-Record* in 2005. Today, Stacy seems to still carry a torch for Jeremy Jones. "He'd never hurt no one," she tells me. "Not a soul." But many records, transcripts, and victims would disagree with this sentiment.

"He was the type of guy you'd keep close like your enemies, because he'd stab you in the back just like that," says Cowboy. "Everything about him was black. His eyes, his hair, all of it. His soul was black. Just had one of 'em faces, that shit-eating grin. Couldn't trust him. We all knew he was a rat fiend."

Jeremy scratched his arms, biting into a pear and leaning his head on the other side of Cowboy's motel door. From the next room, the mother attempting to solicit men to have sex with her daughter came out to see who was there, only for Jeremy to hiss at her like a snake until she went back inside, locking the door behind her.

"Cowboy, I'm dying out here," Jeremy said as he stretched out his arms and curtsied to no one. "Dry as sun-bleached bone, baby." Jeremy tossed the pear's core and kicked it with the top of his sneaker so that it landed on the roof of an already-paranoid Cowboy's room.

Amped up on meth and on day four of not sleeping (all fear from day three onward), Cowboy nearly took the door from the hinges as he ran after Jeremy and chased him for a good quarter mile north on a lightless section of Route 66 toward Miami ("My-yam-uh"), Oklahoma. No one noticed Cowboy in nothing but boxers and cowboy boots running after Jeremy Jones in the early-morning hours, not that they'd tell you if they had. Then again, there is little that hasn't been seen before around the Frontier. One man would say that he remembered the echo of Jeremy's rapscallion laugh as the pair ran into the darkness, soles slapping on the road's surface. Another said that Jeremy was in distress.

Moments later, Jeremy was arrested for public drunkenness and possession of drug paraphernalia when Ottawa County deputy Joe Corley pulled up to him. Corley had merely been patrolling when he saw Jeremy running in his general direction, as Cowboy retreated near naked into the shadowy fields nearby. Sometime between Jeremy's outrunning Cowboy and the deputy's pulling up, Jeremy became agitated, paranoid, and lost his sense of time. He was on the verge of hyperventilation and pie-eyed. It was said that Jeremy was out of his mind, yelling, "He's going to kill me. Cowboy's going to kill me!"

As stated in the arrest report from that morning by arresting officer Joe Corley:

> Subject was running down highway with another subject chasing him. Once I made contact with him I observed a very strong odor of an alcoholic beverage on his breath, bloodshot eyes & slurred speech [scribbled out/initialed]. While patting him down [scribbled out/initialed] a [scribbled out/initialed] used syringe was found in his sock. After Miranda [being read his rights], he admitted to using the syringe to inject meth earlier in the evening.

This arrest report, filed with the district court of Ottawa County, was filled out on the morning of December 30, 1999, the same morning as the Freeman fire. The charges: "Public drunk, poss of drug paraphernalia." Jeremy remained in the Ottawa County jail with an order to sleep it off for several hours, until being bailed out by bail agent Mike McVay at 10:23 a.m. for $1,160. In theory this ruled him out as a suspect.

Coincidentally, according to my interview with him, OSBI agent Steve Nutter was at the Ottawa County Sheriff's Office when he got the call about the fire in Welch in the next county over, putting him in the same place as Jeremy Jones that morning.

On the small blank line left for the time of incident in the arrest report, the arresting officer had written: "06." This had then been scribbled out and replaced with "0359," and unlike the other sections of the report that had been altered, this had no initials of endorsement.

"I advise you to tread carefully on your project," arresting officer Corley, reportedly now living destitute in the state of Florida, publicly posted on my Facebook wall after two years of not responding to me. "It has many dangers. I know I am very careful with what I say and to whom I say it."

It will be the last time I hear from the man.

For the next five years, this incident with Jeremy Jones was never examined as having any relation to the murders of the Freemans and the abductions of Ashley and Lauria. Nor was there a reason that it should be. It went unexamined, and there really wasn't any reason to look hard into Jeremy Jones.

That is, until a man named John Paul Chapman brought the morning up to authorities down in Alabama, over seven hundred miles away, in late 2004.

20

THE BALLAD OF JOHN PAUL CHAPMAN

In 2001, Welchans were still nervous in the wake of the Freeman murders, still *shook up* by the idea that whoever had done this was still out there, lurking in the tall grass of the prairies, perhaps even walking among them. A lack of updates, and a marked absence of any apprehended suspects, cast a long shadow over the wide-open ranches west of Welch. "I feel silly for saying this, but I felt really paranoid," says Missy Dixon, another one of Lauria's cousins and a close ally of Lorene and Lisa. "I was scared out of my mind."

But the families and friends were also hopeful. No remains had been found, so maybe the girls were still alive.

It was early January 2001, not long after the first anniversary of the Freeman murders. A man named John Paul Chapman studied a date of birth and social security number scrawled on a bar napkin once he had safely boarded the Greyhound bus that took him through the haunted hills of Arkansas's Ozarks. The napkin had been given to him by a bartender out of Joplin, Missouri.

Today, you will find virtually nothing about John Paul Chapman. He was a man most women found handsome; he'd say that he wanted to leave his past behind and put Oklahoma in the rearview mirror. Back home, he had three charges of sexual battery from 1996, to which he pleaded guilty, thereby reducing them from a rape charge and affording him probation. "He was a very determined man," says former girlfriend Sherry Davis. "When he sees something he wants, he'll find a way to get it." Even while recounting her horrific rape, for which Chapman was charged, she manages to show kindness toward him, nodding to the earlier days that came in shades of lovesick pink in her memories. "I suppose I wouldn't be the woman I am today had it not been for him. He used to be so kind and charming, always opening doors for me, wining and dining me like no one had before." Sherry explains that once his addiction to meth took hold, he had trouble staying true to who he really was, that he "very much lost himself," becoming paranoid and violent, constantly lying to her. In fact, this is the general consensus of the women from his past: that he was a darling of a man until meth took its hold.

Also on his rap sheet are a second-degree burglary charge and a felony possession charge, both from 1996. Then, on his very last day of probation, he was charged with a new rape and jumped bail. He hopped on the Greyhound with not much more than what was on his back, and that bar napkin in his pocket. Chapman's next stop, Tuscaloosa, Alabama, where the red trollies rang and the *Bama Belle* paddle-wheel riverboat of the Black Warrior River attracted many Bamers in the western part of the state, just over an hour east of the Mississippi state line.

The twenty-seven-year-old held dreams of living happily ever after on a beach, and headed south. He was a stranger to most places there, but had met with some distant friends of his family, as arranged by his mother in those early days before he embarked on a rather nomadic lifestyle. A hyperactive man by default (he was later diagnosed with attention deficit disorder [ADD]) and never one to be unemployed, Chapman found work in no time. He explains that his time in Tuscaloosa was a transitional period, and that he was still planning to move farther south to plant roots.

"But then one day, I'm not there. I'm at work, and they call me saying the US Marshals or some bounty hunter was there looking for me after I skipped bail in Oklahoma, so off I went." Tuscaloosa became just the first of many passing towns.

Chapman, nicknamed by most as Oklahoma, could happily talk his way into any home, onto any one of the many couches where he'd lay his head between odd jobs that kept him occupied. After all, he claims to have been raised well, not dragged up, surrounded by men's men who had shown him the ropes when it came to mechanics and guns, hunting and construction; he became a jack-of-all-trades. "There are reports out there that I was abused, this and that, but that isn't true," he once said. "I was a happy little kid." But his drug habits were never really under control, and while he'd hoped for change, that fresh start, a monkey called meth wouldn't get off his back. "Once I put the needle in my arm, I was an evil monster."

Learning that the Oklahoman authorities were on his tail, Chapman headed south toward the Gulf Coastal Plain, stopping in Mobile, Alabama, a French-influenced city known as America's birthplace of Carnival/Mardis Gras. Here, every morning I'm served the best grits I'll ever eat, and a muddy sea breeze sticks to my skin at sunup. Today, it is a beautiful city on the Gulf of Mexico filled with palm trees and hanging Spanish moss, grand cathedrals and live oaks that capture roads and turn them into tunnels. Busy streets are lined with magnolia trees and beaux arts architecture, a proud antebellum picture of the Deep South where the Mobile River opens to the country's ninth largest port. "I call it a big small town," says Paul Burch, current captain of the Mobile County Sheriff's Office.

Our correspondence began while I was still living in Ireland back in 2016, though we'd meet in both Alabama and Oklahoma and continue speaking in between. "There's nothing like growing up and living on the Gulf Coast," Captain Burch continues. And there is something lively about this place. I have danced here a time or two.

Mobile is half an hour east of the Mississippi state line and less than an hour west of Florida's panhandle. Chapman arrived there and quickly made friends with a couple named Kim and Mark Bentley, a church-oriented couple from Turnerville, on the northern outskirts of Mobile. Mark, who had his own construction business, helped John find work.

But despite sweet home Alabama, Chapman still missed his family: mother Jeanne, teenage brother Jesse, and stepfather Tony, who'd raised him since he was two. When I ask Chapman about his favorite childhood memories back in Oklahoma, he replies without hesitation, "Christmas," recalling his uncle towing an entire backseat full of gifts. "I'd look at the labels, and every single one was for me. This one. Then this one. Next. Next." In him I always felt a sense of nostalgia.

As his addiction to crystal meth began to take a stronger hold, Chapman had a falling-out with the Bentleys. Soon, he was sent packing, and he settled in a cheap motel in a seedy part of the Azalea City. There, Chapman's days were seventy-two hours long, and he was getting so high that his vision would break in flashes of black, like his brain was shorting out. "He was strung out," Mark Bentley remembered. Chapman was losing weight, living day to day and high to high.

While at the motel, Chapman met a man named Craig Baxter from Douglasville, Georgia, who'd temporarily left home to find work in Mobile, where he was a plant manager for a mattress company. Though they knew each other for only a couple of weeks, they conversed as though they'd been friends for years. "He had the gift of the gab," Baxter tells me in 2019. When Baxter decided to leave on account of not being happy with the work there in Mobile, and with Chapman nowhere to be found, Baxter left a note on Chapman's motel door: "If you're ever in Georgia, give me a call!"

About a month after Baxter left, in May of 2002, Chapman wiped the blood from his face in his motel room, lit by the jaundiced glow from the outside lights spilling through the roller shades. He used a sewing needle and thread to stitch shut a gash over his eye. "He said he'd gotten in a fight with one of those guys on the streets who sells newspapers to cars," says Baxter. Chapman called his new friend, who wired him forty dollars for gas, and the next day he showed up on Baxter's doorstep, about five-and-a-half hours northeast of Mobile and over the state line in Georgia. From that night, Chapman took up residence in Baxter's basement.

Chapman began to couch surf through Georgia, taking up a job at the local oil refinery, where fellow workers described him as "your guy next door." Despite this, however, he always overstayed his welcome by way of his drug use being discovered, his comings and goings at all odd hours, sometimes bringing strangers home . . . One woman even once claimed rape. Chapman had an air of seduction about him when it was necessary, everyone agreed, but he was a provocateur and a misogynist and tended to alienate the people who'd taken a chance on him.

"Not everyone gets the same version of me. One person might say I'm a beautiful soul. Another might tell you I'm a coldhearted asshole. Believe them both," he once told me. "I don't treat people badly. I treat them accordingly."

Sometime in all of his moving around Douglasville, he met his girlfriend Vicki Freeman (no relation to the Freemans of Welch) at Gipson's, a popular dive bar later closed for offering lap dances without an adult entertainment license and various tax and alcohol violations, including serving to minors. "He caught my eye right away, he was so handsome," Vicki says to me.

Together, in August 2003, Chapman and Vicki moved into an apartment in Villa Rica, near Douglasville, Georgia. "I loved her back then," Chapman will admit, but he also admits this of most of the many women he's been with. The relationship was defined by crystal meth, and police were often responding to one domestic incident or another at their property. Chapman found himself in and out of psychiatric hospitals as a result of meth-induced bouts of psychosis, with one even leading to an attempted suicide in 2004. Though the police ran his fingerprints once he came from the psychiatric hospital to the jail, no red flags were raised.

One month after Chapman moved to Villa Rica, a local neighbor's teenage daughter claimed that Chapman "creeped her out," learning that he knew a lot about her while at a neighborhood barbecue. She and her mother noted that he always knocked on their door, both the front and back, and that when they didn't answer, he'd try to jimmy the doorknob and break in. At one point, they called the police. Some mornings, according to reports, he would sit out in the complex and drink beer while talking to himself. On October 27, 2003, Chapman was arrested for indecent exposure. "I was taking a leak by my truck when I heard someone start yelling at me because my piss is running down the driveway, and boom, *I'm exposed,*" he tells me in eye-roll fashion. Once again, a background check was submitted, and once again, he was fingerprinted. But there were no alerts on the FBI's system. Chapman was arrested a third time in January 2004, this time for criminal trespassing after the neighbor found a box outside her teenage daughter's window that contained a pair of binoculars, tape, and rope. Once again, the fingerprint analysis yielded no match. Soon, after several disturbances, management asked John and Vicki to leave. Today, Vicki claims that she was not aware of John's harassment of the neighbor until after the fact.

According to the *Los Angeles Times*, "[Chapman] was arrested and freed three times in the last several years because the FBI's computerized fingerprint system failed to correctly identify him."

"Once I learned the first time that that system didn't work, that was it," Chapman will say. In fact, Chapman was pulled over by police a recorded fifteen times after leaving Missouri, was approved for several bank loans, and even submitted numerous applications related to jobs, housing, the DMV, identification, and bank accounts without any incident.

Feeling the Georgian heat after his legal troubles, after using up all his favors regarding employment around Douglasville and Villa Rica, Chapman left. He knew Hurricane Ivan was expected to batter the Gulf Coast, surely destructive enough to bring some blue-collar work with it. With what little he had, Chapman returned to Mobile, Alabama, on September 15,

2004, leaving Vicki with a million promises that he'd send for her once he planted roots. Ivan was a Category 5 storm, gaining massive strength in the Caribbean and reaching winds of 165 miles per hour (270 km/h). Lasting twenty-three days, the hurricane killed 124 people and caused $26.1 billion in damage.

Chapman sought out Mark and Kim Bentley in the outskirts of Turnerville, surprising them, knowing full well he'd be able to sweet-talk his way into staying with them. While the couple opted to find higher and drier ground in northern Mobile in light of Ivan, Chapman stayed with the Bentleys' cousin Scooter Coleman, and they kept up with the repairs necessitated by the storm—they put x's made of masking tape on the windows and waited for the power to run out. At this point in time, after searching the bedroom for flashlights and batteries, Chapman stole the Bentleys' .25 handgun. The next day, the Bentleys returned home after the worst of the storm had passed. Their next-door neighbor, forty-four-year-old Mobile-born Lisa Nichols, had also just returned after seeking shelter elsewhere. At some point, she inadvertently caught John's eye.

The next evening, on September 17, 2004, Chapman attempted to rape Nichols "under the threat of violence" and shot her three times in the head. "They couldn't determine how far he got in raping her," says Captain Burch. "But we believe he shot her when she tried fighting him off." In the bathroom of her trailer home, where Lisa Nichols's body lay on the floor, Chapman doused her and the room in gasoline, then lit her on fire.

The evening of the next day, the storm clouds dissolved and the navy blue of night looked glossy overhead, the way it does after hurricane winds strip the heavens of color. Lisa Nichols didn't answer her phone, not for her daughters and not for her fellow employees, who noticed she never came to work that day at the local supermarket. Lisa's two daughters went to her house, only to make the grisly discovery. In hysterics, screaming, the two young women raced over to the Bentleys'. Mark Bentley and cousin Scooter ran over to help while Chapman stayed behind, "showing little or no emotion or willingness to help," according to the Alabama Court of

Appeals. Later records showed that Chapman called his girlfriend, Vicki Freeman, from Lisa's home phone the evening Lisa was murdered, and they discussed their future and his wanting to move her out there from Georgia.

DNA evidence, Chapman's confessions, and ballistics proved overwhelmingly that John Paul Chapman committed the murder.

"There was zero doubt in my mind that John Paul Chapman murdered Lisa Nichols," says Captain Burch. "He enjoyed raping and killing." Once more, Chapman's fingerprints were submitted to the FBI's database, the Integrated Automated Fingerprint Identification System (IAFIS). Still, no alarms were raised.

Had it not been for Chapman's missing his mother, authorities might have never found out his real identity.

"After John Paul Chapman confessed to murdering Nichols, we let him call his mother. My partner back then, Mitch McRae, and I traced the number back to a Jeanne Beard in Miami, Oklahoma," Paul Burch continues. "So we called Miami PD, asked if they knew her, and sure enough, they informed us that her son was a fugitive."

Oklahoma sent over a picture of Jeanne Beard's son, along with his record and fingerprints. They'd long known who Jeanne was, and her son was infamous in the area.

In a *Los Angeles Times* story, which claimed that the Nichols murder, and possibly others, could have been avoided if not for the system's major errors, the FBI said they "regretted the incident" and announced their plans to conduct an internal investigation into the errors. FBI supervisory special agent Joe Parris stated that the IAFIS was proven to be 95 percent accurate, resulting in the arrests of thousands of criminals per month.

"It turned out John Paul Chapman wasn't John Paul Chapman at all," said Paul Burch.

It was soon discovered that the real John Paul Chapman was serving a twenty-five-year stint in a Missouri prison for armed robbery, and that his mother, the bartender in Joplin, readily gave her son's information away when writing it on a bar napkin. "She figured, 'What the hell?'" said Chapman. "Her son wasn't getting out anyway."

This man was facing charges for Nichols's murder, which bore a striking resemblance to the crimes in Welch from five years before: the shots to the head, the arson, crimes that Alabama detectives were then unaware of. As Burch and his partner led the criminal with an alias from the interrogation room back to his cell, the suspected murderer stopped detectives. "I have another thing," he said.

The man who'd just confessed to killing Lisa Nichols was Miami's own Jeremy Jones, who had been arrested near the Frontier Motel in Dotyville after a near-naked meth cook named Cowboy chased him up an unlit section of Route 66 on the morning of the fire at the Freeman home, just fourteen miles east of Welch. He faced detectives. "There's something you need to know about some girls in Oklahoma."

21

THE CONFESSIONS

Police Captain Burch had met me in the lobby of the hotel I was staying at down in Mobile, Alabama, where he handed me the confession tapes of Jeremy Jones. He was kind, and he certainly didn't owe me anything, so I was grateful that he gave me exclusive access. After he handed me the tapes, I raced upstairs to upload the confessions before hitting the road. It is a two-day drive of Mississippi splendor and floating tufts of fog, like driving through sky and heat. Then the pulsating terrain of emerald green Arkansas. Then I'm welcomed back by prairie and autumn, fear and the imaginary taunting of murderers. Then I spend weeks and months in darkness, holing up in my office. Self-inflicted isolation to where I need daily reminders to eat, to shower, to brush my hair. I obsess to the point where I memorize more than twenty-four hours of footage surrounding numerous murders, as disclosed by Jeremy Jones.

When I come to the case eleven years after his arrest in the murder of Lisa Nichols, Jeremy Jones is still the most high-profile suspect in the murders of Kathy and Danny, as well as their daughter, Ashley, and her best friend, Lauria Bible. Jeremy's good looks have gained him fans, despite the horror of the crimes he has confessed to. Some say it's infamy that he wants, though I come to disagree. Every recent update on the case bears his name, and the victims of Welch are small on a long list of people he cops to killing. I spend the next three years watching his confessions, his details of one murder, then another, then another, until he is suspected in up to twenty-one brutal slayings across America's Deep South. I spend days examining crime scene photos of Lisa Nichols's burned body and the mug shots of Jones with scratches across his face from where Lisa tried to defend herself. And I spend three years trying to contact him, only for his lawyer to write me back and politely tell me to fuck off. *We don't swear like that in Alabama.* So I turn my attention instead to his wife, an attractive German woman turned prison pen pal.

It is shortly after a breakfast at Clanton's Cafe (famous, if you ever find yourself in this part of Oklahoma), and I'm due to meet Mrs. Jones in an hour. I've squeezed a lemon slice to death and fingered little drawings in my gravy on account of my nerves. My senses are still adjusting from the darkness of isolation and the darkness of my mind—the hypersensitivity brought on by this curse. The Oklahoma sun turns everything white-hot, and the sound of a truck rolling by physically hurts my body.

I've spent months corresponding with Mrs. Jones through Facebook, and now she's in town visiting her in-laws, Jeremy's family in Miami. We made plans to meet at a closed wedding chapel that the owner was going to "specially open for us." I take my biscuits and get in the car and ready myself to leave. It is a particularly hot day in autumn, when the temperatures stay north of ninety from one end of the day to the other, keeping my anxiety levels at permanent high tide.

Across the street is a large billboard with Lauria's and Ashley's faces, with bold letters that spell the word MISSING. A moment later, just as I'm getting ready to put the car in reverse and disappear onto Route 66, my phone rings. A private number.

"Is this Jax?" A female voice.

"Who is this?" I ask.

"Are you meeting Jeremy's wife?" But I don't answer. I make sure she can hear me breathing so she knows the call wasn't cut. Just before I hang up, the voice continues. "That's not Jeremy's wife." The call ends.

I sit in the hot car and tremble with an indiscernible emotion that squirms between fear and rage. I'm hit with a sudden wave of second-guessing: did I ever say something in our correspondence that I'd now regret? Did I give this person a way into my personal life? Most of all, if that wasn't Mrs. Jones I was speaking to, then who was it? After I do some digging with nervous electricity, two other sources I reached out to proceed to confirm that the recipient of all this communication wasn't Jeremy's wife at all: it was Jeremy himself.

To this day, I have no idea who was going to meet me at the chapel.

Despite the revelation, I stayed in touch with "Mrs. Jones" and kept up with the pretense for three years. I believe Jeremy Jones wanted to see how persistent I'd be, as I'd continually write "his wife" to speak to him (he was, in actuality, married to the attractive blond German; I just don't believe that's whom I was talking to). It was the little things I noticed: the way they both spell "our" as "are," how when Mrs. Jones tells me that she bought a copy of a fiction book I wrote, she sends a picture that shows neither the US nor the German version but the UK version, of which I'd just mailed Jeremy a copy from Ireland. But as it goes, I let truth tellers tell their truths and liars tell their lies.

It was one day in particular when I was just tired of his bullshit that I wrote "Mrs. Jones": "Let's stop the bullshit, Jeremy." I also gave him my phone number.

That day, Mrs. Jones blocked me on Facebook . . . and I got a call from an Alabama prison. And we'd go on to speak hundreds of times after.

"Stranger danger!" he greets me countless times, though I'm still not entirely sure why he nicknamed me this. When we end our conversations, he'll ask for my Irish husband. "Where's my Lucky Charms?"

Not terribly long after his 2004 murder confessions, Jones recanted his admission about killing Nichols. More than once he'll bring up Scooter, the Bentleys' cousin who stayed behind with Jones to keep up with the damage of Hurricane Ivan at the Bentley home. When Scooter was called in as a witness for the state at the murder trial of Lisa Nichols, those following waited eagerly to hear what the witness had to say. But during the course of the trial, right before he was set to appear on the stand, thirty-nine-year-old Scooter was electrocuted to death.

No foul play was suspected.

"Now, there's something you should be looking into," Jones tells me. "It don't seem right, does it?"

Incidentally, the first confession tape, on which Jones confesses to murdering Lauria and Ashley (though he never refers to either one of them by name), was dated five years to the day after their disappearance. Dressed in prison-issue navy blue scrubs, Jeremy Jones casually began confessing to the murders in Welch. He spoke fast for an Oklahoman, enough that I'd have to stop and rewind most of the taped confessions, his accent twangy. He confessed to Mobile County Sheriff's Office detectives Paul Burch and Mitch McRae, men not one bit familiar with the Freeman-Bible case, with no point of reference. Alabama detectives notified then sheriff of Craig County Jimmie L. Sooter and OSBI agent Steve Nutter, who proceeded to travel down south to assist in the interrogations.

"You could look into his eyes, and it was just black, just evil," says Craig County sheriff Sooter the first time we speak in his office in Vinita. At the time of Jones's 2004–05 confessions, Sooter was sheriff, and he was sheriff still during my first couple of years in Oklahoma. "Like evil was just coming out of those eyes, just black."

This would closely echo the statement I'd heard previously from Cowboy when we discussed Jones's arrest near the Frontier Motel: *Everything about him was black. His eyes, his hair, all of it. His soul was black.*

Jeremy spent most hours of the interrogation displaying visible signs of agitation, but he didn't seem nervous. His shaking knees and tapping fingers appear to be part of his disposition. "Get in, get out, light it, and go," said Jeremy in reference to the Welch fire. Every time Alabama interviewers wanted to extract more information from him, he was keen to barter: phone privileges, a marriage license for him and Vicki Freeman, better food. "He always wants something—that's just par for the course," said one investigator. Jones's admissions came with the constant reminder that meth had destroyed most of his memory, leaving bits and pieces that couldn't quite fit back together. Because of this, his numerous inaccuracies concerning the murders of Danny and Kathy were often overlooked. *"I think he [Danny] was still alive after I shot him. Maybe he wasn't. I think he was. But he might not have been. Meth's keeping me from remembering, you know?"*

Jones tells me later that it was "made up," that there were no such instances where he blacked out. "That's what they [the authorities] wanted to hear."

When it came to the early hours of December 30, 1999, Jeremy Jones stated to authorities that Danny Freeman owed his friend Marvin Roden some money, an outstanding debt for methamphetamine. "He was a feener," Jeremy said of Danny Freeman, a common term for a drug fiend. Jones said that while Roden, an alleged higher-up in the meth world who owned a body shop just across the street from the Frontier Motel in Dotyville, never instructed Jeremy to collect the debt, Roden's wife drew Jeremy a map to the Freeman trailer. Jeremy claimed that he became lost on the back roads west of Welch for hours, cruising along unlit dirt drives under the cover of night, until finding the mailbox with the Freeman surname in his headlights. It would have been a chilly and pin-drop silent night just a few days after Christmas, his favorite time of year.

Lauria Bible's, as well.

At this stage in the interrogation, Jeremy seemed to become confused about many of the details. He said he went up the short driveway, when in reality the driveway was quite long, changing his mind only when investigators prompted him with several "Are you sures?" He then said he went up the porch steps. When asked what kind of steps, he could not remember, before fumbling and guessing. "Wooden . . . I think they were metal?" They were in fact concrete.

The cherry on the top of the inconsistencies came when I found out for myself that Marvin Roden, for whom Jeremy was allegedly collecting a debt, had died two years before the Freeman murders.

When authorities asked Jones to give the layout of the house, he consistently offered up wrong details, adding breakfast bars where there were none, turning in the wrong direction to hunt down the couple in the master bedroom. During the course of the interrogation, however, whenever Jeremy had trouble remembering specifics, he and the officers took bathroom breaks, snack breaks, only for Jeremy to return with his story straight and all the information ironed out. But then Jeremy would get distracted or forgetful, reverting back to the discrepancies.

Speaking with Oklahoma authorities Sooter and Nutter when they arrived down in Alabama, Jeremy claimed that his weapon of choice was a pistol. Later, he backtracked and claimed he'd had a rifle. Further down the line, this changed once more to having a shotgun. Over several hours of interrogation, the following exchange was typical:

"I pulled out my pistol and shot them both in the head," claimed Jeremy.

"You remember you used a shotgun, right?" asked one of the investigators.

"Yeah," Jeremy answered.

Jeremy also went back and forth with who died first and when. He claimed that he stood at the doorway, facing Danny and Kathy from the foot of their bed, which wouldn't have been accurate; rather, from the doorway (where Danny's body was later found), he'd have been facing the side of the bed, with the head of the bed to his left and the foot to his right. First he claimed that he killed Danny first, then had to tackle and wrestle with Kathy as she tried to get out of bed. Then he said that he killed her first, that she died instantly, and that he saw the jerk of her body under the covers. He also claimed to have used "twos and fours," referring to the shotgun buckshot pellet size, while the families insist Danny and Kathy were killed with "sevens or eights," which would indicate bird shot from a twelve gauge, as confirmed by the autopsy. Later he would say he used an 1100 semiautomatic shotgun, then an automatic rifle, then a .25 pistol because he wanted to be sure they were dead, none of which was supported by the evidence (based on the damage caused by the one shot each that killed them, there would have been no doubt that their deaths were immediate).

Jeremy peddled the idea that Danny and Kathy were sleeping when the attack began, which was not generally thought to be true. There was the position of Kathy's body, lying over the covers across the bed, with Danny in the doorway, along with the fact that Danny was still wearing his shoes, which were found melted onto his body, suggesting he hadn't yet retired for the evening. Or perhaps he'd just slipped them on upon hearing a noise, a bark, a knock at the door.

The reports from Jeremy on the accelerant he used also changed frequently, from Coleman fuel he found in the kitchen (a popular component in cooking methamphetamine) to gasoline from his own truck. Even acetone was mentioned a couple of times.

As I played the interrogation tapes back, it looked like guess after guess after guess. Despite hours of interrogation, throughout which he claimed not to remember either one of the girls, he suggested that after killing Ashley's mother and father and leaving them in bed, he went from room to room, eventually finding the girls. This would ultimately change (and remain changed) to the notion that after Jeremy Jones lit the fire, he left for his truck, never knowing that there were two girls still inside the trailer until they came running out, screaming. This seemed like a theory that everyone could focus their attention on. Jeremy intimated to the girls that he had just driven up after seeing the fire from the road, and convinced Ashley and Lauria to jump into the truck so that he could take them to the police station. Jeremy claimed that after he turned onto the road in the opposite direction of the highway, the girls became scared as they realized they'd gotten into a truck with the man they'd possibly just heard gun down Kathy and Danny. "I had automatic locks, locked them in."

"There were some issues with the interviews," admits Kansas Bureau of Investigation (KBI) agent Larry Thomas, who'd later become the bureau's assistant director after famously capturing Dennis Rader, known as the BTK Killer, one of the most infamous serial killers in America. "My boss then called down to Mobile and suggested they carefully look into how some of the information was handled." Agent Thomas traveled down to Alabama after one of Jones's confessions pertained to the 1992 unsolved murder of Picher, Oklahoma, native Jennifer Judd, twenty, who was brutally stabbed to death in her home just over the Kansas border in Baxter Springs nine days after getting married. Unable to provide comment on the other crimes that Jones confessed to, as they weren't his own cases, and unable to speak on behalf of the KBI on account of his 2008 retirement, Thomas explains that false confessions aren't an uncommon thing; they're often forged out of a suspect's need for attention or desire for jail amenities; the latter seems to be the case with Jones. "Not always, but sometimes you get an investigator who is so sure they have the right guy, they give away more information than they're getting."

Thomas explains to me the necessity of "hold-back information," details of crimes never made public in the hope that suspects can provide them to authenticate their confessions. "We started to work on it, on this hold-back information, and Jones didn't have a clue as to what we were talking about," says Thomas, recalling his 2005 interview with Jones. "Then, while we were having the conversation, Jeremy would take a smoke break with the Alabama authorities and come back with the information we wanted."

Thomas's suspicions matched my own while I reviewed the interviews for the Welch case. The interrogators seemed happy to accept Jones's mismatching information, his guessing, his tendency to take a leak every time an important detail was brought up.

"They'd send me back [to my cell] with all the files of the victims," Jones reveals. "They'd encourage me, telling me to steer this way or that way. They were holding a carrot on a string for me."

Immediately following his confessions, Jeremy Jones became the next it boy in the world of true-crime sensationalism, checking off all the boxes that turned him from bona fide killer to celebrity: handsome, chatty, a bottomless source of information and confessions. The media and law enforcement alike reveled in it. The press wanted a piece of his charm, and agencies from all across America had cases that showed superstar potential and needed closing. "They saw me as dollar signs and book deals," Jones says, admitting that he never minded, because it gave him better jailhouse amenities.

Even my interview with OSBI agent Nutter corroborated this. "As I recall, the detectives at the Miami [Oklahoma] Police Department were upset with some sheriff's deputies from Alabama that had come up with a journalist and were investigating the Freeman murders," said Nutter. "They said that Jeremy Jones had confessed to it, and they were up there [in Oklahoma] doing some legwork on it. And this reporter was going to write a book about it."

"My personal opinion," retired KBI agent Thomas continues, "was that Jones was obviously coached."

While I feel confident that Jones was lying in his confessions, his information isn't necessarily wasted. By the time I begin speaking to Jones and by the time I lock myself in a dark room for weeks on end to study the confession tapes, I am no stranger to many of these details: Marvin Roden, the Coleman fuel, the layout of the house, down to the finer details falsified by Jeremy, such as frosted tips that Danny Freeman did not have in his hair to worrying about neighbors who actually didn't exist.

Then something clicks. I go back to my phone photos, to the blacks and whites of the graveyard girls at the library, and discover something new.

Jeremy Jones is confessing to the wrong murder.

What Jeremy was aptly describing was another double murder, in a trailer park called Carriage Hills, a frightening drive up the bluffs of Grand Lake o' the Cherokees at the back side of Afton, Oklahoma, just twenty miles southeast of Welch. When I drive through myself, all the locals emerge from the trailers, scattered haphazardly among the hills. Many of the residents show obvious signs of meth addiction as they eye my car. The message is clear: outsiders not welcome. Burned-out cars line the sides of the roads, and windows are covered in aluminum. Babies wearing only diapers wander in yards without supervision. Jones's descriptions of the murders at Welch are a perfect match for the case of another couple shot to death. Another trailer burned. Another unsolved murder, of a couple named Danny Oakley and Doris Harris on February 21, 1996.

Much of what I learn about the Oakley-Harris case comes from Paula Barnett, the sister of forty-year-old victim Doris Harris. We are on our way up to a U2 concert in Kansas City when we talk about Doris. "She was just the most wonderful person in the world," says Paula. Today, she still considers Jones a suspect in her sister's murder, which occurred while Doris and her thirty-seven-year-old boyfriend, Danny Oakley, were sleeping on their waterbed, another similarity to the Freeman case. Both were shot in the head and killed instantly prior to their trailer being set on fire. While there wasn't any evidence at the crime scene in Welch to suggest that the murders there were drug related, the double murder of Danny and Doris in Afton in fact was. "My sister got caught up," says Paula, discussing the fact that Doris's boyfriend was a locally known manufacturer of meth. "But it didn't mean she wasn't someone's daughter, someone's mother . . . my sister."

Even today, some locals still confuse the Freeman murders with the Oakley-Harris murders from three years prior.

Together, Paula and I pore over autopsies and phone records, reports, the things that murder cases are made of, the things lost in the Bible-

Freeman case. And like the Bible-Freeman case, the Oakley-Harris case comes with its faults, most of them arising when authorities found a man named Denny Ray Hunnicutt passed out behind the wheel of a car that matched the description of the car neighbors saw leaving the scene. Hunnicutt had fresh burns up his arms and quickly became a suspect, but he was never charged. And the case was littered with authorities who were known to dabble in scandal, much of which has been documented over the years, including one involving the sheriff back then, who was later ordered to pay more than $13 million in compensation for raping female inmates in 2011. Then there is ADA Winston Connor, who was arrested and charged in 2019 with solicitation for murder, witness tampering, assault with a dangerous weapon, pandering for prostitution, obtaining unlawful proceeds, and racketeering after plotting with a convicted murderer named Slint Tate, who ran a million-dollar-per-week meth ring from prison. Former ADA Connor also faced counts of "conspiracy to distribute a controlled substance, unlawful communication with a convict, solicitation of prostitution and committing a pattern of criminal offenses," according to the *Tulsa World*. I spend a long time researching murders and crimes that became lost in the hullabaloo of corruption and scandal, and back-burner priorities that ended up fading.

Today, criminal charges against the former ADA Winston Connor remain pending.

According to Jones in his Alabama confessions, he ran into Hunnicutt (now deceased) in the parking lot of a bar weeks after the Oakley-Harris murders. Hunnicutt went on to explain to Jeremy Jones how he had been there when the fire was set, having spent the night using meth with Doris and Danny, about which Jeremy played dumb. Hunnicutt told Jones that he'd snuck off to the bathroom to inject meth and a man (presumably Jones) came in and killed Danny and Doris. Hunnicutt hid in the bathroom and was trapped in the fire, waiting as long as he could before narrowly escaping.

There is hold-back information not made public on this case that led me to believe that Jeremy was not lying about what Hunnicutt had told him about the Oakley-Harris case. Hunnicutt was released shortly after his arrest and died in 2006. No one since has ever been arrested for the murders of Danny Oakley and Doris Harris.

"The case was handed over to the OSBI," says Doris's sister, Paula. She says that like the case in Welch, the investigation was headed by OSBI agent Nutter. But to her, "No one cared about two meth addicts." Drug debt was the prominent theory that swirled around the Oakley-Harris murders, and it seemed the couple knew they'd gotten in too deep and were planning their escape: their bags were packed by the front door, with bathing suits and suntan lotion to boot.

With the disappointment brought on by the Shadwick and Glover searches of Wyandotte that yielded nothing about the girls' remains, families and authorities were eager to hear what Jones had to say, and what he had to say didn't stop with the mismatching details of the Bible-Freeman case and the Oakley-Harris case. Jones would confess to several more murders around Welch, many not before heard of by families, cases that would get new attention upon Jones bringing them up.

After confessing to the Oakley-Harris case, Jones confessed to the murder of nineteen-year-old Justin Hutchings, an alleged meth user from Baxter Springs, Kansas, fresh out of rehab who was pushed out of a speeding truck in Picher, Oklahoma, on September 11, 1999, just a few months before the Welch murders and only twenty-three miles away. It was a case also overseen by then Ottawa County Sheriff's detective Mike Eason, who headed up the Shadwick affidavit and conducted the search on his Wyandotte property back in 2001, along with being present for the Glover search.

Jeremy claimed to have given Hutchings a "hot shot," a needle of meth mixed with peroxide, because, according to Jones, "peroxide don't show up in the system." I confirmed that fact with my medical examiner source Darren Dake, who concurred that peroxide would not show up in your basic toxicology screen unless it was specifically being looked for. Between paramedics and witnesses, the Hutchings death was a strange case not looked at as a homicide until after Jones's confession, though the manner of death was listed in the autopsy as unknown and the cause was toxic effects of methamphetamine. There was an ominous note found on the body that read "Disciple 13," and after being pushed out of the truck, Hutchings was dragged into a house, stripped naked, and covered in ice, which was how he was found by paramedics. Even the medical examiner alluded to the rumors of poisoning, noting in the autopsy that "the rumor circulated that . . . he may have been injected with cyanide and/or some other substance by another person." But I speak to nearly a dozen people who all say that they know exactly who did it: one notorious man I find operating between several meth circles in the area, and that person is not Jeremy Jones, though I'm easily able to establish a relationship between the two. In fact, even though it wasn't investigated initially as a homicide, it was a wide-open secret within the community that Hutchings had met with foul play. "Good luck proving it," one of the firsthand witnesses, a man who watched Hutchings die, says to me with a smirk. And even though several witnesses tell me who did it, today the case remains unsolved.

"The double murder in 1996 of Oakley and Harris and the 1999 murder of Hutchings were horrendous," says current Ottawa County sheriff Jeremy Floyd. "When I took office, I made it a goal to review these cold cases, along with many others. Cases involving the taking of human life should never be archived or forgotten," which these seemed to be. I ask him about the current state of affairs. "Cold cases are followed up on frequently, especially if we [the sheriff's office] receive new information and/or tips." Floyd further explains how the Oklahoma State Bureau of Investigation has also "recently established a cold case unit in 2019. In conjunction with this new unit, technology, and following up on leads, I pray we can solve these cases." He looks longingly into the dying fire in his living room. "Those families need closure."

For all these small communities, for amber waves of grain, there is no shortage of murder in northeastern Oklahoma. Jones also confessed to the

1997 double murder of Harmon Fenton, thirty-three, and Sarah Palmer, nineteen, of Commerce. They were a couple who were heavily involved in methamphetamine and were reported missing. A month later, their decomposing bodies were discovered just over the Kansas border in the bed of a pickup truck in an abandoned shed, up in an unincorporated town called Melrose. It was a brutal murder in which Fenton was shot once in the abdomen, presumably left to watch as the murderer(s) used his girlfriend, Palmer, for target practice, shooting her in various parts of her body—seven times front and back—, strangling her, stabbing her, breaking her bones, and possibly raping her. Despite my efforts to investigate this case, I had to step away after a man confessed the murders to me and threatened to do the same thing to me if I kept nosing around. Based on his documented history, I took the threat seriously enough to step down after issues of stalking and this suspect's calling me in a fake woman's voice to try and arrange meetings. None of this does a thing for my nerves.

Investigators soon dismissed Jeremy Jones's claims to have killed the couple, when they learned he was incarcerated in Oklahoma at the time of the murders, only to be released a couple of days before their decomposing bodies were found.

The Fenton-Palmer case remains open with Kansas authorities today.

Every one of these cases had one thing in common: the families of the victims uniformly believed the investigations had been halfhearted or botched, and the blame tended to fall on the victims themselves for becoming involved in the local culture. As Jeremy Jones continued to provide authorities with vague details of these various killings, there was no denying that there were a lot of bodies surrounding the meth circles that intertwined with one another. Furthermore, it gave way to the possibility that Jones's relationships with the people involved could have given him the opportunity to hear something from one of the many outlaws he associated with. Connections could be made between Jones and every one of the victims and suspects he named and didn't name, many of them associated with the likes of the Glovers and the other outlaws in Wyandotte, where authorities searched for the bodies of Lauria and Ashley in 2001. I wondered if he'd heard the rumors and possibly something about the whereabouts of the girls. If the New Year's party accommodated dozens of meth-addled criminals who came to take turns on the girls, and with Jeremy Jones closely tied to the men who came forward, could he know something?

If Oklahoma was a beautiful woman, then this case was a scar on her face. It hurts the heart when I am swimming through sunsets so spectacular and so wide that they're like drowning in color, and welcomed by prairie afternoons when the wheat meets me with a wave that smells like sunshine and youth's foolish first love. All my years here in Oklahoma, like my writing, will be a love-hate relationship.

It becomes easy for me to be drawn down these rabbit holes, investing every waking moment researching and investigating each one of these cases. Some bring death threats that I'm still too scared to talk about. Some bring new friends who come to see me from Oklahoma. But I have to focus. God willing, I have time to return. But for now, I have to be here for Ashley and Lauria and remember this story is theirs and not his.

We can't lose focus. Lorene's words reverberate in my head.

Today, Jeremy Jones is suspected not only of the murders in Oklahoma, but of many others across the South, and despite many agencies traveling to Mobile, Jeremy Jones was convicted only for the capital murder of Lisa Nichols in 2005, along with rape in the first degree, sexual abuse in the first degree, and burglary in the first degree.

He was sentenced to death and continues to call me from death row. *Stranger danger!* Over the years, I've carefully studied several murders in which Jones remains a suspect. I became close to the families of his alleged victims. I visited them in their homes. I'd learn, and I'd grow and harden all at once.

"Jax is stressed," Jeremy Jones tells my husband. "Here's what you do. Go draw her a bath. Give her a nice massage with some rose petals. She'll love it. All women love it." He can paint scenes of romance without any effort, rather hopelessly. In the years that we'll talk, I'll maintain a certain distance. Despite all the detestable things that came from his interrogations, I'd heard for too long of the women who fancy him, the love letters in prison, and the bullshit. I'm not too proud to think I'm immune to anything I don't understand.

I have yet to meet a person familiar with the Bible-Freeman case who doesn't associate it with Jeremy Jones.

"I mean, I knew *of* him," Paul Glover Jr. once told me. "He wasn't a stranger to me or nothing. I knew of him, but he never ran."

It was known that Jones was associated with Paul Glover Sr. and many of the criminals of Wyandotte.

Every conversation and every investigation into violent crime in the state at that time told me one thing: Jeremy Jones knows something about every terrible thing that took place in Oklahoma. And more important, he may have known the perpetrators who took the girls. So when he turned his attention to the Welch case, I knew I had to listen—even if it meant picking through countless layers of misdirection and deception.

I lie awake at night, thinking about whether the girls could smell Jeremy's sweat in the cab of the pickup: the choking stench of the chemicals dripping from his pores, panic. Did Ashley watch her home burning in the rearview mirror as they drove into the night? Was this when the girls realized their fate, racing through the flickering darkness of the passing forests as they headed to their death? Is this the stretch of road, or this yard, or that hole where their bones will one day be found?

Jeremy's story changes multiple times, but ultimately he settles on the iteration wherein the girls ran from the front of the trailer and jumped into the truck with him just as he slammed the door to leave the scene of the fire (another confession had him taking the girls at gunpoint and forcing them into his truck). This narrative, however, is not supported by the physical evidence, which indicates that the path of the accelerant started at the woodstove next to the front door. The fire would have blocked their route, so they would have had to leap through the flames in order to make their way to the truck from the front door. According to Jones, after locking the girls in his white '91 Ford pickup, he sped through the back roads toward Miami and came to a stop in Galena, Kansas, about forty miles northeast of Welch, one of many mining towns Jones frequented in his youth, where he alleged he used to sell dope with the Glovers. Located in the Tri-State Mining District, Galena was named for the galena ore that came from its land and it is lauded as the oldest mining town in Kansas.

Jones claimed to have parked by one of the mines in Galena, increasingly alarmed about what he was going to do with the girls. They had seen his face. There was no turning back. He said that after forcing them out of the car at gunpoint, all three of them were crying in the headlights of the truck, near the edge of one of the bottomless cavities. Jones claimed that he shot one, and when the other tried running, he shot that one twice. He had never been able to discern which girl was which. He said he dragged them into the mine. Jones said that he never heard a splash, not even when he threw railroad ties in after them to cover them up. He denied any sexual assault.

During the investigation, neither Jones nor any of the authorities bring up Jones's arrest at the Frontier Motel in the early hours of the morning of the fire.

Today, people dispute whether Jeremy Jones could have realistically set the fire in Welch, traveled to Galena to murder and dispose of the girls, and circled back to the Frontier Motel in time to become embroiled in his argument with Cowboy. OSBI agent Nutter, who helped conduct the interview about the Welch case down in Alabama (along with the cases of Oakley and Harris, Justin Hutchings, Fenton and Palmer, and others), did not believe Jeremy would have had the time, claiming he would have only had a "twenty-minute window" to get high (though this was a detail more linked to the Oakley-Harris confession), dispose of the girls, and return to the motel. Sheriff Sooter, however, was convinced that Jones was responsible, insisting that "he had plenty of time to start that fire."

"I think that's why Sooter didn't work the case well in the end," said Danny Freeman's stepbrother, Dwayne. "He had it in his mind that Jones did it, and that was that." But because Sooter didn't have any law enforcement background prior to his being elected to office, some questioned the veracity of his beliefs.

Based on the arrest report from the morning of the fire, the time of arrest initially began with "06," but this was crossed out and rewritten as "0359." The repeated instances of amended documentation were a consistent source of fascination in the case, but this change wasn't hugely telling without a firm sense of when the fire in Welch actually started. Due to the natural inability to remember all of the details after so many years, or unable to offer any official expertise related to the science of fire, or even because the answers were unknown to them, everyone from the OSBI to the local sheriff's offices to the victims' families told me to refer to the fire marshal's investigative report. But, as I came to learn, no such investigation took place, according to the Office of the State Fire Marshal.

> I can find no record.
> We were not called to do an arson investigation.
> We did not investigate a fire in Welch.
> No such request was made to the State Fire Marshal's Office.
> No.

Without a fire investigation having been conducted, so much remains unlearned about the murders in Welch, including, but not limited to, the possible involvement of Jeremy Jones. Between the varying answers of the families, the local men of the Welch Volunteer Fire Department, and law enforcement, the time when the fire started ranged in a large window between ten p.m. on December 29, 1999, and near dawn the next morning. Many factors had to be considered, such as the currents of air inside the trailer, the arsonist's common trick of lighting a candle and letting it burn down to the accelerant (which could delay the fire for hours as the culprit made his or her escape), the kind and quantity of accelerant used, and all the other things that contribute to an arson investigation.

In the wake of Jones's confession, he sat with authorities, drawing maps and discussing the specifics of the mines and sinkholes in the Galena area.

Six months later, on June 29, 2005, authorities examined the pits of Galena. The wind was hot that day, the kind that feels like it's the only thing keeping your skin from burning. The effort constituted the largest search for the girls to that point, with thirty-five members of law enforcement, including state and federal agencies, combing the grounds with dogs and the wells with cameras in wind-kicked dust. "What we are looking for is worse than looking for a needle in a haystack," said Sheriff Sooter in an interview with the *Oklahoman*.

In my own meeting with Sooter, he tells me that there are "several thousand miles of mines under the ground. They go all over northeast Oklahoma into Joplin, Missouri, into Kansas, and so forth. There are running rivers underneath, in the mines. And the thing is, if the bodies were in the mines, the temperature in there is a constant fifty degrees, I believe. So if the bodies were in there, they wouldn't be as bad as you think." Then, just as the searches began accruing media attention and Jones's own profile was raised, Jones changed his story for the last time.

With no signs of the girls, Jones recanted all of his confessions, claiming that he only wanted better food and phone privileges. And above all, he was hoping for extradition so that he could go back to Oklahoma, where his family was.

Today, he denies involvement in any and all of the murders he was ever suspected in.

"I didn't think he did it," says Lorene. "But we know he was tied to some of the earlier suspects." Lorene still believes that Jones may very well know something about Lauria's and Ashley's final days, that he might have information about the much-discussed New Year's Eve party. "All of them, all those drug people, are intertwined," Lorene continues. "I think Jeremy's heard things. But the bottom line was he was free for several years before his arrest, four years. You can learn a lot in that time, just reading the papers."

"You know, back then, I wasn't thinking ahead," admits Jeremy Jones, who now claims he feels regret for giving false confessions. "I wasn't thinking about how this can affect someone's mother." Today, he says he is sorry. "I just hope Mrs. Bible will forgive me one day."

Lorene, however, says that Jeremy Jones has never reached out to her.

In the end, no charges were filed in any of the Oklahoma murders to which Jeremy Jones confessed. And despite the highly public buzz surrounding the charismatic death row inmate, there were no significant leads between his 2005 confessions and my arrival in Oklahoma in 2016. And even though no significant suspects came to light for the next eleven years, a new fact was about to come to light, when a woman named Winnie came to Lorene with information.

It would take the families seventeen years to learn about the last person to possibly see the car transporting the girls and their captors in the early-morning hours on the day of the Freeman fire.

SECTION 4

LATER LEADS

22

THE EDGES OF OKLAHOMA

December 30, 1999
The Morning of the Fire

Where the local historical maps are scribbled in black because even the archivists of the town consider this nowhere land, deep in the hinterlands of the Neosho River where cowboy country ends and Indian territory begins, there lived a young couple. Deep in the country, it's a place known only to locals, far enough from any town limits to happen upon by accident. It's in these little no-name towns of Oklahoma that time seems to have stopped: traditions reign supreme, and its people continue to live unaffected by the revolutions and trends of the outside world. And happily so. These are the places for people who want to be left alone, where the pecan trees twist tighter and the homes lie camouflaged against thick, dark briar.

It was only a few hours before Kathy Freeman's body was found on the morning of December 30, shortly before three a.m., when Winnie (traditionally named Awinita, Cherokee for "fawn") became restless by way of TV reruns in her farmhouse. Even the early-rising farmers were in the thickest cycles of sleep. Winnie was already an hour off her shift at the local casino, but the phantom beeps of the slot machines still tinged in her ears, and insomnia kept her in its vise.

Still in her waitress uniform, she stepped outside, hoping the cold air would be enough to make her at least want to change into her pajamas and crawl into bed. She crossed the yard, a small property landscaped with frostbitten spices and winter-dormant flower beds. She walked toward the edge of her flat property by the country road, lit by a lone yellow spotlight on a telephone pole. Winnie took in the chill and looked out to the noth-ingness of the grasslands ahead and heard the deafening silence of the winter's night.

According to *The Old Farmer's Almanac*, there was visibility of 9.9 miles, which, if it had been light, would have allowed Winnie to see the chimney smoke of her closest neighbors some five miles out. But then the wind dropped, and the sound came of a roaring engine in the distance closing in. It was unusual to spot a car around here, even in the day-time, but at this ungodly hour, and with no sign of headlights to accom-pany the noise, it was just unnerving.

Winnie's gut rippled with fear; she stepped back off the edge of the road and took shelter in the darkness, sewn into bushes of juniper. She held her breath as the spotlight washed the 1980s model car in silver and yellow for a moment. Not far from where Winnie stood camouflaged, the car suddenly stopped, the driver braking hard enough to create a large cloud of dust that further hid Winnie, but kept her from seeing clearly. In that moment, she thought she'd been spotted. While the car still ran, one of the doors opened so the interior light glowed through the dirt and the dinging sounded to alert of an open door: a scuffle, a screech of a female, a deep roar from a man's throat. The commotion lasted all of a few sec-onds, but Winnie knew fear when she heard it, and the indecipherable voices relayed to her that something was very wrong. The door slammed shut, and the lightless car left as fast as it could.

As the car raced away from Winnie's home, the taillights exploded into life just before it disappeared into the overgrown backcountry where the moonlight didn't touch, illuminated hazy red in the dust. Winnie stood frozen for several moments, trying to discern by its sound which direction the car was heading, until the last echoes faded entirely. As stiff as the winter branches at her back, Winnie reached into her bra to pull out a cigarette case. The scrape of her Zippo was loud in the silence, and Winnie cupped her hand around the glowing smoke and darted back up the steps of her home, unable to shake off the unnerving sense of fear and rage that came from the voices.

In the kitchen, she sat by herself in the dim stove-top light, waiting restlessly for Noah, her husband, to wake up. Her ashtray was overflowing when Noah finally bounced down the stairs, dressed for the day. He dropped a kiss on Winnie's cheek and went for the coffeepot. "What's the matter? Couldn't sleep again?"

With circles growing darker under her eyes, she looked up. "I saw something this morning." She couldn't stop replaying the memory, second-guessing what she saw.

Noah turned to her and cleared his throat, only then noticing the pile of cigarette butts in an ashtray on the breakfast bar. "Everything OK?"

"A car full of people," she answered. "The headlights were off, and I heard a girl's cry. And a man's yelling."

"Maybe just some kids gallivanting around."

She looked across the room and out the window toward the sounds of the morning birds. "Maybe . . ."

Noah, late for his job all the way in Tulsa, took her hand and gave it a shake. "You look tired, honey. Go and sleep for the day. Those night shifts aren't doing a thing for your nerves anyhow."

She gave him a closed-lip smile, a brief reassurance as he took his lunch box from the countertop, gave a quick pat on his wife's head, and left the house.

But word spread around Oklahoma quickly, and before long, there wasn't a soul who hadn't heard about the commotion happening over in Welch. As conjecture swept through the community in the following weeks, and the missing-persons posters sprang up all over town and on local TV, Winnie made a realization, with a sinking heart, that the car she saw could have been driven by the man or men who had taken Lauria and Ashley. It was the right time, the right direction, and in all her years on those country roads, she'd never seen anything like it.

Years later, Lorene Bible, never having heard of this event, caught wind of Winnie and drove over to meet the woman herself (Lorene investigated all parts of her daughter's case). According to Lorene, Winnie and her father called the Oklahoma State Bureau of Investigation back then to report what she'd seen. The OSBI assured them several times that they'd send someone out to take Winnie's statement.

When I spoke to Nutter and asked him about this witness, it didn't ring a bell. "I don't remember that," he said.

According to Lorene, no one went out to take Winnie's statement, as promised, not until Lorene reported it herself to authorities in 2016.

23

ANOTHER AVENUE

2016

I spend a chunk of my life investing every heavy ounce of emotion in the pursuit of one theory only to be forced to jump to the next until my head starts to spin from the number of suspects: from the drug circles of Wyandotte that included names like Chester Shadwick and the Glovers, to the confessions of suspected serial killer Jeremy Jones. I've fallen into an ocean of blood, and on some days, I feel like I'm floating on my back, doing my best to go with the currents with open eyes and open ears; I learn slowly that fighting the tides leads to more frequent panic attacks. And all the good things I once knew about myself are drifting away in those tides—my sanity, above all. But navigating her way through the waters alongside me is Lorene, through the bones of winter and the flesh of summer. She has spent decades chasing leads, fetching the false hope thrown her way and bringing it back without fail. This is her life's purpose.

The prairies remain empty, without answer, never changing.

"[Sheriff] Sooter seemed to put his eggs all in one basket, and that was Jeremy Jones," said Danny Freeman's stepbrother, Dwayne Vancil, one of many who considered Jeremy Jones low-hanging fruit for officers wanting to get this case finished with as quickly as possible. "Between that and Nutter not doing much, it quieted down after Jones. The case just went into limbo." Dwayne went on to share his resentment that Sooter had no law enforcement background prior to his being elected to the sheriff's office. "It's like taking a carpenter to work on your car."

"It slowed down after Jones," admits Lorene. "There were more minor leads, leads that we the family looked into. But it was mostly quiet for the next eleven years."

Discreetly between the more significant leads, the Freeman family legally declared Ashley Freeman dead in 2010. The decision largely stemmed from Danny's father Glen Freeman's desire to take ownership of the land in Welch where he keeps to himself today. Ashley, being the sole heir, had the right to inherit the land after her parents were killed, but with no sign of the girls surfacing in the case, the Freemans felt they had to move on.

But for the Bibles, declaring Lauria dead isn't an option.

"Hope is all we have," says cousin Lisa.

Come 2016, there is a fresh generation on the case, now led by OSBI agent Tammy Ferrari and DA investigator for District 12 Gary Stansill. Stansill comes with the Freeman-Bible case being a special interest of his after his 2010 retirement as a sergeant for the Tulsa Police Department, where he was acting supervisor of the Sex Crime Unit, as well as the Child Crisis Unit. After retirement, upon learning there was a position open at the district attorney's office, Stansill took the job. In an article for the *Claremore Daily Progress* titled "Back on the Saddle," he describes crimes involving children as being the hardest. "They're the most emotionally difficult ones to work." Stansill seems to acknowledge that this case needs special attention, that it requires the mentality he's acquired over the years from his work with children. He once described working on the Freeman-Bible case in an interview with the *Tulsa World* as akin to "having four jigsaw puzzles dumped into one pile and being asked to sort one out." For anyone familiar with the case, this is plain to see.

For both the Bibles and the Freemans, the case seemed—finally—to be in good hands. A new team. A new season. A new direction for the investigation, perhaps.

When I spoke with current OSBI agent Ferrari, she was open about her frustrations with the Bible-Freeman case, citing that most tips were from anonymous sources and came so vague that they were hard to follow up on. She also discussed the obstructions brought about by witnesses getting older or passing away, often from addiction. "I don't know if it's going to take a dying declaration from somebody or what, but I definitely want to solve it," she said.

Ferrari also expressed her hopes that the girls might still be alive. "I would never want them to be held captive out there, God forbid," Ferrari started, making reference to Elizabeth Smart. "But to be alive somewhere, that would be wonderful for us to be able to find them and return them to their families. There's that possibility, and I would hope for that."

"By now, I know the girls have passed away," says Lorene matter-of-factly in the bleachers at her grandson's baseball game. "You hope that after so many years your child will come home and it'll all be all right, but if that's not the case, then I have to bring their bodies home." I have come to know Lorene well enough to know that there is nothing cold or cut off in her resolve; she is guarded, she is wary, and who can blame her?

I ask Lorene about the eleven-year space between Jeremy Jones's confessions and my meeting her. "I just do the best that I can. I follow tips. I speak to people. I listen."

In addition to the newer generation of investigators, the Bibles create a Facebook page titled "Find Lauria Bible—BBI," on which tips began to pour in almost immediately. "We saw it as a new opportunity, a new way to bring exposure to the case, and a way for people to reach out to us," says Lorene. "It's another avenue. We will take any avenue we can to help find the girls." It is successful in creating a new burst of interest.

"The page was started in 2016," says Lauria's cousin Lisa, who helps Lorene run the page. "There's been so much exposure because of it, getting beyond this four-state area and reaching all over the world. It especially became vital for people who didn't want to go to police." She explains that some of the people reaching out to the "Find Lauria Bible" page are integral witnesses who, in the initial days of the fire, were ignored by law enforcement.

One such witness was Winnie, the insomniac who lived out in the country and witnessed what very well could have been the getaway car speed by. In 2016, Winnie reached out to the Bibles via the Facebook page. "She could have seen the car that the girls were transported in, which came from the direction of Welch, where the Freeman trailer fire was," says Lorene. "I believe her." Lorene, the one-woman investigation team determined to track down her daughter, went out to visit Winnie to hear her account directly. Convinced her information was genuine, Lorene demanded that the new authorities get out there and take down Winnie's statement.

It's this pattern I see throughout the investigation: Lorene leading the charge, carrying out all of the initial legwork before authorities get involved.

Other sources who begin to come forward prefer to use Facebook to contact the Bible family because they are cautious about dealing with the police directly. Lisa explains that many of the people offering information are still active in the drug scene and fear arrest. "Locally, people know there've been issues of trust between us and law enforcement, so they trust us by default. They've long heard us announce that their tips are confidential, and that's important to them. Sometimes, these people are afraid." Overall, social media proves to be "a blessing."

As soon as the Bibles published the Facebook page in January of 2016, the tips began arriving thick and fast, some sound, others clearly not. As they sifted truth from fiction, the tips that appeared the weightiest and most consistent all pointed back to Chetopa, Kansas.

"The thing that really steered the case back to Chetopa was a tip to the 'Find Lauria Bible' page," said Lisa.

Here, the case seemed to go full circle, back to Chetopa's own Charles Krider, Danny's best friend, who'd kept his cattle on the property at Welch and regularly visited the trailer to smoke grass.

24

CHETOPA

1999

I am back at the edge of the Freeman property, outside looking in, up a cold hill and at the blackened smudge against the leaden sky that is the burned trailer. It is 1999 and most signs of life are nowhere to be found. The barn cats are lost and the cattle of a family friend stand waiting. The bursts of laughter once belonging to the girls aren't even a memory here. I don't know why I miss them.

Only a few days after the fire, an unwashed, callused man named Charles Krider took his truck south of the Kansas–Oklahoma state line. He came from Chetopa, Kansas, which sat just above the border, and headed toward Welch, which sat just under. He drove down to the Freeman property, where the remnants of a crime scene that had been picked apart down to the bones stood unattended. His route there was no different from what it had been in the days before the fire, when he would go to visit his best friend, Danny Freeman, with a bag of grass, like he had a hundred times before. Back in 1999, there was a large round dirt track toward the middle of the driveway so that you had the option of turning east to a barn long before reaching the house. Charles took the right-hand

227

turn and crawled past, avoiding the path that ran close to the trailer's remains. The old guns that the families had spread across the yard remained, now cold. The suspension squeaked as the old truck bounced in the potholes, and he kept his eyes straight ahead. At the request of Dwayne Vancil, Charles had come over to fetch the two head of cattle that Danny had been raising for his friend, since his quarter-acre corner property in Chetopa lacked the space.

Charles lifted his sunglasses and skimmed his eyes across the pastures for his red cattle. His fingers were shaped like spoons, and the cold months chapped his lips. "Look at big mama cow and big daddy cow," he said as he spotted them across the property.

Near the barn, Dwayne helped Charles round up the cattle and load them onto a stock trailer behind his truck. Danny's stepbrother had long heard a lot about Charlie, but never met him personally until then. They exchanged phone numbers. "He was a little emotional, crying," says Dwayne. "But it felt forced." A few days later, Dwayne made the trip back up to Chetopa to meet with Charles, who came out of his house on Walnut Street to speak with Dwayne in Dwayne's truck. "I was there to ask him about his and Danny's dealings," says Dwayne. "I knew the two of them were into growing pot, but it was for their own personal consumption."

Charles and Danny discovered their love for smoking weed while working together at a welding company called Wiseda, and they wound up exchanging their own homegrown plants to see whose was better. After one particular trip to Louisiana, when Danny took his wife and two kids to visit relatives, he returned to find his "mother" plants had died. He turned to Charles for a favor, as he'd once traded plants with him, asking to have some of the females back. "This is how we ended up in business together," says Charles.

"I knew they'd dealt together in the past," says Albert Lynn, the younger friend of Danny's who'd join him on gigging trips on the river at night. Albert denies ever knowing Charles Krider personally, but when I ask him to think back to the time around Danny's death, Albert says that he believed "Danny was doing his own thing" separate from Charles by that time.

Despite claiming to be Danny Freeman's best friend, Charles wasn't considered a suspect in the immediate aftermath of the murders. He received a brief visit from then OSBI agent Steve Nutter, and then appeared to drop out of the picture.

"We started questioning some of Danny's coworkers at a welding shop up there," said Nutter in our interview, claiming that the men of the mining machines all told him that he was best to go and talk to Charles in Chetopa. "He cooperated," Nutter continued. "[But we were] never able to get enough to write a warrant."

Chetopa (pronounced "sha-topa") is a peculiar little town, one of "rural omens and barnyard prophecies," as one friend puts it, another town where everyone knows everyone else's comings and goings. It's seemingly wholesome, a town of about a thousand people raised on the same Neosho River that courses down through to Oklahoma. In my back-and-forth over the years, most of the residents I talk with speak plainly of evil, giving credit for bad men to the devil and the merits of good men to their personal Lord and Savior. "If you don't believe in Jesus and the devil, just wait till you hear those missing girls' voices from Charlie Krider's old place," says one random local. "You'll become a believer then."

It's as slow as most small towns in Middle America are, but with an edge of superstition mixed with fervent religious devotion that rests on the thin white line that draws out Oklahoma's never-ending horizon. Folklore and superstition are rampant. God forbid the roosters crow before midnight to summon the bad weather or the moon shines on your face while you sleep to make you go insane. And maybe that's what happened in Chetopa. Maybe the full moon showing over the town as it slept gave birth to monsters.

All I have to go on regarding Charles's appearance are his mug shot photos: a bald man with a long, untamed beard marbled with olive green hues that become whiter the closer to his chest they get. His brown eyes are stark against his blue prison jumpsuit, and he stares into the camera as though he knows exactly who'll be looking at these pictures later.

Charles's and my correspondence begins while he is in prison, and much of the conversation revolves around him and his relationship with Danny. "We became good friends because of our mutual interest in the growing and consumption of a certain plant that God made and we used," he starts in one of many letters. Because our letters are monitored, he doesn't use words that can implicate him in a crime. "I would call Danny Freeman my best friend after knowing him and his good family for many years—some of the best people I have ever had the good fortune to know in my lifetime."

By Charles's own admission, he and Danny were in the marijuana business of "marrying the male plants with the female plants." There isn't a tinge of regret to this. "To start off, the Freemans were not my neighbors," Charles corrects me. "I met Danny Freeman when I went to work at a large welding shop in Baxter Springs [Kansas]—they built large, mining haul trucks for the mining industry. I worked the evening shift and he [Danny] was a lead man for the day shift." Wiseda was one of several places where Danny found employment when the migraines caused by the gun-cleaning accident parted in his head like storm clouds, long enough for the man to do what he could to make a living.

Charles speaks highly of Danny, claiming to know Kathy and the children only loosely; they were very much in the background. "Danny and I smoked a lot, but he wouldn't do it around his kids." He says that Ashley and Shane were usually away at school ball games or off with their friends. "I was there every Friday evening when I knew the kids would be gone, sometimes on Saturdays." While this became a routine, he'd also occasionally stop by midweek to check on the cattle he kept on Danny's property, equipped with his own bag of the grass that bonded them together. But then he alludes to the fact that in the two years leading up to his murder, Danny began to use methamphetamine.

"I will never lie to you," Charles tells me in one letter. But while meth is brought up often, no evidence of the drug was found at the crime scene in Welch, and in all my conversations with those closest to Danny, Charles is the only person to claim to have seen Danny use meth. "I am willing to bare my soul to you if you are out for only the true facts."

According to sources, Danny and Charles each had their own fair-sized number of crops. "Danny grew marijuana in Welch, and Charles grew it in Kansas," Lorene tells me. "That way if one got caught, it wouldn't affect the whole crop because of the state line between them," where a jurisdictional conflict would arise. Despite living in separate states, there was only a ten- to twenty-minute drive between the two, making them nearly next-door neighbors in the deep, dark country.

I ask Charlie why he thought the OSBI started to suspect him, and he figures it stemmed from the deathbed confession of a man named David A. Pennington, a name I'd heard thrown around when looking into the drug scene in Chetopa, but not a name I'm especially familiar with. "The OSBI visited me a few months ago, telling me that David Pennington had made a dying declaration," Charles writes from prison.

But according to Charles, the dying declaration never came to anything.

"I and an FBI agent interviewed him. I think on the third day," said OSBI agent Nutter in regard to Charles Krider, asserting that it never really led to anything substantial. "But then he came back on my radar when he was arrested for murder."

It is a snowy afternoon in Chetopa, Kansas, and everything is muffled and still. In the car, I follow a local man known as R.H. east out of the town, coming to a stop on a rural road where a spectacularly golden dusk spills over into a frozen creek and the icy howls of the westerly wind. Squinting hard from the overpass into the shadows of the creek, I make out an old wooden train trestle wrapped in ivy and dead overgrowth. Its dozens of legs are crooked and long, like the teeth of the man who brought me here. "That's where Charlie Krider dumped her body." The local points with a yellow fingernail. He takes a few steps back and looks up the dirt road like it's done him wrong. He leans on a sign made illegible by rust and riddled with bullet holes. "I'll keep a lookout if you wanna go over." We're somewhere in between the unassigned lands outside of Chetopa: maybe ghost town, maybe unincorporated, but nameless, in any case. I try to imagine the train trestle when it had life and connected to Picher once upon a time. Instead it was here where, fifteen years ago almost to the day, the partially clothed body of fifty-eight-year-old Judith Shrum was found.

Later in the evening, after I leave the overpass, I meet with Karen Cook, Judith's daughter, and Karen's husband, James, in the blackjack hills of Wyandotte where they live, about 36 miles southeast of Chetopa. It's that winter kind of quiet that paints the darkness a peculiar moon blue and turns the wind into a stinging grain and an ominous warning. I go to listen to Karen's memories of her mother, and in typical Chetopa fashion, they come with the mention of pecans. "We'd collect them from all around the yard and sell them so that we had Christmas money," Karen remembers. Like Lorene, she smiles at my pronunciation of "pecan." And it is no wonder, since Chetopa is the self-proclaimed pecan and catfish capital of Kansas.

In 2004, Judith Shrum was a cafeteria cook for the Chetopa school district where her killer, Charles Krider, worked as a janitor in the mid-nineties and where he had attended school as a kid. Widowed by her husband's sudden heart attack a year prior, Judith was a woman of church potlucks and crocheting, with shelves of knickknacks delicately placed and dusted around her home. "She loved her grandbabies," says her daughter; Judith had two grandchildren. But Judith was also young at heart, with short sandy blond hair, bright blue eyes behind gold-rimmed glasses, and gold studs that sparkled from her double-pierced ears. "She was a nurturer, always taking care of someone. That's just who she was." Her close friend Mary had made it a point to visit Judith often in the wake of Judith's husband's death. But on January 19, 2004, Mary reported her missing after going to her house, as previously planned, and receiving no answer at the door or on the phone. Mary thought it peculiar: the front door was unlocked, and Judith's phone and keys had been left on the kitchen counter. Calling her friend's name, Mary made her way down the hallway, past the wedding photos and Judith's own pictures from Glamour Shots and into Judith's bedroom. While nothing major seemed out of place, wet towels had been left on the floor.

Concerned that Judith could have been depressed as a result of grief, police sealed off the house and began a search. Four days later, a young local boy stumbled upon her half-naked body in the shallow creek bed some ten miles away. Judith had been strangled to death.

It didn't take long for Chetopa police to name Charles Krider as a suspect; the Chetopa police chief himself claimed to have seen Charles driving in the area that night and reported his suspicions (DNA taken from a pubic hair in Judith's shower would later implicate him). Charles claimed that on the night of her murder, he had watched a football game at a friend's house and was home by nine p.m., before venturing off to go hunting for beavers at eleven p.m. and returning at two the next morning. He also claimed to have his own tilling business, admitting that he at one point had tended to Judith's garden prior to her disappearance.

Charles Krider was found guilty of second-degree murder.

But even before Judith's murder, locals and shopkeepers thought Charles to be "unusual," and "weird," and this was the general consensus in Chetopa. I have a habit of asking anyone I run into in these little flyover towns—a cashier, a diner, a neighbor—what they've heard, and several recount how Charlie used to walk around at odd hours in the dead of night wearing nothing but his overalls. A couple of former coworkers say he was caught more than once masturbating at the local welding company. "He's the guy you hold your breath when you see him walking past, hoping he don't see you," says one man. Despite all this, Charles seemed to come from a good, God-fearing home, a unit consisting of a successful brother, a mother now in her eighties, and a father, once a manager at the local charcoal plant, who had passed on.

"Be very careful up there [in Chetopa] asking questions," Charles writes me from prison. Even though we spend a couple of years corresponding back and forth, there are cards he keeps close to his chest. "There are people there connected to the ones [murderers] I will not speak of until I'm out. They are not to be messed with in any way. There have been people found killed in barns and old silos, and those are the only ones that have been found."

Speaking with Charles is the first time I really feel like I'm getting somewhere with this case. In spite of the vagueness and the wishy-washy statements, there is a hunch, a feeling that maybe, if for the first time, I am looking in the right direction, that the family is aimed in the right direction. But when I speak to Lorene about her own hunches, she is as stoic as ever, maintaining, once again, that there are other avenues she has to pursue. "Another day I look for my daughter."

"There are old mine shafts and air vents to the mines that I think *they* have used for years to dispose of things," says Charles in reference to the men he refuses to speak of. "*They* are the people you don't want to meet."

Charles Krider fills his letters with promises of crucial information and of the identities of killers and of all the dirty secrets at the heart of Chetopa. "It will have to wait until I am out," he writes as he expresses fear for his elderly mother, who must continue to live in Chetopa.

25

THE SEARCHES OF CHETOPA

Come to the old Charlie Krider place and look in the well." This was the extent of an anonymous tip to the Bibles on Facebook, but it strikes a chord with Lorene, who hadn't heard the name since the murder of Judith Shrum. It is the winter of 2016, and the words bring the first real buzz to the case in over a decade, since Jeremy Jones's false confessions from Alabama's death row. Lorene keeps the tipster's identity safe, not just from me but from authorities. She is a steel trap. "I went there to Krider's well and checked it out," Lorene tells me. "Once I found the well, I told authorities I'd gotten a tip. I didn't say who I got it from, but I was going with or without them." Once again, Lorene takes it upon herself to investigate, so it's second nature, never an instance of grumbling.

At the time of the Freeman murders back in 1999, Charles Krider's residence was a large two-story farmhouse near the center of Chetopa. It was a clapboard house with peeling white paint tinged with the faintest shade of foxglove purple, in old-fashioned Midwestern style, on a block of smaller houses that seemed to shy away from its stature as one of the oldest houses in the town. After the house was sold, soon after Charles's arrest,

Chetopans watched from their front yards as the building went up in flames in the middle of the night, casting everything else in Chetopa into darkness. The fire was so big and bright that it could have been seen from the ghost towns nearby, had those of the living world occupied them. Following a brief investigation, it was ruled an accidental electrical fire, and the case was closed.

By 2016, there is nothing left of the corner property, which stretches from one block to the next. All that remains on the otherwise vacant lot is a small yellow shed that contains items belonging to the current owner, and on the other side, a large square slab of concrete on the ground. Underneath that is a brick-lined well narrow enough that if it had been used to hide the bodies of the missing girls, they would have first needed to be dismembered.

On January 15, 2016, the backhoes were on standby, along with a large group consisting of officials from two states: the Labette County (Kansas) sheriff; a Labette County Sheriff's Office detective; the Chetopa police chief; two representatives of the District Attorney's Office District 12 (Craig, Mayes, and Rogers counties in Oklahoma), along with their investigator, Gary Stansill; OSBI agent Tammy Ferrari; and two anthropologists from the Office of the Chief Medical Examiner. A pop-up blue canopy was erected, the land around them sticky with wet leaves and that after-rain, earthy smell thick in their nostrils. For the first time in over a decade, since the empty searches of Galena instigated by Jeremy Jones, the Freeman and Bible families reunited with the same hope that had aligned them from day one: finding the girls and bringing them home.

The search brought with it a swell of media attention, beyond the few loyal reporters who'd stuck with the Bibles since the early days of the case. As the crowds gathered in their colorful fleeces—with the exception of Lorene, who wore black—they huddled, fixing their attention on a small screen that streamed live as authorities used what the *Parsons Sun* local newspaper called "a long extension pole, similar to what supports a camping tent" attached to an underwater camera to start exploring the bottom of a well once owned by Charles Krider. Moving delicately under the black water, the camera skimmed the sides until it reached the solid bottom made of a concrete base twelve feet beneath. The authorities slowly stirred the two to three inches of sediment, hoping to capture any little thing: a piece of clothing, a ring, perhaps a bone.

The three-hour search, to everyone's simultaneous disappointment and relief, yielded nothing.

OK, what's next? Lorene remembers thinking. *This tip didn't pan out, so what's next?*

However, the search on Charles Krider's property, unbeknownst to the wider public, seemed to open the floodgates for new leads. Bystanders jerked their necks for Lorene to go over and they sent messages through third parties to the girls' relatives as they lingered in Chetopa. "We had people coming left and right, talking about where the girls' bodies were," says Lorene. The impregnable collective silence in Chetopa began to come apart, with neighbors coming forward to share what they'd heard, what they'd seen. "They were talking about Charles Krider, and then other meth cooks and dealers from the area, like a man named Phil Welch," Lorene says, referring to the religious meth cook who had also lived in Chetopa but had parked his meth-cooking trailer in Picher at the time of the Freeman murders. "And two of his friends, Ronnie Busick and David Pennington." They were said to follow Phil Welch wherever he went, a pair who'd also been reared right there in Chetopa. Suddenly, the families were inundated with information.

By summer, I am no stranger to the latest rumors that have arisen in the wake of the well search—one of them being that Charles *didn't* dispose of the girls down the well, but rather that they are under the basement where his house once stood. There, in the discolored grass, I can see the square left after the house burned down. In 2013, after the fire, the owner of the property had men with bulldozers push what remained—all the burned parts and furniture and debris—into the basement, and cover the junk pit with dirt.

The current owner, and several other people, consistently mention that beneath this rubble, there is rumored to be a square concrete slab on top of the concrete floor. It is the belief of several Chetopans that there you'd find the girls' bones, but they very well might be just the small-town rumors one finds around a town like this. I have little to go on and no photographic evidence of the basement floor, but as the theory becomes compounded by one tip after another, I want to pursue a second search on the Krider property, even if authorities deem the tip weak, which it was. I hate the idea of never knowing, and in my zeal, I hire a local man with a backhoe to dig when no one else cares to. Alongside a cameraman I'd personally hired out of Brooklyn to help me here in the Midwest, I contacted local Kansas authorities and all the necessary people to ensure we weren't risking hitting underground mains and lines. But it is this very decision that causes the OSBI to stop speaking to me, and for this, I am regretful. Though I can look back and see that this may have been a foolish decision based solely on my impetuous nature, I can't say that I fully regret the decision to look here.

Until I have published this book, Charles Krider will never know that this search was my orchestration.

While the crew sets to work on burrowing into the heart of Chetopa, which takes up most of the day, the cameraman and I decide to send his own underwater cameras down the well. I remember the feeling of getting on my belly, facedown in the well with the father of Lauria Bible, Jay, standing over me, in the event that we discovered his daughter's remains in the black water. We divide our attention between the echoes of our voices down the well and a small screen as the cameraman directs the camera's movements like a surgeon, bobbing in and out of the water. When we look at the footage later on, it is unnerving trying to inspect every speck of something that floated by and hearing our own muffled voices from under the water. Was this Ashley's and Lauria's fate?

Like the search team before us, we find there is nothing here.

People and objects around me move with my pulse in my sight, and dark shadows strike from the corners of my eyes. Each of the 105 degrees adds a beat in my heart, and I can't distinguish the sounds of locusts from the sounds of the snakes in the trees and the sounds of the sun. Hypersensitivity. I look up at the rustling elms, spellbound by the white-hot light piercing from the trees like a million little eyes in wait. I can hear heat and taste the black water that the backhoe scoops from the basement just by looking at it. With the Bible family nearby, the arm of a digger scoops for what feels like days, and Lisa, Lauria's cousin, stands clutching a silver cross at her chest. We all pray silently today. Together, we watch the backhoes scrape and rev under the inky water, while locals arrive with their own water pumps to drain it. Each bend of the machine's arm unearths old hamper baskets, a shower curtain, the odd shoe and pants. Large piles of mud and glass are excavated and dropped in sloppy piles onto the grass, where we sift for answers with our hands and the toes of our boots, mindful of broken glass. And just as we begin to wonder if we'll ever reach the bottom, there it is: the concrete slab, which before now I wasn't even sure existed.

"People might think it's an emotional roller coaster from where they're sitting, but I don't feel it," says Lorene Bible, who can move on to the next tip as fast as she can zero in on one.

Though half of me can't wait to hightail it out of Chetopa, the other half can't look away from the gaping hole in the ground, the basement of a convicted murderer. I feel like Chetopa is where I need to be. Through the anxiety, the panic attacks, the suffocating heat, and the palpable danger of the place, something keeps pulling me here.

Tip after tip came in to the Bibles, all saying the same thing: everything you want to know is right here in Chetopa.

26

REVIVAL

1999

In 1999, the fumes of meth moved over the plains. It was early and the morning stars shone against the unfolding of sunrise. It could have been Picher. It could have been Chetopa. Today no one is sure, but in this part of the world, life is divided in half: cutthroat skies on top and black and blue below, mud and prairie violets. A scar that ran across its middle, the horizon, held motherless men, the very men private investigators found in the ruins of Picher. Their leader, Phil Welch of Erie, Kansas, the religious fanatic found at the edge of a ghost town. It was one of many trailers where Phil held his sermons, where memory was short and suffering was long. Still tacked to the wall, a missing flyer with Ashley's and Lauria's pictures.

Today there is nothing here, but if I stay in this grassy lot long enough, I can hear "Nothing but the Blood" and a sermon on its third day, no matter where. In Picher, Phil Welch's trailer was bulldozed or swept up by an EF4 tornado. On the outskirts of Chetopa, his home was struck by lightning and burned to the ground.

"He was as evil as they got," says R.H., the man who led me to where

Chetopa's Charles Krider disposed of a school lunch lady. It was a town where everybody knows everybody, and R.H. knew them all. "He [Phil Welch] had one of his girlfriends hanging by her wrists in his closet, and he kept whipping her with the belt, just whipping. She was screaming and Phil said to me, 'Don't mind her. The bitch loves it.'"

Phil Welch fancied himself an ordained minister and demanded that the living room of his home be vaulted instead of finished like the other rooms. "He said it would make a good chapel," his landlord once said to the *Tulsa World*. "There was always gospel music playing. Always."

"He could talk for days while high," says a relative of Phil's. "And he was intelligent, as if everything he said was at the edge of something profound." At the root of his babbling was bullshit. However, there was no denying that Phil cast a spell over his small congregation of followers, including two men named David Pennington and Ronnie Busick.

It always seemed that Phil Welch was at the top of the food chain, only keeping company with people he could have dominance over, and that was most people; for Phil feared no one and nothing. Most that I speak to, including a family member named Rhonda, recollect horror stories about Phil Welch's former family: the wife he beat and the four children they had. They are stories laced with cattle prods and bullwhips, of sexual abuse against his own biological children. He implemented impossible rules that relatives weren't aware of. Eating a slice of pizza that Phil had mentally declared his own meant a whipping and sleeping outside; having butter at supper not melted to his liking meant taking a hammer to his wife's fingers, one by one.

I come to learn that there was a cop who lived next door, one who heard the beatings and watched the meth cooks for years. When asked why he did nothing, "I am sorry," he answered. "I had a wife and kids." Even the law was afraid of Phil Welch.

"When he flew into his rage, it went for hours and hours, all through the night," says Rhonda, who explains that Phil would make his children beat up a mentally challenged neighbor kid, lest he beat them. "He thought it was the funniest thing in the world." Even years before the Freeman-Bible murders, he was a meth manufacturer and dealer, perhaps one of the first in the Midwest. "He'd go out to the barn for hours." Phil used to cook there. "Then he'd come back with nosebleeds and get into one of his lectures and talk for days. I mean, days. And you couldn't get a word in edgewise."

I sit through countless tales of horror.

It wasn't hard to see how a man who demanded such power could get the likes of Pennington and Busick to follow him anywhere he went.

David Pennington and Ronnie Busick were more of your miscreants, raised under the shaking heads of disappointed Chetopans who expected nothing more than trouble from the boys, poor boys, boys of angry fathers and neglectful mothers. Those in the area knew enough that if Pennington and Busick walked into a bar, you were best to sit on the other side and avoid making eye contact. "I knew they was dangerous," says one local. "But if you didn't bother them, they didn't bother you."

"I just didn't make eye contact," another says. "Just kept my head down when I seen them driving by."

Today, people refer to the men as though they were wild animals, and they even kept themselves in such a state. Ronnie, the fairer one, was always crazy eyed, with a mane of salt and pepper that poked in all directions, while David was your mouth-breathing, thin, and dirty kid whose clothes never fit him right. Both carried with them long lines of felonies, most involving drugs and domestic violence.

Chetopa was one of those towns that died by night, though it wasn't uncommon to see the likes of Welch, Busick, and Pennington, or any of the other meth heads of the area, rolling their trucks at night, stealing cattle and bales of hay. But even if farmers knew they'd taken their things, not a God-fearing soul went up against Phil.

"This is what you do if one of these rancher types pulls a gun on you," several people would hear Phil Welch say before he'd go into demonstration, noting the importance of breaking the clavicle. "There's nothing like seeing a man's face once you've disarmed them. Power. That's power." Phil habitually sucked on his teeth between sentences while high.

I thought about one of the more overlooked facts in the murders of the Freemans, and that was the collarbone that the medical examiner had noted was broken right before Danny's death. Could Phil Welch have disarmed Danny?

Pennington and Busick listened with meth-induced concentration, maybe too afraid of Welch not to listen. The three men gathered by the kitchen stove, cooking up a fresh batch of methamphetamine as Phil ranted on about something that he'd fixed his attentions on, talking until he had no voice. Often scripture, what he'd adamantly call "church." And Pennington and Busick, claiming to love the Lord, nodded, trying to listen over the gospel music that Phil played for days on end. Until Phil turned to them with that black-eyed, intense gaze, bringing lines of crystal under their noses, carrying on with out-of-context, askew verses of the Bible. Together, they partook of meth.

"He would talk about 'By his stripes be healed,'" said Phil's relative Rhonda. "Then he'd whip one of the kids with a switch." His children, now adults, still carry the burns and the scars of his beatings on their backs and their legs.

Another relative recounted an event that saw Phil Welch take his twelve-year-old son and strangle him under the water in a bathtub until the boy lost consciousness. Welch proceeded to lift the nearly lifeless, soaking-wet body from the water and place him on the floor, spending a few minutes trying to revive the boy. When he finally came to, Phil pulled his face to his. "Now you know what it feels like to die."

As the three men got high and brought twisted versions of Jesus Christ into their nonexistent hearts, a young boy walked in.

"When Phil yelled for you to c'mere, by God, you went," said one of the relatives of Phil Welch.

The boy R.E. was the young son of one of Pennington's girlfriends. He came into the kitchen, where the men huddled around a short stack of Polaroid pictures.

"Wanna see something?" Ronnie called out to the boy, looking over at Welch to suss out his reaction, which came across as approving. Beside him, Pennington chuckled. Busick slapped the boy on the back of his head, grabbing the scruff of his neck and rubbing his nose in the photos.

"We got 'em," commented Welch. "We got 'em good, didn't we?"

In the photographs were two of Phil's victims, gagged and tied to chairs, Phil lying beside them.

"I remember that about Phil," Rhonda continues. Sources say he used to take pictures, even of his own children, whom he'd sometimes have stand naked in the living room just to humiliate them. He'd sometimes go as far as cutting their clothes off with a knife. While his relatives got dressed, he'd jump from behind the door and get a shot of them naked before running off, laughing with entertainment.

The boy R.E. closed his eyes when having his face shoved in the photos, the way a dog has his nose shoved in shit. In the pictures were Lauria Bible and Ashley Freeman days after the fire.

And they were alive.

27

"THIS PLACE IS ATE UP."

It has been more than a year since the basement and well searches of Charlie Krider's property in Chetopa turned up empty. I spend months living on the Grand Lake o' the Cherokees. Floating docks line the lake, and the smell of gunpowder becomes a pleasant fixture in the air when I am writing my notes or transcribing interviews in a hammock. I watch the seasons change and the hills distill campfire smoke. I lie about who I am to neighbors and spend the odd hour enjoying slot machines and learning to cook over fire until the cold months come and the nights stretch long.

In the lead-up to this reckoning, I wrestle with darkness like a dog with a bone. In trying to understand this world, the people who make up these communities, and the terror that lurks on the fringes of their lives, I speak with child-rape victims who have since grown and given their lives over to drugs, and addicts with their faces disfigured by knives as a result of drug debt. I receive phone calls from someone who just breathes on the other end in the middle of the night. And maybe this doesn't seem so ominous if you're normal, but I am mentally chained to a bed, listening to the ebb and flow, the breathing of darkness.

A text from a source tells me to "get out of there now." And panic comes when my down-to-earth, calm husband starts closing every blind of our home and packing our bags to leave. As one blind closes, I see the shadow of a figure outside that is my fear.

"I'm getting the fuck out of this place," he yells.

"I'm. Not. Done!"

I call Lorene Bible, barely able to breathe in the grip of a panic attack. Lorene has long been dealing with the characters I fear, and she listens patiently that night and calms me down. "Go into a room," she says. "You're going to stay away from the windows. You're going to breathe. Then you're going to hang up with me and call the sheriff." She talks me down for a good amount of time until the panic recedes.

For the first time, listening to her maternal words of comfort, instead of trying to see Lauria through Lorene's eyes, I finally see Lorene through Lauria's. It is a bloodred stitch that keeps this story from falling away, and it is called mother.

The next morning, while we were waiting at an airport in northwestern Arkansas, our flight was canceled. Then another. Only for us to learn that our connecting flight from New York to Dublin was canceled on account of a storm. As it went, something kept me here in Oklahoma.

I stayed, nerve-filled nights and the occasional shooting star. And while I am here with death and despair on my mind, it is hard to deny Oklahoma's red-faced beauty, its butchered red skies and the way the wheat offers you the chance to see the wind. It is in these moments of relative peace, while I look out over those spectacular frames of the Midwest, that I stop and reflect on the lives of Lauria and the Freemans, and feel my resolve harden. I have to tell the girls' story.

I try to hold on to that sense of purpose and certainty while driving north, sweaty palms and all, to meet Charles Krider up in Chetopa not long after his 2017 release from prison. September clings on firmly to the summer heat, and the air is thick, swirling slowly like treacle. Pecan farmers move about in the hot morning fog that hovers just above the earth.

They move in and out of the twisted trees of the groves, armed with buckets, floating like ghosts.

This time of year, I hear the nuts dropping to hit the earth, like the tapping of fingers anxiously waiting for a cool breeze. Many in the area recall wearing metal cans on their heads as children to hear the thundering of hickory beat on their makeshift helmets. Every memory is accompanied with a smile and the stories about the old harvesting traditions of their late grandparents. In Kansas, tradition is everything, and nostalgia tends to be more forgiving than history would allow.

I send a *should anything happen to me* precaution to my sister.

Charles is on parole and can't cross state lines. We choose to meet at Veterans Park in Chetopa, just on the Neosho River and full of picnic tables and canopies. As I pull up, I see he's already here. I feel faint with anxiety, but while every limb tingles, and though my stomach is cramping enough to make me cry out in pain, I've learned a few tricks over the last year that feel like small pieces of armor.

Use a pen from a hotel I'm not staying at.

Remove my wedding ring an hour before to hide the line.

Always have an exit strategy.

After a year of prison letters, then phone calls and texts, I spend the next several hours speaking face-to-face with Charles Krider.

He is cleaner than in the mug shots I've seen: where his facial hair back then was wild and discolored, it's now neat and tinged with shades of blond and red. He is calm and ready to talk, but beset by intermittent bouts of blame for most things that have gone south in his life. "My ex-wife was the one that did that dig," he says, referring to the second excavation, which—unbeknownst to him—I helped conduct. Or maybe he does know and is stringing me along. I manage to remain impassive. "She's always out to get me," he continues.

The truth of it is that the searches of Charles Krider's property in 2016 proved to be a dead end; there was nothing beneath the concrete slab at the bottom of the basement but undisturbed soil. As I am beginning to recognize in this case, the frequent, persuasive misdirection often leads everyone back to square one.

"Next," says Lorene.

But there is still an undeniable momentum to the attention falling on Chetopa, and as more people in the area start to reach out to the Bible family via the Facebook page, the two families' sights, as well as my own, remain fastened here in the southeastern corner of Kansas.

"This place is ate up," says Charles as we sit opposite each other on a picnic table. He wears mirrored sunglasses, so it's like speaking to my own reflection. I try to focus on what he's saying while reminding myself to breathe down to my belly (inadvertently shallow breathing, as anyone with anxiety can attest to, can make a person feel like they're at the edge of passing out, and I am in no rush to be unconscious around a convicted murderer). "People keep secrets here."

He is also better spoken than I imagined from our e-mails; his real-life voice is gruff, different from the voice I'd associated with him when I read his words. His forearms are sinewy and strong, that prison hardness formed out of bitterness and time. Throughout our correspondence, I'd pictured him as heavyset, and I spend the first section of our meeting re-calibrating my view of the man. Despite all the rumors I've heard, he never strikes me as *weird* during this meeting in the park, and he is respectful and kind, pardoning himself the few times he lets slip a cuss. Before now, Charles was little more in my mind than an amalgamation of rumors and pieces of gossip I'd absorbed from locals, and he confounds my expectations. I've long since adjusted to the stoicism and reserve common to the people in these communities, and Charles is no different: he never smiles or shows any emotion.

Speaking at length about Danny Freeman, we touch on Danny's fears of the local deputies from the Craig County's Sheriff's Office back in the nineties. "If they would have treated him like a decent human being," Charles starts, before readjusting his line of thought. "I'm sure they treated him differently because of the way things are down there [in Welch]. I'm pretty sure they knew what he was doing, but they were so dirty, they didn't know what *he* had on *them*."

Charles explains that after Shane's death, Danny was engulfed in grief; he describes how when he'd go to visit Danny, they'd smoke up, and Danny would just sit and obsess over Shane's autopsy, talking about how to proceed with a lawsuit against the county. Charles and I discuss the possibility that Danny might have let the lawsuit go, had he not believed that the police were trying to cover it up—that perhaps a mea culpa from the sheriff's office could have pacified him and prevented the subsequent war, even if shooting officer David Hayes was on the right side of the law. "Maybe then it wouldn't have gotten to the point where he [Danny] wanted to kill anybody."

Charles confesses that Danny Freeman asked him to be his ride when Danny, according to Charles, went over to kill David Hayes. "'If you hadn't've told me,'" Charles told Danny. "If Danny hadn't've told me what he was doing, I would have driven him anywhere, but knowing he was going to kill that man? I said, 'No way. If you hadn't've told me, Danny.'"

I spend the morning talking about the drug rings in the area until I feel comfortable enough to steer this conversation back to the one thing I really want to know, the thing he had promised: the identities of the men he had refused to speak of while in prison.

The heart of what I want to hear from Charlie is something I first heard from current OSBI agent Tammy Ferrari when I asked her about her own interview with Charles. "He just went back to the same stuff," she said. "Says he was very good friends with Danny . . . feels whoever is responsible for it needs to pay the ultimate price." But then Ferrari gestured to something that didn't tend to feature in the narrative I'd heard countless times from the wider community, something that only those closest to the investigation had caught hold of. "He talks about an incident where some people came up to the [Freeman] residence, like a week or two before the fire."

This had also been brought up by Danny's father. "Some guys came here to try and threaten Danny, and Danny was having none of it," said Glen Freeman. "Danny told one of them, 'Don't bring that killer here ever again.'" But Glen couldn't recall any names. "I just know it was someone he knew who'd brought someone dangerous, and there might have been a few of them." Relatives say that Danny chased the carful of people away under the threat of a shotgun. Some suggest he fired a warning shot.

I think about the used shotgun shell that CCSO deputy Mark Hayes found in the driveway on the morning of the fire, the one he begged Nutter to take into evidence.

When I tell Lorene about this piece of information, the shotgun shell is news to her. However, she was fully aware of the rumored incident in which Danny chased a carful of people off his yard.

"Danny called Kathy after they left," Lorene said. She went on to explain that Kathy was at her parents' house when Danny called to tell Kathy about the incident, and that Kathy was rumored to tell Danny that she feared those men, that she wanted her husband to have nothing to do with them.

"We don't know if they have anything to do with the fire," continued OSBI agent Ferrari. "But we'd like to."

"It was the Sunday before [the fire]," continues Charles. "I went over and saw Danny was upset. So I asked him what was wrong, and he said, 'Well, I had some problems this week.' So I asked, 'Well, why?'"

According to Charles, Danny said, "A pickup pulled in, had three people in it. They were very adamant about buying my whole crop." This will be something Charles insists on: that Danny Freeman began selling his marijuana in exchange for meth, two drug worlds that operated rather separately from each other. This divided those involved on the details of the case: some are convinced he sold marijuana to pay for his legal costs for the lawsuit pertaining to Shane's death, while others—those closest to Danny—are firm in their belief that his dependencies never exceeded the pot plants he'd sown for himself. Throughout my research, there are small variations. To this day, the details of Danny's alleged marijuana and meth businesses remain without specifics, though it's possible that whatever trouble Danny found himself in might have had something to do with these dealings and run-ins . . . possibly murder.

Charles continues. "Danny knew two of them, and one of them had just gotten out of prison." But when it comes to actually naming the three men, Charles becomes fidgety, visibly a little tongue-tied. Some sources claimed Danny even said, *Get that murderer off my property.* "Jax, the way people operate around here . . . there's always people in the shadows. And they're in the shadows because of a reason."

I leave Chetopa that afternoon after several hours of talking (much of the conversation revolved around Charles's declarations of innocence and his being framed), but my gut says to keep looking here for the same reasons it tells me to run away. There is something about this town and the men in it that just doesn't sit right with me (though little does, in this case). It is an eerily fascinating place: many people come out of their way to find me, claiming to know something about the girls, but then they refuse to say more out of fear. Countless people talk about hauntings, saying that they can hear the girls from holes in the ground or have spiritual visions of their murders. Chetopa's main street (Maple Street) has dilapidated water mills and abandoned storefront windows with messages written in dust and an old lady peeking out from her lace curtains at the sound of my boots walking up and down the road. And by God, the best pecans you'll find.

I return to the town again and again, right up until the fall of 2017, when Lorene abruptly tells me to stop talking to certain people in that area.

I go back to the lake house after speaking to various people in Chetopa. It smells like Halloween; crisp, like faraway fire and rotting fruit. I sit alone with a cigarette (I've since quit) on the second level of the floating dock as the sun starts to double over into the lake. Small fires ignite around the foothills. I'm in a difficult stretch of the investigation, and I'm swallowing down the distinct feeling of defeat and menthol when I receive a call from Lorene.

Lorene's call comes soon after my questioning a man who, unbeknownst to me, is in the scopes of the newly formed team assigned to the Freeman-Bible case (consisting of OSBI agent Ferrari and DA investigator Stansill). I ask her why. Then she tells me, on behalf of DA investigator Gary Stansill, to stop my current line of inquiry so as not to impede the investigation.

"They made an arrest," she tells me.

I gasp at the same time a fish jumps from the water. In my silence, Lorene states that authorities have been working closely with counterparts in Kansas to build a case against the man in question during the short time they had him incarcerated for unrelated drug charges. Lorene's silence, and now mine, is essential in the state's early stages of making a case. Along with a few others, Lorene slowly started to let me into the BBI.

I duly stay silent for the next seven months until an explosive break in April of 2018, when authorities announced that they've made their first arrest in relation to the murders in Welch.

SECTION 5

THE ARRESTS

28

THE ARREST

The days around the public announcement of the arrest are rugged for the Bibles and the Freemans, two families scarred over the years by enough dead ends to drive an average person insane. They'd walked through fire, and raced from one end of the earth to the other. At any given moment, you can ask Lorene Bible how long it's been since she last saw Lauria, and her answer will always be in terms of days.

Three months after I learn about the man they arrested and are covertly investigating up in Wichita, a discovery is made with promises of progress in the case. On December 29, 2017, exactly eighteen years from the day that Ashley Freeman and Lauria Bible were last seen, the *Tulsa World* published an article detailing how newly elected Craig County sheriff Heath Winfrey discovered a box containing old case notes while moving into his office earlier in the year. As quoted in the newspaper, DA investigator Stansill told reporters, "Winfrey has provided investigators previously unknown notes and documents he discovered referencing the Freeman/Bible case that was left from the previous sheriff administration."

As in the alleged cover-up of Shane Freeman, the current Craig County

Sheriff's Office seems eager to place the blame on its predecessors. And while I speak with former sheriff Sooter several times after this discovery, he refuses to speak publicly about his thoughts regarding the box and doesn't return a comment for the record. Although I've never adhered to Sooter's belief that Jeremy Jones was responsible for the Freeman murders, I've long felt his heart was in the right place, that his choices didn't stem from corruption or selfish need, but perhaps he lacked the proficiency needed for such a high-profile case in a system where the role of sheriff came down to nothing more than a popularity contest. Nevertheless, this box is an uncomfortable footnote to his time in office.

"These notes and documents have proven to be extremely valuable," continued Stansill, though the contents remain unknown. "This information has produced leads that have produced additional leads." Naturally, I wonder how such crucial information could have sat in an office through one to two sheriff administrations and nearly two decades unnoticed. Without knowing who authored these mysterious documents, it is impossible to place the blame where it belongs, but perhaps that is the point.

While remaining silent on whom they'd arrested, Stansill does admit that he and another investigator have "interviewed several people who have knowledge about the shooting deaths of Danny and Kathy Freeman and the disappearance of the girls."

Devotees of the case become elated at the news of a potential breakthrough, but Lorene Bible refers to the timing of the announcement as a "ploy" designed to be publicized on the anniversary of the girls' disappearance. "Winfrey found the box in February, but they didn't release the info until December, ten months later."

According to Sheriff Winfrey, it was just after taking office at the beginning of the year that he stumbled upon the box while moving his stuff in. "It was just sitting on the shelf," he tells the *Tulsa World*. "We weren't digging for it—we just found it." Together, Winfrey and Stansill share their optimism and hopefulness over the publicly unknown contents of the notes, claiming that the information helped move the case forward.

"It wasn't anything new," Lorene Bible disagrees, maintaining that it was the tips that arrived through social media leading back to Chetopa that really put the investigation back on track. "It was just a smoke screen to get the girls' faces out there and get people talking." It seems to be the administration's hope that it could encourage people to come forward with information that would help authorities with the case they were trying to build against the criminal they'd arrested. "If it were something of real value, they wouldn't have sat on it for a year." Lorene contends that the contents of the box are information she'd long known about, tips she'd personally submitted. But it is her goal to keep the story thriving so she goes along.

Others think of it as a gambit: local-boy politics and shifting blame. Lauria's cousin Lisa perceives it as a way for current investigators to get credit for doing the hard work that had really been conducted by relatives. "I thought it was tacky, even the timing," she says. "The box didn't have anything to do with the direction the case was going in, but they sure wanted to look good." In fact, the Bibles frown on the way the CCSO has approached the case as of late, sharing their disappointment that the new sheriff, Winfrey, took over a year to mention the case publicly or attempt to speak with the Bibles. The family found this especially disheartening not only because they had known Winfrey since they were all kids in Bluejacket (Winfrey was between Lisa and Lauria in age), but because the Freeman-Bible case was, and is, one of the more notorious horrors to happen in Craig County's history.

Heath Winfrey is a stocky, dark-haired man with a high-arched brow and a goatee. While new to the position of CCSO sheriff, he has a sturdy background in law enforcement and a strong understanding of the drug problem in the area from working with the Oklahoma Bureau of Narcotics and Dangerous Drugs Control. Although his career only began in the early 2000s, he was a new graduate from Bluejacket High when he first heard about the fire. He and his buddies were hunting west of Welch on the morning Kathy's body was discovered. "We had heard that they were hunting for Danny, and he'd ran off with a girl," he tells me.

"I could understand how he was busy, how budgeting was an issue. These were things he told me down the line," says Lorene. "But he could have explained this earlier; he could have approached me earlier. The Bibles and the Winfreys have known each other since we were kids." But Lorene also seems to suspect he knows that if the case is solved all these years later "that it's coming back on the door of the Craig County Sheriff." In all my time with her, Lorene keeps her focus resolutely on moving forward to find the girls, but in moments like now, I see glimpses of her anger over the way the case had been handled, and I can't help but wonder how much she blames law enforcement for failing her family. "After we find the girls, everyone knows this is going back to them."

The case is a test in patience, and above all, I have learned that nothing comes quickly. The harder I work, the longer the days sprawl; I'm living in a perpetual state of "We're about to"s and "Any day now"s, waiting for impending searches and press releases. "You learn not to get your hopes up," repeats Lorene.

There are days when I swear we're right there, days when I'll bet a hundred bucks on a suspect. There are hunches and instincts and dreams and nightmares that I believe are worth betting my life on. And then nothing. So when the discovery of the crate of notes in the sheriff's office is announced to great public excitement, I find myself pausing, cautious, waiting for more news. I learn why Lorene doesn't buckle up for the emotional roller coasters.

By April 2018, four months have dragged since authorities rekindled the hopes of the community with their news of the mystery box. It's been seven months of sitting on the secret of the criminal they arrested in Wichita and held on drug charges; the suspect's identity remains unknown to the public, as authorities continue to build a case against him ("They're going to announce him any day," I hear consistently throughout those seven months).

Between Ireland and Oklahoma, I am with my family in New York, eating ice cream and about to sit and watch a movie when out of the blue,

Glen Freeman calls me. "Something isn't right, Jack," he says, regarding an unusually large amount of rumors clouding about. Within moments, I begin to hear the same thing from several people, leaks: that after the weekend, authorities plan to release the names of three men in connection with the murders of not just Kathy and Danny but of Lauria and Ashley as well.

On the morning of the press release, I sit at my sister's kitchen table with every nerve in my body hardening to electrical wire. God curse the day when I thought I'd ever drink decaf. I stay in constant touch with Lisa and Lorene. I text a dozen people at once, making calls, getting calls, inundated with requests for updates. I relay messages between so many people that I eventually shut everything off and leave open on my computer only the tab for the live press release, as media outlets set up their equipment in a room at the Vinita fairgrounds, where Lauria and Ashley had hoped to present their show animals at the county fair in the new millennium.

Beside me is a familiar shadow called anxiety. A killer who smacks his teeth over my shoulder.

While the general public doesn't know the details of what's about to be announced, everyone knows they're about to learn something of game-changing significance about the Freeman-Bible case. Livestreaming, I see some of the reporters I've gotten to know over the years as they set up their cameras and microphones; everyone knows they're here for more than your garden-variety rumor. "Check one, two"s and feedback, and the room fills with static and whispers, which I can hear clearly, even from my sister's kitchen table.

Inhale for four seconds, hold for four, exhale for eight. Accept. Let the storm rage. Breathe. The killer fades.

But as the journalists set up, the families are being prepped at the courthouse only a couple miles away in Vinita: there were Lorene and Jay; Kathy's parents, Celesta and Bill Chandler; Dwayne Vancil and his father, Glen Freeman; current district attorney Matt Ballard; Investigator

Stansill; OSBI agent Tammy Ferrari; Craig County sheriff Winfrey; and several more members of law enforcement and Bible relatives, including Lauria's cousins Lisa and Missy. There, before they leave for the fairgrounds to brave the lights and reporters, authorities explain exactly what they are going to announce, what they aren't, and make sure everyone is on the same page. In the private room reserved for the meeting, verbal spats erupt between the families, filling the hallways of the courthouse. Everyone is at their boiling point.

About fifteen minutes before the announcement, as the families are en route from the courthouse to the fairgrounds, I receive an out-of-the-blue Facebook message from "Mrs. Jones," the woman who claims to be the wife of Jeremy Jones on Alabama's death row (he still does not admit that this was ever him). "Hi, Ann," says Mrs. Jones, using my real first name. "I am in a restaurant in Miami, OK and somebody told us the news in regard to the Bible-Freeman case. Just wanna leave you a quick 'Thank you.' If it wasn't for you, this wouldn't have happened." (It's worth noting, I take zero credit in any of this.)

I call Mrs. Jones's bluff and tell her that I too am in Miami, but she declines to meet. I wonder how in the hell he got ahold of this information before the rest of the world. I suspect it's Jeremy's vague way of expressing gratitude.

From New York, I watch the press conference begin. Spokeswoman Michelle Lowry of the district attorney's office prefaces the announcement with some housekeeping rules and asks that the focus be only on the case, essentially requesting that audiences avoid asking questions pertaining to the errors of previous authorities. She then introduces District Attorney Matt Ballard, a finely dressed and surprisingly young man in patriotic red, white, and blue who delivers the statement.

"For eighteen years, the community in Craig County and many members of the media have followed the case of the deaths of Kathy and Danny Freeman, the mysterious disappearances of their sixteen-year-old daughter, Ashley Freeman, and Ashley's friend sixteen-year-old Lauria Bible, and the arson of the Freeman family home," Ballard begins. "Yesterday, there was an arrest in the case. OSBI investigator Tammy Ferrari and my SVU investigator Gary Stansill, through incredible police work, identified three perpetrators."

Cameras flash as he goes on, his face inscrutable, the pinstripes of his suit ramrod straight. "Today, charges were filed against Ronnie Dean Busick, who by law is presumed innocent of the charges. Mr. Busick is charged with acting in concert with two other men as follows: four counts of first-degree murder for killing Kathy Freeman, Danny Freeman, Ashley Freeman, and Lauria Bible, two counts of kidnapping for the abductions of Ashley Freeman and Lauria Bible, and a final count of first-degree arson for setting fire to the Freeman home."

This announcement marks the first official report that the girls are dead.

"The other two perpetrators as named in the most recent course of the investigation are Warren Phillip Welch II, more commonly known as Phil Welch, and David A. Pennington." It is learned that both men died, in 2007 and 2015, respectively.

Ballard confirms that both families were briefed on the details uncovered by Ferrari and Stansill, that both the Bibles and Freemans have "learned these young ladies' final days were certainly horrific." Ballard also expresses his hope that this new information will help people finally come forward, the general belief being that others in the community know where the girls' bodies might be found. He cites an affidavit that will be made available after the press conference, "revealing the girls were kept alive for an unknown number of days following the fire."

After the OSBI assistant special agent in charge, Aungela Spurlock, makes a statement commending the OSBI's work and their varying methods of investigation, and acknowledging the families' hard work and perseverance, the floor opens up for Craig County sheriff Heath Winfrey.

"Since taking office fifteen months ago, there's been the goal in our administration to help bring those involved in these crimes to justice and locate Lauria Bible and Ashley Freeman," he says, dressed in a gray police uniform accented with gold pins and black trim. "We will not stop working until bringing Lauria and Ashley home."

For the authorities making these statements, it has been eighteen years since the girls were abducted from the scene of a violent crime. For Lorene, it has been 6,690 grueling days of not knowing where her flesh and blood went.

I knew this was the only likely outcome, but confirmation of the girls' deaths falls like a hammer's blow. One of the more gut-wrenching aspects of the conference is the multiple references to Polaroids. "There was physical evidence in the form of photos," says Heath Winfrey.

It was something that was also raised by DA Ballard, who claimed that "Polaroid photographs of the girls and their final days were seen by multiple people, and Welch, Pennington, and Busick made many statements to many people over the course of their lives."

Before I can read the twenty-nine-page affidavit, sure to describe in detail what led to the naming of these three men, I watch Jay and Lorene approach the microphones. They look older than when I last saw them only weeks before, the way men look after long stretches of battle. But in them is a unity rare to see in a couple that has suffered so deeply and consistently, who have lost a child under the worst imaginable circumstances. They look tired, and tearful too, but they are unbreakable.

For the first time since I met her, Lorene softly cries as she begins to speak. "This does not stop until we bring the girls home," she starts. "I do believe there are people out there still afraid to talk because they're fearful for their life." Lorene pays tribute to a new generation coming forward, the sons and daughters of killers and witnesses, many of whom live or have lived in Chetopa, Kansas, and the now ghost town of Picher, Oklahoma.

Jay is dressed in denim, and his face is already wet with tears as he takes the podium. "The Lord has answered a lot of prayers for us," says Lauria's father as his voice begins to break. "We've missed her for a long time, but we're going to bring her home."

Lorene steps forward again, allowing herself to show some of the emotion she typically saves for private moments. "I was told earlier today that sometimes I seem kind of hard," she admits, pointing to Jay beside her and acknowledging how it's usually Jay who is perceived to be demonstrative. As her voice begins to waver under the strain of holding back tears, she manages to stop herself. "I fight. That tearful mom will be there when I find my daughter. But until then, how hard? How hard do I have to fight? I need to know—because it's been a fight." No one in the audience speaks a word. There is no rush of reporters asking questions, no clearing of a throat, not even the sound of a deep breath. When Lorene speaks, the world listens, and after a moment of silence, Lorene gestures wordlessly to open the floor.

Every subsequent answer is delivered with control and resolve; Lorene doesn't play the part of the grieving parent some commentators expect to see, but she is a source of empowerment and determination with a single mission in mind. I once told her that I could never cope the way she did, had that been me, but she looked at me and told me that anyone will do anything to get their child home. "I'm a storm to be reckoned with," she continues to reporters. "You can come with me or I'm going on my own. . . . Lauria turned thirty-five on the eighteenth. So she's been gone more than half her life. I need a place where I can say, 'That's where my daughter is.' I used to go to the Freemans' driveway and put out wreaths, but it's just a driveway. When you lose a loved one, you could go to a cemetery. I don't have that. And that's what I want."

While the remains of Lauria and Ashley have yet to be found, it feels like a day of mourning, of paying respects to two beautiful girls who, as we are all coming to learn, lost their lives at the hands of monsters. I thought I had become inured to the darkness of this case, but reading the affidavit, learning about the dozen people who kept silent and the statements to authorities that were never investigated, I become horrified anew at the missed opportunities that blighted the investigation.

The affidavit identifies witnesses only by their initials, though it doesn't take much for those closest to the case or longtime residents of Chetopa to figure out who they are. The DA's spokeswoman explains the decision to redact names as a practical necessity: "The reason for this is they are co-operating witnesses, and because of the nature of the crimes and the ongoing investigation there is a need to protect identities, and that will remain the practice going forward."

29

RONNIE DEAN "BUZZ" BUSICK

Despite the arrests of Ronnie Dean Busick and the deaths of Phil Welch and David Pennington, the subject of the three men had always been a touchy one for locals. Even today, I will meet many people who still fear Phil Welch in death. So when I speak to Busick's niece Dawn for the first time, the borders are clearly drawn as to what is allowed to be on record and what strictly isn't.

Dawn recalls being a child in southern Kansas, running through the purple and cream iris beds of her grandparents' yard. The home provided by Dawn's parents seemed in a perpetual state of disrepair, and she was happy enough staying with Gramma Nadine and Papa Alpheus on the weekends in Chetopa. Her father's parents were *shrewd* antiques dealers who tried to help her hone the skills required to spot genuine pieces versus the fake stuff; Sundays were busy with yard sales and flea markets, sticky with the week's pecans rounded up to make turtles and brittle. She was a towheaded eight-year-old who'd feel the grief of losing her *pistol* of a grand-mother. "Lung cancer," Dawn tells me years later. "I can't remember how many times they went in and took pieces of lung. She was tough as shit, though, took years to die. Even the active-dying part took days, and we kept vigil. Gramma Nadine's last words were 'Well, shit, I can't even die right.'"

It was the day of Gramma Nadine's funeral, and Dawn took on the job of washing and presenting the dress her grandmother would be buried in. She ran around the "jumbly, weedy" property where old and dark outbuildings were filled with rusty machinery. "Somewhere in all of that was Papa's still." Grandpa Alpheus had been a bootlegger into the 1940s. But as she explored the yard in search of the impressive apparatus, she found her uncle Ronnie with his back against one of the sheds. Before him, an albino woman with only a few teeth left to her smile, as though they rattled about in her head, on her knees for Ronnie. Dawn says that Uncle Ronnie caught her eye, then winked. He pointed at the woman giving him head, gave Dawn a thumbs-up, and jerked his head as a gesture of saying *C'mere* to the eight-year-old child. "Well, I ran like hell."

The home in which Ronnie was raised sat crookedly where a few dirt roads end and furrow into deep, wide ditches, becoming dense with wild radish and prairie aster. But Nadine took pride in her flower beds, bringing color against the dull and dated wallpapers and grime-stained carpets of inside, features that had never changed over the decades since Alpheus built the house himself in the forties or fifties. His daughter (Ronnie's sister) had her husband build hers next door; the several small homes where the Busicks lived looked run-down over the years of weathering storm after storm, just a short two-mile walk from the state line. When Ronnie was a child, the porches had been full of junk, washers, and wringers, so he and his older brother and sister would have to use the back door, where cacti grew among collections of Kewpie dolls and ceramic hobo clowns looking down at their pants with sad faces. The kitchen's and the hallway's windows were filled with antique glassware, so that the light painted the whole house in carnival red. "Nadine fried three meals a day and smoked like a chimney, and the ventilation wasn't that great," says another relative. "The walls and everything that didn't get used had its own flocked wallpaper made of dust stuck to grease and tar."

Today, Dawn seems of high intelligence, the kind that comes with a touch of crazy, and she talks fast with the frequent use of the word "fuck." "He actually never touched me, but when I was no longer a child, I'd call him 'Uncle Bad Touch.'"

Ronnie Dean Busick spent much of his life in and out of jail, mostly for drug convictions, but the home of Nadine and Alpheus would forever be his home base. Relatives say that he was "slippery-eyed clever," but also refer to him as being as dumb "as a box of hair." It is the general consensus that he was equal parts bumbling and conniving. And when the sixty-seven-year-old man was arrested in Wichita on a parole violation, then later extradited from Kansas to Oklahoma on murder charges, no one who knew him entertained the idea that he was higher in the food chain than the likes of Welch and Pennington.

"No one was surprised to hear about all of this," says one relative of Busick's. "Sure, they were surprised it was someone they knew, but not that he could do it."

For Dawn, one of the most memorable things about growing up with Ronnie Dean Busick coming in and out of the home was a specific cowboy belt buckle he sported—one with a cartoonish depiction of a woman with her legs spread, viewed from the explicit perspective of a gynecologist, and her bubbly breasts and nipples in the background, with a "long, hard dick and hairy balls" aimed for her, ready for penetration; on the top of the buckle were the words *I'd Rather* and on the bottom were the words *Than Eat*. Ronnie Busick wore this belt even to his own mother's funeral. "Of course, growing up with him around, in the times he wasn't in jail, he'd catch me staring at it," says Dawn. And how could she not? "He'd call me over and measure my head against his waist and say, 'Honey, if only your head was flat, I'd marry you.'" He was referring to a place for a man to set his beer while receiving oral sex.

Fortunately for Dawn, her parents never let him be alone with their daughter, noticing the sideways glances he'd give her or the way he'd stare for long, uncomfortable moments. Gramma Nadine, who usually had

Dawn sleep on the couch, would have the child sleep on a cot right next to her and Alpheus's bed on the occasions that Ronnie returned home from one stint in jail or another. Even after Ronnie's brother died in 2009, Ronnie always called his brother's wife, who was described as timid and sweet, perhaps the only woman kind and patient enough to put up with his yarns, no matter how squeamish they'd make her. They were often uninhibited tales of sex and urges, bragging about "picking up women and fucking them." On one notable occasion, Ronnie said of the girls in his life, "If they don't want to give it up, then by God, I fucking take it." But in the mercurial fashion of meth addiction, he'd say in the same breath, "If only I married a sweet little thang like you, I'd never get in any of these messes."

Tom Pryor, the private investigator who found the insurance card on the Freeman property a few days after the fire in Welch, had had his own encounter with Busick when Pryor was still the police chief in Chetopa. "This is how stupid he is," says Pryor, explaining that it was during Busick's "younger years" in the 1970s when Pryor went to inquire about Ronnie's sister on Nadine and Alpheus's homestead. "Ronnie came from the woods or the back of the trailer, ran inside with a big bag of pot, and goes straight into the bathroom, right where we could all see him because he didn't even close the door behind him, starts dumping it all into the toilet right in front of us."

Relatives also mentioned the art of dowsing most revered by the Busick clan, a family in which water witching was used to sense the natural resources offered underground in Chetopa. "Grandpa Alpheus was a dowser and dug the gas well on the property my dad and Uncle Ronnie lived on, and it was about a hundred feet from the gas stove in the house," says Dawn. "So, he's [Ronnie] standing at the stove and cooking up a big, fat batch of meth, and there's a knock at the back door. He yells, 'Come on in!' and the deputies did."

Though the son of a bootlegger and a dowser (the practice of divination is largely shunned and was once viewed as satanic in small American towns like Chetopa), Ronnie was also known for being loose-lipped, a man who couldn't keep a secret. "That's why I don't think he knows where the girls are," says one relative. "He's too dumb and had too big of a mouth."

The man described by unsurprised relatives versus the man that is walked into the Craig County jail is a clear juxtaposition: the wild, silver-haired and -bearded man with eyes so dark that you couldn't see your reflection in them, and now the fat old man with no hair on top, stringy in the back down past his shoulders, and walking with a cane, without which he is hardly able to move on his own. In a video recording from Lisa Bible-Brodrick's phone, you can hear those who loved Ashley and Lauria the most shout out to Busick when he comes down from Kansas, ushered from the truck with DA investigator Gary Stansill and Craig County sheriff Heath Winfrey at either side.

"Do you want to tell me where my niece is at?" yells Lorene's brother as soon as Ronnie exits the SUV.

"Huh?" Ronnie asks.

Lorene's brother repeats himself from the other side of the metal gate.

"I wish I could," answers Ronnie, hardly audible. "I don't have a clue."

"How do you *not* know?" calls out a reporter.

"'Cause I wasn't there."

"Are you afraid to admit what you'd done?" another woman calls out.

"I didn't do nothing." Ronnie crawls from the car to the back doors of the courthouse, feebly limping. His sideburns are thick and white, as is a long horseshoe mustache.

"He puts that limp on when the cameras are on," Lisa tells me. "When we see him in the courthouse, he walks just fine. He's pathetic."

Most of the 2018 affidavit issued by the district attorney's office, which consists of the statements of twelve people, revolves around Phil Welch, said to have been the mastermind behind the Freeman murders, purportedly the consequence of drug debt related to methamphetamine and/or a drug deal gone south. However, one 2017 interview has a confidential witness called R.H. tell of a time he spotted Ronnie Busick on Maple

Street in Chetopa. Knowing that Ronnie was staying up at his parents' old place, the home he had inherited from Nadine and Alpheus, R.H. stopped and gave Busick a ride and offered to buy him some potatoes and such, saying that Busick "appeared about to starve to death," according to the affidavit, and that Busick knew R.H. to be a "soft touch for a free meal."

As it turned out, R.H. would be the very man who kept the lookout when I followed him to the old abandoned train trestle east out of town, where Charles Krider dumped Judith Shrum's body. *I'll keep a lookout if you wanna go over.*

According to both my conversation and the affidavit's information about R.H., Busick started "running his mouth" about his involvement with the Freeman murders and the girls' abductions while on the way to the grocery store, telling R.H. that the girls were tied up in a trailer in Picher, "where they were raped and tortured." When I meet with R.H. after the press release, he tells me that Busick admitted the girls were kept alive for several days, but says that he [Busick] was not the shooter of Kathy and Danny, though he stayed behind with David Pennington to light the trailer on fire.

"Had I heard about the fire and the missing girls when it all happened? Sure I had," R.H. says as we sit together in the kitchen of a mutual acquaintance. "Hell, I knew Danny [Freeman] from working together. Pretty good guy, actually." But R.H. cannot confirm any drug involvement with Danny. "We never went on any picnics or anything."

R.H. and I discuss his encounter with Busick, reviewing what was already spelled out in the affidavit. He added that it was about two years after the girls went missing. "He started mouthing off, bragging about what he did to them two little bitches, how they had them taped up, raping them, torturing them, messing with them and stuff."

The term "them two little bitches" rings familiar, echoing what Phil Welch told private investigators when they found him in Picher.

Busick continued talking to R.H. as they drove. "And they ain't ever gonna find them bodies neither." At that point R.H. slammed on the brakes and yelled at Busick to get the hell out of the truck, not far from the Busick property on the train tracks.

"Did he seem remorseful?" I ask.

"He was smiling ear to ear," R.H. tells me. "That bothered me for years." R.H. claims he went straight to the police department there in Chetopa.

R.H. says that the current investigators found his "name scribbled on a piece of paper" (it's insinuated in the affidavit to have been discovered in the mystery box in the Craig County Sheriff's Office). R.H. told current investigators that all of his information should be on record, but they said they could find no records. "Well, I just don't understand that," R.H. says.

With the inability to locate R.H.'s statements, it seems there are now two states that lost important documents related to the Bible-Freeman case.

When Agent Ferrari and DA investigator Stansill interviewed Busick in 2017, his statements contradicted those of witnesses, including wishy-washy admissions that he'd known Welch and Pennington. He spent the majority of the interrogation in silence, not moving when investigators kept accusing him of the four murders, though I can't imagine that there was much happening in his head. He spent most of the time with his eyes lost on the reward poster that agents set before him—one that offered the fifty thousand dollars collected from a Freeman-Bible fund-raiser in Welch, and on each side were two bold school photographs of Lauria and Ashley in color. Perhaps, in spending hours staring at the girls' pictures, Busick hoped they'd come back to life. . . . Perhaps he was silently remembering their time together.

It was a copy of the same poster that Phil Welch had tacked to his trailer in Picher.

With his cheeks sagging and a blank expression dull across his face, Busick contended, "I'd tell you where they was if I knew."

"Well, who did know?" asked Stansill.

"I'd probably say Phil, and probably Dave," he answered, stating that when he'd ask the other two where the girls were, they'd keep it "hushed up."

"You think they had something to do with it?"

"Pretty sure Phil did."

In the end, Ronnie Dean Busick would resort to staying mostly quiet.

As of September 2019, Busick still sits in the Craig County jail, having spent months being evaluated by those assigned to see if he is competent to stand trial. The defense argues that he might be able to plead guilty by reason of insanity on account of his being shot in the head back in the 1970s.

"The family always used that as an excuse, every time Ronnie did something wrong," says one of his relatives. *Oh, don't mind him—he was shot in the head years ago,* they'd say as if it explained his peculiar ways, the sideways looks at children, and the fights he'd find himself in.

"He was caught in bed with some fella's woman," says Lorene Bible. "Got himself in trouble and got shot."

"I really don't think he does know where those girls are," says Dawn. "And I hate that so much. I hate to think of those girls' bones settling at the bottom of a water-filled mine."

Lorene, however, has her own opinions. "He knows," she delivers with the familiar silence, unwilling to share her secrets. "He knows." While my own, amateur guess would be that Busick does not actually know where the girls were, I'd learned better than not to believe Lorene.

Though Busick denied any involvement in the murders of Kathy and Danny to investigators, he confessed that he "became suspicious [of Pennington's and Welch's involvement] after they found the insurance card." Even simple Ronnie Busick surmised that "it didn't take a rocket scientist" to figure out whose car was at the Freeman trailer that night, and the mention of the insurance card left behind came back to him in the initial days after the murders.

The insurance card, in fact, is central in the evidence that led to Busick's arrest and the naming of Pennington and Welch posthumously in the murders.

In the first few days after the Welch fire, Private Investigator Tom Pryor walked back up the incline of the driveway, past the dogwoods and bois d'arcs where Ashley and Lauria had collected food for the goats only days before, and asked around for who was in charge, at least on an official level. After a moment, he found Agent Steve Nutter. Introducing himself, Pryor held out the card. "This might be of some interest to you. Might be nothing, but every little thing counts in these things, don't they?"

30

THE INSURANCE-VERIFICATION CARD

This 2018 affidavit is how the public first hears about the insurance card found on the property of the Freemans by private investigators Tom Pryor and Joe Dugan, the card supposedly presented to and refused by OSBI agent Steve Nutter. This valuable piece of evidence is what led the pair to the likes of Phil Welch, whom they found singing on the side of the road near the chat piles of Picher. But the card also opened most of the doors in Chetopa for the private investigators, who chose to follow up on the card in the first days of the millennium, so that when the later generation of investigators assigned to the Bible-Freeman case reinterviewed many of the ignored witnesses (including Tom Pryor himself), it seems as though they're the last to learn about the card.

"We knew about it right away," says Dwayne Vancil. "We thought it had been followed up on."

"One to two days following December 30, 1999, a search party found an insurance-verification card belonging to E.B. near the crime scene," the affidavit reports. According to records, on January 3, 2000, less than a week after the fire, the FBI interviewed E.B., the then girlfriend of Phil

Welch, who claimed to have no idea as to how her insurance card wound up on the Freeman property. The affidavit, while it never admits the mistakes of past agents, does acknowledge that "Affiant Ferrari could not locate the insurance card in the evidence file on the Freeman case which should have contained a list of all physical evidence to the case." An FBI lead sheet from January 2000 referenced E.B.'s insurance card, though the FBI had only briefly come onto the case on account of a nearby spree killer on the run and the heavy possibility that whoever had the girls had crossed state lines.

"Then they were gone, just like that," says Dwayne Vancil.

It is revealed that on January 9, 2001, just over a year after the fire, OSBI agent Steve Nutter interviewed T.W., another girlfriend of Phil Welch's, one who, in the four months after the fire, began living with him in his Picher trailer, where she overheard all three men refer to the people "who were killed in Welch," people who owed them drug money. T.W. stated that "Pennington and Busick set fire to the home." The OSBI interview with Nutter also mentions that the reward poster with the girls' faces on it was "nailed to the wall" at Phil Welch's trailer, and that T.W. had "seen several Polaroid pictures, which Welch kept in his soft leather briefcase." T.W. said she was certain that the girls in the photographs, who were held captive against their will, were the very girls in the reward poster. The Polaroids showed Lauria and Ashley, with their "hands tied and mouths gagged," and a distinctive bedspread identified by T.W., who easily recognized it from the time she had spent living with Phil Welch. T.W. also made reference to Phil Welch's former girlfriend E.B., confirming that Phil Welch had kept the ex-girlfriend's car, the same ex-girlfriend whose insurance card was discovered at the scene of the crime.

Following up on T.W.'s information six months later, OSBI agent Nutter interviewed E.B. for the first time since she'd been interviewed by the FBI a year and a half earlier. It seems that the notes of the FBI regarding the first interview with E.B. had not been factored into the Oklahoma side of the investigation. In June 2001, E.B. confirmed to OSBI agent Nutter that Phil Welch lived in two homes, in Chetopa, Kansas, and Picher, Oklahoma, but she had "no idea how the card had gotten to the location where it was found." While she denied knowing Danny Freeman, she claimed that Phil Welch in fact did know him. E.B. explained that she left Phil Welch a few months after the fire due to his physical abuse, which would be brought up by almost everyone who knew the man, horrible accounts of beatings and rapes.

Eighteen years later, the insurance-verification card is a barefaced fact looking me straight in the face. There is the sudden realization that had it been followed up on, there is a strong possibility that Ashley and Lauria could still be alive today.

According to Private Investigator Pryor, the insurance card was not collected as evidence until investigators took it off him in August of 2017. The affidavit states that "Pryor reported to law enforcement about finding the insurance-verification card, but they did not take possession of the card." Pryor confirms to me that it was Nutter who denied taking the key evidence. For those close to the case, it's nearly impossible to learn of these disasters on top of the already well-known mishandling when authorities failed to find Danny's body and when there were no efforts to search for the girls.

But the shocking and infuriating facts of witnesses ignored or not followed up on and the card that could have led them all in the direction of the missing girls and their captors aren't the only shocking missteps in the course of the investigation.

"After finding the card, I traced it back to E.B. and her car, the car that Phil Welch used to transport them girls," PI Pryor tells me, further explaining that he got to speak with E.B. personally, until the mention of Phil Welch scared her into shutting up. "And guess what happened."

According to the information provided in the affidavit, Pryor found the car reportedly driven by Phil Welch to the Freemans on the night of the murders in a salvage yard in Picher, Oklahoma. The affidavit reads: "Pryor stated he reported finding the vehicle to law enforcement and requested they process the vehicle. Pryor reported he was told the vehicle had been through too many hands to be processed [for evidence]." If true, then I wonder if this case met with either the most inept or the most corrupt collection of law enforcement agencies ever seen in American history. For all we knew, it could have held crucial physical evidence that proved the girls had been in the car, evidence that could have led investigators to the men who took the girls before they took their secrets with them in death. And who was to say there wasn't a clue inside that could have led authorities to the girls' whereabouts?

Either way, the refusal to follow up on the car wasn't the last of it, and in reading the district attorney's documents, I know I'm not the only one whose face becomes red with rage, whose guts get sick because of the failures of others.

The affidavit also reports that current authorities reached out to PI Joe Dugan, Tom Pryor's partner, and in learning that he'd passed away in 2009, they spoke with Dugan's relatives. "Joe Dugan's relatives reported that Joe Dugan had a box of investigative material pertaining to the Freeman case," the affidavit says. "After his death, relatives of Joe Dugan took the investigative material to the Craig County Sheriff's Office. The sheriff's office refused to take the material, and it was eventually destroyed by Joe Dugan's relatives."

While the glaring miscarriages of justice are overflowing, from one state into the other, from one decade into the next and the next, the newer generation seems more hell-bent on fixing the wrongs made by past investigators, starting with reinterviewing some of the old witnesses.

31

DAVID "PENNY" PENNINGTON

I remember one of my letters from convicted murderer Charles Krider, the fellow marijuana businessman and best friend of Danny Freeman whose basement and well were searched to no avail in 2016. In the letter, which I received from prison, Charles mentioned David Pennington two years before Pennington's name went public, and that Pennington had made a deathbed confession that pointed to Charles.

But after the 2018 press release that named the three men, Charles denied knowing Pennington at all, despite growing up in the same small town. I wondered to myself if Busick, Pennington, and Welch were the three men that Charles refused to speak of, the men Danny chased off his property.

It is troubling to see the relatives (and survivors) of the murderous trio, Ronnie Busick, Phil Welch, and David Pennington, get the brunt of the public's outrage. The public sometimes ignores the fact that relatives of murderers are often victims themselves, and this is what springs to mind the first time I speak to Jerri Shelton, the stepdaughter of accused killer David A. Pennington. "He was the only man I knew as a father," she tells me. While admitting the fact that David had been tied up in meth addiction, she says that he cleaned up and "became everything to us."

Also a lifelong resident of Chetopa, David Pennington was a big-eared boy raised on the river, catfishing for as long as anyone could remember. Even fellow Chetopan Charles Krider's elderly mother would mention, "Pennington and Busick knew all the farm ponds," elaborating that Pennington talked about fishing all the time in the doctor's office where Mrs. Krider worked. She, along with most who knew the Penningtons of Chetopa, knew them to be as poor as church mice. "As boys, he [David] and his brother would come by my home—they didn't have much in life," Mrs. Krider explains. "I'd give them food and whatever I could for them to play with. His dad beat their mother and the boys, then left town and became a preacher but the boys would have nothing to do with him. As he [David] got older, he'd cut hedge wood for me." And while David's life choices weren't surprising to those who knew him and watched his health deteriorate over the years, many believe he came to change his life for the better in those later years before dying in 2015. Mrs. Krider even has her own testimony to that, saying that David Pennington came to the doctor's office and told her he'd given his heart to the Lord. He even professed this by singing her a hymn.

David's love for fishing carried all the way up until he got too sick to do it, succumbing to COPD "and numerous other diseases from the drugs he sold and did," according to Jerri, which led to his dying at age fifty-six. Upon a doctor's suggestion, Pennington used to sit with a bag of deflated balloons in his pocket, blowing them up as an exercise for his lungs between fixes from his oxygen mask. While his life was cut short by the demons of his past, Jerri maintains that he was the best grandpa to her children that anyone could ask for, since becoming sober ten years before his death.

"He did meth for so long, he couldn't breathe," says Pastor Raymond Whetstone when I speak with him and his wife in their Chetopa home. "We'd buy him inhalers. He lost all his teeth from meth, his stomach swelled up . . . but it's our job to accept them where they are."

Up until his later years, when he couldn't even make it to the bathroom without passing out, David was just another man who worked odd jobs between drug deals and cooks. "He was either welding or cutting wood—those were his big things, even when I was a kid," says Jerri, who would have only been ten years old at the time of the Freeman-Bible murders. Because David had a work history similar to those of Danny Freeman and Charles Krider, who had both held welding jobs there in Baxter Springs just twenty miles east, I ask Jerri Shelton if her father worked at Wiseda. "I think so," she answers. "Me and my mom was just talking about that, and she said there were a few different companies he worked for back then, so most likely."

I get the chance to speak with Jerri in her Missouri home, a dialogue punctuated with photos of her father fishing or with his grandchildren on his lap. While she insists that her father's life changed "drastically" with sobriety, she also admits that she spent much of her childhood removed from the home upon the state's intervention due to drink- and drug-fueled Saturday nights and bursts of domestic violence between David and her mother. Recollecting their past, and the couple's inevitable separation years later, Jerri maintains that "he loved her with all his heart and soul, to the very end." While David Pennington was reported to be seeing several girls at once, there seems to have been a special place reserved for Jerri's mother, whom he married a couple of months after the murders in Welch.

I sit with Pastor Raymond and Nancy Whetstone, a lovely elderly couple. Pastor Ray still leads Chetopa's Faith Baptist Church, where Pennington and Welch were regular attendees. "I would always find Pennington's wife after David beat her," says Nancy, who helped Jerri and her mother move to a safe house days after the fire. "David Pennington stalked me, stalked me by driving by my house over and over while my husband was away on a revival. This would have been the weekend this all happened," says Nancy. "That's the only time I really ever felt fearful during the time with the men." And even though Nancy explains in detail how David "beat the tar" out of Jerri's mother, even the devout Whetstones were surprised that David could have helped wipe an entire family clean off the face of the earth. But Phil Welch was another story.

It is rare to hear about David Pennington without the mention of Phil Welch. They liked to hole up, bouncing between several ramshackle homes and trailers to manufacture and use drugs. Even years before the murders, Pastor Whetstone walked in on them smoking marijuana, only for Phil Welch to cast a devilish smirk. "He looked right at me and said, 'This is what Jesus died for, Pastor.'"

David Pennington's stepdaughter also nods to Phil Welch as contributing to her father's newfound and fanatical devotion to God. "Phil was such an intense person," she says. "He [Pennington] got really into religion. They were singing religious songs together, doing church services at Phil Welch's home, that kind of thing. Don't get me wrong. That's not a bad thing, but it was really, *really* intense."

David Pennington started attending Whetstone's services irregularly in 1976, when Pennington had only "been doing marijuana, I think," according to Mrs. Whetstone. Over the decades, Nancy was very involved with Pennington and the woman who'd become his wife, even after they were married by Pastor Whetstone in the Picher trailer on February 1, 2000. "He'd stomp her or throw a cup that would gash her head open, really serious stuff," says Nancy. The pastor's wife tells of how her son had to come over with a gun to protect her when David was demanding to know where Nancy had taken the girls the weekend after the fire. "But she'd always call him and go back." Eventually, David Pennington took Jerri and her mother and moved them very near to Phil Welch's trailer in Picher, as though gravitating toward the man. Since these men spent more time where they cooked than where their families were, it could be said, and often is said, that David and Phil lived together.

Phil Welch's influence on some edged dangerously close to cult-leader status, and David Pennington didn't seem immune to his spell. Pastor Whetstone pointed to his own head and then to his chest. "He had the Bible here, but he didn't have it here," he said, regarding Welch's claims of being an ordained minister and holding his own church services in the very trailer he'd cook and sell methamphetamine in. "He'd be so religious but did such terrible things." Pastor Whetstone had known David for years because he had been raised in the same small town. Phil Welch came from Erie, Kansas, about forty-five miles north of Chetopa, where he was primarily raised, though his family moved around often. It was when Pastor Whetstone was doing jailhouse ministry that he first met Phil Welch, at the Labette County jail in Oswego, Kansas. "He was as mean as an old rattlesnake."

While the Picher trailer was gone forever, either because of demolition upon the exodus of Picher's civilization or because of the tornado that ripped through those hanging by a thread, Phil Welch's other home, his last, was struck by lightning and destroyed. "It wasn't even a big storm, just a small cell," said the landlord to the *Tulsa World*. "As though the storm came straight for that house."

I go to the ruins of Welch's last home and sift through the burned and rusty debris, far and deep in the Kansan country near the unincorporated town of Hallowell. Here, where he died from complications of ALS in 2007, I find an old Bible.

"He was scary when you looked at him," says Jerri Shelton. "He didn't even really have to say anything to you. He could just look at you, and it made your stomach turn." She goes on to address the fanaticism that came with Welch. "He would come over and do Bible hymns. I don't know if it was drugs with my dad or what, but it was almost like a cult following. You know what I mean? He thought he could exorcise demons, and he [Welch] was intense and out there. He was extremely scary."

"I remember him reading books on witchcraft and demonic stuff," says a relative of Phil Welch. "He thought he was holy or divine enough to be above it, that none of it could touch him. That the devil couldn't touch him."

Even one of Ronnie Busick's relatives who acknowledges having had a brief affair with methamphetamine back in the day admits to being on the wrong end of Welch's attentions. "Those eyes . . . I'd believe any horrible story anyone could tell," she distantly remembers. "Let's just say he'd like to watch, sometimes give instructions. Laugh. When it got good, he'd sit forward with his elbows on his knees, and those fucking eyes." She says Welch was a sexual deviant who performed unspeakable acts of abuse that included foreign objects and multiple people he could control, "suggesting various contenders for the next round of 'will it fit.'"

"When they said Phil's name, I wasn't surprised," says Jerri, which seems to be the sentiment of everyone who personally knew him. But one of the most damning things to come from David Pennington's stepdaughter is the mention, for the first time in about seventeen years, of a New Year's Eve party, which she brings up unsolicited during our first conversation. While never mentioned in the affidavit, the rumors of the New Year's Eve party, which in the early 2000s ran rampant throughout the Wyandotte meth circles some thirty-five miles away from Chetopa, still hold water for the likes of the Bible and the Freeman families.

"Remember when I said all these drug people knew one another?" Lorene asks. "Over state lines, over the years, they're all connected."

"He always said he regretted going to that party," Jerri casually starts, remembering that her stepfather was home "before the ball dropped."

This night, when he returned from the alleged party, was only days before the pastor's wife helped Jerri and her mother escape to a safe house, giving David his reason to stalk Nancy. "When he came home [from the party], he kept me and my mom in the house for days. He was scared. And of course, he was high and had found religion in the wrong person. Phil was that person." Jerri further explained that Phil believed he was a true prophet of God. In an event that seemed "out of character for him," Jerri remembers it being the only time she saw her stepfather truly scared, locking them in, perhaps locking others out. "Anytime my dad talked about that party, he referred to it as *that* party," she continues. "He always regretted going to it. I don't know if that's when he maybe became involved as far as the girls went. I'm not sure, but he regretted it. . . . He wasn't the same after." She says that while the details of the party were never disclosed to her, David became paranoid in a fit that erupted when he came home that night, and he began "throwing stuff in our fireplace."

"I think it ate on him," comments Pastor Whetstone, who would later conduct the funerals of both David Pennington and Phil Welch. "There were some bad things in his heart."

With Pennington's name released in 2018, there comes the affidavit's longest statement, stemming from an interview with a young man called R.E. As it goes, R.E. is the person who opened up the can of worms and helped direct the entirety of this investigation back to Chetopa. He was the boy forced by the three men to look at the Polaroids of the girls.

The affidavit makes reference to a 2005 interview of R.E. by former OSBI agent Nutter and a KBI agent. But R.E., like others, was dismissed.

It was a quiet night in 2017; Ottawa County sheriff Jeremy Floyd was just leaving the office, turning his lights off and taking his Stetson with him. But just as he was leaving through the back emergency exit, he found a scraggly gentleman under a lamppost, waiting. A man who knew to keep his cool, Floyd approached R.E., who appeared jittery and anxious. "So I invited him inside," said Floyd.

"I know the person who killed the girls," R.E. started. "Phil Welch."

According to the affidavit, R.E.'s mother dated David Pennington at the time of the Freeman murders and the abductions of the girls. He stated that though he talked to authorities in the past and told them what he knew then, authorities didn't put any stock in the young man's confessions due to his lifestyle and the people he associated with. Having lived around this Chetopa/Picher crowd and the likes of Pennington and Phil Welch over the years, he said that he was terrified of Welch.

R.E. explained to authorities that back then, he had to sleep with a kitchen knife under his bed, and would wake to his phone ringing in the middle of the night. "Don't you say a word," Phil Welch would growl before hanging up. Like others, he spoke about Phil's coming over to the house to cook dope with Pennington and to sing Bible hymns. He described Welch as "evil."

In 2017, R.E. confessed to authorities, including Sheriff Floyd, DA investigator Stansill, and OSBI agent Ferrari that both Welch and Pennington had admitted to killing the girls. He also said the pair claimed it was all over drugs (though he couldn't be certain as to whether or not it was over debt or a deal gone bad). He admitted that his mother would "get beat" by Pennington "over this stuff." In one standout incident, Pennington and Welch bragged over the Polaroids they kept of the girls like a trophy. R.E. perceived the men as being so prideful, in fact, that they shoved the photos into his face, near giddy.

Out of respect for the families, and to avoid sensationalism, the DA's office does not detail all that is included in the photographs. From what I learn through some of the confidential witnesses and law enforcement, the photos include the very things that the mind tries to protect you from.

As written in the 2018 affidavit, "R.E. stated he heard there was another person with Phil Welch that night [the night of the Freeman murders]. . . . R.E. stated David Pennington and Phil Welch were 'laughing' about the girls being in a mine shaft and they would state 'good luck in trying to ever find them.'"

When asked if either Pennington or Welch indicated how the girls had died, R.E. replied, "Yeah, they were raped and violently strangled to die."

Before the new investigators' 2017 interview with R.E., they'd also spoken to his mother, L.E., back in 2016. She confirmed that she had in fact lived with David Pennington at the time of the murders (while it was maintained that he also kept his home with Jerri's mother and spent most of his time with Welch). L.E. told authorities that she had to hide from Pennington based on Pennington's numerous confessions to killing the girls and his threatening that if she ever left him, he'd kill her too. She told authorities it was a "bad drug deal. . . . They decided to take the girls and have fun with them. Know what I mean?"

According to L.E., Pennington told her that "one of the parents" (presumably Danny Freeman) was buying drugs from Pennington when the "girls walked into the room." She said that Welch, Pennington, and Busick were responsible, each one having sexually abused the girls. While she claimed not to know where the girls were, she said, "They may be at the bottom of a pit," where Pennington said she'd end up too if she ever told.

L.E. passed away before the release of this affidavit.

Neither mother nor son, L.E. and R.E. respectively, was a stranger to the car that was reportedly used to drive to the Freeman trailer on the night of the fire and then used to take the girls out. According to the affidavit, "L.E. reported that a car belonging to a woman who Phil Welch was seeing was used and that the woman's 'ID' was found on the ground." And in regard to her son, he also knew about the card, saying he'd heard both Pennington and Welch talking about it, fearful that it would be the piece of evidence that could lead back to them.

Even Pastor Whetstone and his wife know about the insurance-verification card, believing that authorities must have known. "Everybody here knew about the insurance card for years," says Nancy. "People talked about it all the time, starting shortly after the murders. Why did no one follow up on it?" I have no answer.

Another associate of David Pennington, J.B., said that three to six months before he died, according to the affidavit, Pennington said he "knew more about the murders than what he was letting on to people about it." J.B. also claimed that "everybody already thought David Pennington was involved in it anyway." This witness also pointed toward Phil Welch's girlfriends E.B. and T.W. as having information.

Yet another witness, J.R., claimed that he walked into a friend's trailer, where he observed his friend, along with Busick, Pennington, and Welch, looking at several Polaroids, and while they scrambled to hide the photos from J.R., this witness claimed he was able to see one of them in David Pennington's hands; in the photograph were Lauria and Ashley "duct-taped to a chair with their hands bound." Having heard the men on several occasions talk about the girls, he recalled one saying, "Yeah, we got them, didn't we?"

A fifth witness, a fugitive who'd only speak in brief moments to current investigators on the phone due to a warrant for his arrest, told Agent Ferrari that "David Pennington spilled his guts" and that Pennington got drunk and said that he "and that Welch dude" were involved. This witness also claimed to know the pair as meth cooks. When this on-the-lam informant could finally be interviewed in jail after being arrested in 2018, he told Stansill and Ferrari that he heard Welch, Pennington, and Busick talk about the murders often, referring to the girls as "them two little bitches," as though it were some kind of inside joke. He also claimed that it was a "robbery gone bad," that Danny Freeman owed the men "a bunch of money," as stated in the affidavit.

"I remember the ten-year anniversary [of Ashley and Lauria going missing], and they had a thing about it on the news," recalls David Pennington's stepdaughter, Jerri. "And I had looked over at him [David] and said, 'It's really sad that nobody has found them yet.'"

"They're at the bottom of a mine shaft with water running through it," he abruptly answered, saying that he knew a guy who used to dump cattle in it. He shifted in his stepdaughter's silence. "At least that's where I'd look."

Jerri tells me that she hadn't been contacted by authorities, not even after the press conference that named her father as one of the murderers. Instead, it was Jerri who reached out to the Bibles herself. "They have the most right to be angry," says Jerri, in regard to the public's anger, which is often misdirected at her. "They don't lash out. They don't say terrible things. It's really amazing how strong they are."

"This solves nothing," Lorene contends. It seems this flood of information, as officially released by the district attorney's office, offers little to no solace to a woman whose only purpose is to find her daughter. "This is about bringing the girls home, and until then, it's not solved."

The affidavit discusses several more men and women and women's children who lived for years under the threats of Phil Welch, Ronnie Busick, and David Pennington. I collect hundreds of pages of records pertaining to Welch, including arrest records that document assaults, batteries, burglaries, child abuse, domestic violence, terrorist threats, and more. Several of these reports revolve around the very witnesses of the 2018 affidavit. When one of his former girlfriends tried leaving him, Phil Welch chased her down. Witnesses say he threatened to slit her children's throats and dump them in mines: they'd "end up like the girls." Witness after witness saw Welch lying with the girls in the photos.

I come up from reading the affidavit feeling angry and empty. My belly fills with disgust at the thoughts of the men, these girls.

Today, Ronnie Dean Busick is still awaiting trial. By law, he is presumed innocent until proven guilty.

David Pennington and Phil Welch died in the course of the investigation.

Charles Krider is not currently a suspect in the Freeman murders and continues to reside in Chetopa.

While the investigation feels on the right track, for both the Freemans and the Bibles alike, who all believe that the three men named are in fact the ones responsible for the murders, a division remains; and the mention of police involvement is inescapable.

"Now, he [Ronnie] did not know a damn thing about who *really* wanted it done," says Busick's niece the first time we speak, offering the information without prompting. "He would have been kept in the dark about that. . . . The whole 'It was a drug deal' sits wrong with me. As soon as it happened, everyone knew what had gone down, because everyone knew about the court case coming up."

I ask for clarification. "Are you referring to Danny Freeman and the potential lawsuit against police?"

"Yup." From there, she chooses to go off the record.

I even asked R.H., who knew all three men, why, even now that Busick was in jail and the other two men were dead, people in Chetopa are still too scared to talk.

"Law enforcement," he says straightforwardly. "A lot of the younger generation is listening to the older generation. Keep your mouth shut. There's things I couldn't be paid a million bucks to make me say."

At the end of the interview, R.H. and I stand up. Together, we walk outside, looking next door to where David Pennington lived with Jerri and her mother at the time of the murders.

"There were people who weren't scared of nothing who were terrified of that guy Phil," he says.

"But he's dead now."

R.H. lights a cigarette. "Thank the Lord."

This is where my research has to end, a line drawn in the white dust of the poisonous chat. Like those who loved Lauria and Ashley the most, I feel like I can dig forever. I even feel guilty for not having an ending for this book to give the families. Because while the men who did this are no longer able to commit more horrific crimes, I'm not sure anyone's any closer to finding the girls. Sure, I know it feels like the end is near, but I know the families have felt like this a thousand times before. As Lorene will say, it's best not to get your hopes up. I believe hope is all a person needs to survive most anything, but I see how it can also make a person mad.

32

LIKE LIGHTNING

Today

It is a year since the first arrest. My trips home are fewer than my visits to Oklahoma, where I'm always welcomed back by the shadows and the grip of fear masked in the nourishment of the prairie, where dawn's lines of color fluctuate like the sea, looking back to a shore made of stars. She is not mine to visit. I am hers to take. But every time I pass the sign that welcomes me to Oklahoma, I swear I hear the breath of Ashley blowing out her candles, a breath that matches the wind on the grain. And Lauria's laughter laced in, something playful, a reminiscence of youth. A mother and father's slow round of applause. The blood of murderers' veins that runs cold like the rivers that cut through out back by the dam.

It all fades to the silence that belongs to the prairie when the wind pauses, then revs back up with the unchanging taunts that keep the answers close to her chest: somewhere out there, Ashley and Lauria remain.

I feel a certain honor to have seen the case come this far. Through the ups and downs and the ons and offs, where every red herring in the four-state area comes like catfish (for every suspect I mention, there are more who didn't make the cut). It is dizzying, it is emotional, it is frustrating, and sometimes it is terrifying. But it feels like everyone is making progress. The news of the naming of the three men brings forward a new wave of people and information, and helps narrow in on where authorities believe the girls' remains could be found today: the scourge that is Picher on Oklahoma's beautiful figure.

But while focus stays on the abandoned superfund site, the families and the authorities accept all tips, from everywhere.

As late as January 2019, I follow a rumor back to a former member of law enforcement. Not expecting much, I leave with a CD that holds a recording from the early 2000s of a deathbed confession, the elderly father of a suspect trying to point authorities to where the girls' bodies are. The leads still flow, and the families still listen.

"Why now?" I ask the former member of law enforcement who gave me the CD.

"I have my reasons," my source says, alluding to concerns of police corruption.

In typical Lorene Bible fashion, I learn not to get my hopes up. The grim reality remains that Lauria and Ashley might never be found, that even if precise coordinates are provided, the mines are a largely inaccessible maze filled with moving water that could have flushed the girls' bodies thousands of miles, into any one of several neighboring states. And though the Bibles concede this, they will never give up.

"Lauria's grandparents died before we could find her," Lorene tells me. "Her grandpa, on his deathbed, asked if there was something more he could have done to find her." Hearing about the loved ones making promises to glean information from heaven and get it back to Lorene in this life nearly breaks my heart.

During the course of my writing this book, Celesta Chandler, Kathy Freeman's mother, also passes away.

For the first time in about a decade, I even watch Dwayne come back publicly to the case. "This crime was too vicious, too personal," he says to reporters, never convinced that the motivation for the murders was drugs.

He also expresses his anger. "We knew all three names in the first few days of the fire," he says, referring to Busick, Pennington, and Welch. "We told Agent Nutter, and he said, 'No, they had nothing to do with it.'"

No one in the Oklahoma State Bureau of Investigation, the Craig County Sheriff's Office, or any other agency related to the case has made an official comment on the missteps or negligence or corruption of the investigators of old.

Like I tell those back home about what I actually do in Oklahoma: 99 percent of my job is gaining trust. It's only after the arrest, in the summer of 2018, that Dwayne shares with me documents that have been kept out of the public eye since DeAnna Dorsey clutched them on the talk show taped in Los Angeles days before her 2002 murder.

In my hands for the first time is Shane's autopsy report.

In my hands is the signed statement of CCSO's Mark Hayes, brother of shooting officer David Hayes.

In my hands is the signed statement of CCSO's Jim Herman.

In my hands is the signed statement of CCSO's Troy Messick.

In my hands is the signed statement of CCSO's Charlie Cozart.

Delivered are the promises of a video taken by the Freeman family of Shane's body, as Dwayne helped prop up the boy's corpse in the basement of the funeral home, motioning toward the suspect bullet wound on the side of Shane's chest.

According to the autopsy report, Medical Examiner Donna Warren's finding was that the slug entered and exited the back of Shane's upper left arm (in and out through the triceps). It then entered the torso about two inches right of his left nipple. The slug never hit the bone of his arm, but went through his chest through the fifth rib and hit his lungs and heart. The slug remained lodged in Shane's body and was extracted by the ME from the muscles of his back on the opposite side of where the bullet entered at a slightly downward angle.

Based on the entrance and exit wounds at the back of the arm, and the path of the burn as the slug grazed the side of the chest, the Freemans believe that Shane was in the physical position of attempting to run away. However, when I speak once again to coroner and teacher Darren Dake, he insists that the autopsy report does not definitively imply whether Shane was in such a position.

But, to repeat Danny Freeman's words in the *Tulsa World* shortly after his son's death, "We might not know everything."

Today, there remains a great divide.

"I'm a little bit reluctant to even talk about it," says David Hayes to me after three years of my pleading, the first time he ever speaks publicly about the shooting. "And it's not because of you."

When I speak to David Hayes, now the captain of police in neighboring Rogers County, he sounds remorseful over the shooting death of Shane—not regretful that he shot him, but regretful that he had to shoot him back on January 8, 1999.

On that cold and windy late afternoon, David Hayes drove west of Welch, where people are few and the skies are low. With rumors flying that the Red Light Bandit was armed, David Hayes was the first to arrive, and when he turned onto the road, his patrol car was facing Shane. "Things happened pretty fast," he tells me.

Believing it was going to be a routine deal, Hayes observed Shane sitting in the disabled pickup on the side of the road. "I wasn't expecting trouble," says Hayes, who took with him his state-issue twelve-gauge shotgun, got out, "and ordered him out of the truck and on the ground." Shane didn't appear nervous, nor did he seem frenzied. "He was distant," Hayes remembers.

I wonder if perhaps Shane was crashing after his manic crime spree, maybe accepting. Or maybe he was just young and naive, hoping to go to jail. Maybe he wasn't thinking at all.

"He hesitated a little bit." David Hayes pauses, his voice thick with disappointment and his words carefully chosen. "I wish he would have tried talking to me." Instead, Shane exited the truck, closed the door, but didn't get on the ground as he'd been instructed. Instead, he pulled his jacket to the side and brought up the very pistol he'd stolen from the Bibles' house the day before.

In a second that stretched on forever, when looking down the barrel of the pistol that Shane held up, "Time slowed down," recalls Hayes. "And I thought to myself, 'I can't believe he's making me do this.'" Hayes claims to have felt the presence of God around him. "Everything was calm."

David Hayes shot Shane at exactly 4:20 p.m., just seconds before backup came. The second officer would be Troy Messick, the very officer who'd later deliver the news of the fire to Lorene Bible in McDonald's and would respond to the Bibles' discovery of Danny's body. He was also the man who reported Shane as a runaway upon Danny Freeman's insistence after the phone-cord incident.

Deputy Hayes, however, thought he'd missed the boy, seeing that the shot of the twelve-gauge didn't knock him off his feet. Shane slightly turned and headed for the rear of the truck, doubled over. But when David looked through the truck's windows from the same spot where he had taken the shot, Shane didn't reappear on the other side, having fallen at the rear of the truck. "He was dead by the time I reached him."

According to the signed police statements before me, Shane died at 4:20 p.m.

Messick arrived at 4:21.

Lieutenant Jim Herman arrived at 4:33.

Undersheriff Mark Hayes arrived at 4:37 with Investigator Charles Cozart.

And Sheriff Vaughn arrived at 5:24.

These are the men who stood in the cold and saw dusk through to night, with a lifeless teenager at the center of their focus. These are the men who would first arrive at the boy's home when it burned down less than a year later.

I ask David Hayes specifically if he thought this was a suicide by cop.

"I have no doubt," he answers. "I have no doubt that that's what took place." Some had surmised this in the past, claiming that Shane chose this way out in lieu of returning home, as social workers, and his father, were trying to have him do.

We also talk about the alleged stalking by Danny Freeman, which warranted the allegations of other officers wrongfully arresting Danny and threatening him and his family. To my surprise, David says he had no firsthand experience with Danny's stalking. "I don't know he ever stalked me," says David. "I know he came to my house one evening after that [Shane's death], and I was notified. And he [Danny] was intercepted by another deputy and taken to the sheriff's office." This is the event detailed in the letters written by both Kathy Freeman and her mother, Celesta Chandler.

I ask David what went through his mind when, fast-forwarding a year later, he heard that Kathy and Danny had been murdered.

"It was unbelievable." And though he'd taken a polygraph test to determine whether or not he had knowledge about the Freeman murders, he never personally heard what the results were. Like his brother, Undersheriff Mark Hayes, he knew that Agent Nutter sought him and other members of the CCSO as potential suspects early on in the case.

"Living with this has been tough," he says. "But I did what I was trained to do, and my conscience is clear." His one hope was that the story could finally be put to rest.

"No gun visible," the Freemans continue to repeat. "No gun visible."

Standing in the isolated section of a road today where seventeen-year-old Shane gasped his last breath, I see where the prairie meets the hills, and the wind becomes trapped screaming in my ears. A silent prayer on my lips tastes like the dust of the road, and I close my eyes and imagine the withdrawing echoes of a shotgun blast around me. There's neither a cross nor a flower from Ashley that remains twenty years later—no evidence of anything at all happening here. I think of my husband's words when I said how I've connected most to Shane. *Maybe that's because you were just like*

Shane when you were his age. I survived the blooms of youth, but I struggle to let go of the idea that one movement, justified or not, intentional or not, could have cut this boy's life short forever.

I listen to a car in the distance taking long minutes to arrive. "You need any help?" the driver asks. And suddenly I think of the several locals who stopped and asked Shane the same question shortly before his death. *No, thank you; help is on the way.*

"No, thanks," I answer before introducing myself. "Did you know Shane Freeman?"

"Sure, I remember him," the driver answers. "The boy ran like lightning."

33

NO END

In 1999 and on into the nights of a new millennium, a small gray trailer tucked itself away amidst what felt like the endless chat piles and turquoise pools of poison that had bubbled up from the ground in Picher. Carried by a white wind were the sounds of gospel hymns, scratchy from a hand-me-down Victrola found in the left-behinds of the chat rats who were forced to abandon their homes. The music blared all night, for no one here slept. Sound didn't carry like it did in the prairies. Instead, it was stifled by mountains of toxic waste and the threats of men who kept close to the meth sessions and deluded sermons.

"I still have nowhere to go and pay my respects," says Lorene, who no longer visits the end of the Freemans' driveway. Now we bring flowers to a grassy section in Picher where there's not a single sign of life but for the remembrances accumulating from friends and family. "I virtually have the doorstep of a killer to go to." And not even a doorstep is left.

I ask the families how they keep the darkness from consuming them.

"Lauria was a beautiful and precious soul," says cousin Lisa. "To allow the darkness in any of that, it would be tarnishing her memory."

Nine months after the naming of Ronnie Busick for the murders of

Lauria, Ashley, Kathy, and Danny, I sit in The Cow, a small restaurant in Welch. The restaurant is dark and quiet, and I am the only one here as I wait for my order to be wrapped up. I watch the snow come in sideways on the empty street. It feels something like coming home. Something about Oklahoma will stick with me forever.

I can hear where there should be music playing, and sitting in front of me is the familiar shadow, the fear. I ask it if it wants to sit next to me, and in this way, the panic attack is diverted, and the fear fades away. It is because of this approach, largely learned by watching people who suffer more than I can imagine, that my panic attacks disappear.

"The darkness is always there on the sidelines, but we cannot let it in," says Lorene. "That's defeat. I will not be defeated."

My food arrives, and I take the affidavit with me.

But there is one more interview brought up in the affidavit, and it is with Phil Welch himself. In the February 2003 interview, "Welch stated prior to the murder of Freeman and his family, Phil Welch moved to a residence approximately 3/4 mile north of the Freeman residence."

In the affidavit that only provided so much of this interview, Phil Welch "indicated that he met David Pennington in Chetopa and they became friends." When learning that the insurance card leading to E.B. was what led to him, he explained that he and E.B. had already talked to law enforcement. "He did not know why the insurance card was removed from the vehicle or why it was found near the crime scene."

Another failure by those who literally had the killer right in front of them.

"You know what I wonder?" Alabama death row inmate Jeremy Jones asks me after learning about the card himself. "I wonder if they [the girls] tried getting out at the end of the driveway there. The card just blows away. Hell, maybe they threw it out on purpose."

We might not know everything.

I pack my darkness, and I leave. As the snow comes down hard, I step out onto the sidewalk, looking across the street to the Welch firehouse, where the fire engines sit silently and the gentle clink of the American flag hitting the pole keeps on overhead. I taste the snow in the air as I head west, making my rounds to see Glen Freeman over at the Freeman farm, where I'm always sure to stop by whenever I visit. Passing the Sherrick ranch belonging to the couple who called in the fire in 1999, I continue up the road to the Freemans' like I have countless times before. Past the familiar ramshackle white house that sits between the Sherrick and Freeman properties. I remember sitting in the Sherricks' home and asking them about the traffic that went up and down the road.

"Do you know who lived at the other house?"

"No," they answered. *"No idea."*

If not for the truck parked in front of the house, I wouldn't suspect anyone lived here. So I stop, then knock on a broken door until the current tenant meets me.

"Hey, I'm sorry to bother you," I begin, introducing myself. "I was wondering if you had heard about the crimes up the road back in 1999."

"You want to know when Phil Welch lived here, don't you?"

I stand frozen. The affidavit was incorrect, and Phil Welch didn't live north of the Freemans, but south. He lived here. "Yes." I clear my throat.

The tenant confirms that Phil Welch's time there did in fact overlap with when the Freemans lived up the road. He tells me that Phil lived out in the sheds (though meeting the landlord later on, I confirm that he did not live in the sheds, but in fact cooked meth in them). The snow comes down as I nose around the several collapsing sheds in the back, full of junk and weeds and broken wood and rusty nails. But as I look around, out to a panoramic view of hills fading into the grayness of falling snow, something strikes me: the sight of Glen Freeman's trailer down the way.

If I were Phil Welch, I could cook dope with the Freemans' home in my view. When I get in my car and measure the distance, it is only eight-tenths of a mile away. *Well, shit.*

I drive farther into the backcountry than ever before to meet the landlord, getting lost over and under the Kansas state line in the myriad of no-name towns. On my way back from meeting the kind elderly woman, the undulating roads and dense forests create stomach lifts and darkness. Dusk makes blind spots, and just before the last flare of the day is extinguished, I happen upon a mailbox that reads "Welch."

I stop the car and weigh the idea out for a minute.

Up a long and steep driveway are a house, a bonfire, and the shadow of a man moving back and forth outside. But at the foot of the driveway is a KEEP OUT sign on a strip of barbed wire that's been disconnected from its posts and laid across the ground of the driveway. I leave the car on the road and slowly walk up, the familiar bogie that is anxiety swirling in the pit of my stomach. I try to wave to the man, but he doesn't see me, taking hauls of firewood in a wheelbarrow between shed and fire, and I fear calling out in case of dogs. I keep my distance and stand still, taking off my black jacket in the freezing cold so that maybe the white of my Metallica tee can catch his eye. It does.

The man takes his time to walk over, and I wonder if he's seen me the whole time. He comes as slow as the dusk here to conceal the virtues of daytime, in coveralls and the smell of fuel, and when the man comes close enough for me to see, I swear to God I am looking into the eyes of Phil Welch.

All I hear is the heartbeat in my ears, and I feel the sudden need to run back down from where I came.

"Forgive me," I start. "I saw the name on the mailbox."

The man, an identical match to Phil, is his estranged brother, a man who cut ties with him decades before. We speak for a while, shivering in the cold until I can't feel my toes, but he doesn't go on record. Behind us, the sun sets, taking my shadows with it. And once again, I find myself in the pitch-black hills of the prairie.

I take everything I have and pack it in the rental car, preparing to head back to the East Coast, but it's far from being my last time in Oklahoma.

On the seat beside me, the many writings of Lauria Bible as I cut through the countryside:

> *I have a special spot down by the old duck pond. . . . I love that in the evening, when the bold sun is setting with its colors glaring at the water how it glistens as the big, powerful, yet calm wind tosses the water around. . . .*

Oklahoma changes me forever, and more often than I care to admit, I still talk to Lauria and Ashley, looking to ghosts for reassurance and the silent request to be found. I still return, having made new relationships and the plans to forever keep my ear to the ground, my door always open. Sometimes I just enjoy the drive from the East to the West: when red sunset lingers over the fields after long days, my hair tangling in the thick, hot wind of a speeding truck. I'll trace my hand over the passing fields and a dirty fingernail along the horizon, remembering all the things that teenage girls live for: *the carefree heart, the white-trash kiss, reckless love.*

"The sight of it all helps me get my mind off the world and all my worries," Lauria's words end.

"This doesn't end until I find my child and bring her home," Lorene contends twenty years later. Because while I end the book, this story still continues, and so do the families. There is an immeasurable hope kept by the families in spite of the painful possibility that they might never find the girls.

But like I learned on my very first visit to Oklahoma: the prairie has her way.

ACKNOWLEDGMENTS

It should come as no surprise that most of my thanks belong to Lorene Bible, whose strength and determination continually inspire me each and every day. Without her, many would not know this story. I cannot thank Lorene, and many others, enough for opening their hearts and homes to me and allowing me into the most painful parts of their lives. I recognize that my presence wasn't always easy on you, and I love you for your patience. For Jay Bible, whom I so respect and admire for sharing his heart with me. To Lisa Bible-Brodrick, the woman who unexpectedly became one of the greatest friends this Yankee could ask for, and the rest of the Brodrick gang, who are crazier than a pit full of whistling raccoons (or something or other). To Missy and the rest of the Bibles and Leforces, who stay loud and strong as Lauria's voice across generations and time. The unity and perseverance of this family are nothing short of astounding, and I have been blessed to get to know you all.

I have so much gratitude for those on the Freeman side of the family, who I've come to just adore so much. To Glen, who holds a special place in my heart, thank you for your trust. And to Dwayne, whom I can sit and talk to for hours and hours, conversations I cherish. To Chris and Huey and our times between Welch and Louisiana, and to Lonny. Thank you all for letting me into your lives, even when it hurt, and for helping me understand so much.

To Celesta Chandler, who passed away before I could finish this book: may you finally know peace. And to Bill, may you too find peace. I will always remember the love you had for your family.

To Jeremy Hurst and Kat, thank you for your kindness. To Sheena, a true friend to Lauria and Ashley and one of the sweetest women I've ever known, thank you for being a beautiful soul over the years. To Justin Green, for sharing so much about Shane and your guys' unbreakable friendship. To Aaron Roper for his abundant information and tourism, and his family and friends for their warmth (and tasty ribs). To Sheriff Jeremy Floyd and Melissa, for opening your home and for always lending your support. To Cowboy, who could always show me around Oklahoma's nooks and crannies and bring a smile to my face. To R.E., whom I've come to just adore as a friend. To Jerri Shelton, for your trust and your unending sweetness. To Tom Pryor, for your openness. To Ally Lynn, for letting me in. To the Sherricks, for allowing me to be the first person you publicly shared your story with. To Tiffany Alaniz of Fox23, who's covered this story since its genesis and is a woman who always helps. To Sheila Stogsdill, for the same. To coroner Darren Dake of the Death Investigation Training Academy, who I'm proud to call a friend, and Priya Banerjee, MD, board-certified forensic pathologist—thank you, guys, for your patience and guidance. To retired NYPD sergeant Joe Giacalone, who taught me so much about law enforcement. To Paul Burch, for your overwhelming help. To Larry Thomas of the KBI for his expertise. To the Cooks, who cared so much for Judith—thank you for being amazing. To Paula Barnett: I love you to pieces. To Sherry Davis, for being a gentle soul over the years. To the Whetstones, whose godliness and goodness bled into these pages. To "Rhonda," whom I never thought I'd get the chance to meet, but am so glad that I did (I believe you are just amazing). And to "Dawn" for overcoming so much.

ACKNOWLEDGMENTS

To Ken and Sara Clark for all your graciousness and accommodation. To Anita at the casino (you know why). To the guys and gals at Stephen David Entertainment, who made it possible to achieve a lot of my research. To Dean Bridges and the Cowboy Church, for all you've done for me. To the historians and archivists of Vinita for being so helpful and accommodating with keeping history alive. To the staff members of the Bluejacket and Welch high schools, especially Shellie Baker, for showing me around. And a special shout-out to Clanton's Cafe, home of the best food you'll find in Oklahoma. Thank you all from the bottom of my heart.

For the sake of protecting people's privacy, a huge thank-you in general to everyone who let me interview them, both for this book and otherwise. I want to share my gratitude with all the men and women in Wyandotte who spoke to me about this case for the first time. Most of you should know who you are. To those in and around Chetopa for allowing me into your lives and overcoming fear to speak out. To my sources on and off the record at the Craig County Sheriff's Office and the Ottawa County Sheriff's Office, as well as the agents and staff from the DA's office and the OSBI, who offered their expertise for the sake of my writing this book, and for the sake of keeping this story alive. Thank you, all.

Now I leave Oklahoma to direct my admiration toward the people near and dear to me, for those who saw me bear the writing process. Starting with my husband, John David, thank you for never letting me give up, no matter how hard I tried. I love you, and I hate you for it. To my sister, Jessica, my best friend and the person who knows me better than anyone (S/O to Roger, and Mandy and Sarah!). To my in-laws back home in Ireland, Ber, Paddy, and Sarah, for all your incredible support over many years. To my mother, who died while I was writing this book—thank you for passing the writing genes to me and not to Jess. To my father, Vik, and Linda, thanks for being you. To my dear friend Amit "A.A." Dhand, the Harper Lee to my Truman Capote—here's to the Harrys and Freedoms in all of us. And to my dear friend the judge Jim Szablewicz, for so much help in the legal realm. To Tom Saum and Joey Slavinski and the rest of the

Scooby gang back in New York for helping me through the rough patches of my mind and for being the first ones to land on when I needed a break.

Lastly, the women behind the publishing curtain, starting with Emma Finn at the C&W agency in London for being the first person to take a chance on this book. To Zoe Sandler at ICM in New York. You guys are the greatest. To Sarah Hodgson of HarperCollins UK, who's always believed in my writing ability. To Jen Monroe at Berkley and Penguin Random House USA, who I've come to appreciate and adore. To Kathryn Cheshire at HarperCollins UK for being a great editor. To Caroline Lamoulie at Plon (France), my French partner in crime. Thanks for working so hard to help get this story published. To everyone at the publishing houses who had anything to do with this book. I could do none of it without you.

And of course, to my children, who will always remind me that there's beauty and light, even when the world goes dark. You are the reason I write and I love you all THIS much.

Please follow the case on Facebook at **Find Lauria Bible**, as run by the Bible family, for photos, information, and more. Tips are always welcome.

Tips and information can also be submitted to the Oklahoma State Bureau of Investigation: **1-800-522-8017** or **tips@osbi .ok.gov**.

Donations are also welcome on GoFundMe, **Lauria and Ashley Scholarship Program**, dedicated to local scholarships at the girls' respective schools.

There is a $50,000 reward in place.

INDEX

313